GROUP INTERACTION
AS THERAPY

CONTRIBUTIONS IN SOCIOLOGY

Series Editor: Don Martindale

New Perspectives on Organization Theory: An Empirical Reconsideration of the Marxian and Classical Analyses
William L Zwerman

Garrison Community: A Study of an Overseas American Military Colony
Charlotte Wolf

Small town and the Nation: The Conflict of Local and Translocal Forces
Don Martindale and R. Galen Hanson

The Social Shaping of Science: Institutions, Ideology, and Careers in Science
Roger G. Krohn

Commitment to Deviance: The Nonprofessional Criminal in the Community
Robert A. Stebbins

Capitalists Without Capitalism: The Jains of India and the Quakers of the West
Balwant Nevaskar

Black Belonging: A Study of the Social Correlates of Work Relations Among Negroes
Jack C. Ross and Raymond H. Wheeler

The School Managers: Power and Conflict in American Public Education
Donald J. McCarty and Charles E. Ramsey

The Social Dimensions of Mental Illness, Alcoholism, and Drug Dependence
Don Martindale and Edith Martindale

Those People: The Subculture of a Housing Project
Colette Pétonnet. Rita Smidt, Translator

Group Interaction as Therapy

The Use of the Small Group in Corrections

Richard M. Stephenson

and

Frank R. Scarpitti

Contributions in Sociology

Number 13

Greenwood Press

Westport, Connecticut ● London, England

Library of Congress Cataloging in Publication Data

Stephenson, Richard Manning.
  Group interaction as therapy.

  (Contributions in sociology, no. 13)
  Bibliography: p.
  1. Corrections. 2. Group psychotherapy.
3. Rehabilitation of criminals. I. Scarpitti,
Frank R., joint author. II. Title.
HV9275.S73   365'.66   72-830
ISBN 0-8371-6399-4

Library of Congress Catalog Card Number: 72-830
ISBN: 0-8371-6399-4
First published in 1974

Greenwood Press, a division of Williamhouse-Regency Inc.
51 Riverside Avenue, Westport, Connecticut 06880

Manufactured in the United States of America

To Our Wives Phyllis and Ellen

Contents

List of Tables

Preface

The history of purposeful intervention in personal and social problems has been long and, in most cases, unproductive or disappointing. Innovation and bold experimentation have often been turned aside in favor of tradition or for fear of consequences. Imaginative intervention has frequently been based on vague hunches or impressions in the absence of firm knowledge or broad theory upon which to build and test a program. Research, designed to explore intervention processes and evaluate results, has been largely absent.

The program discussed in this book attempts to attack some of these deficiencies. Avowedly experimental, based on theoretical considerations concerning the etiology and maintenance of the behavior to which the intervention is directed, and accompanied by comparative research evaluation, this program is designed to intervene in the processes of delinquency and, by making use of them, reverse and change behavior to more acceptable and law-abiding dimensions.

The general considerations upon which the intervention is based and a discussion of their implications for a program of corrections are presented in Chapter 1. Chapter 2 describes a particular program, known as Essexfields, as an example of one among several instrumentations of the guiding principles and objectives of this form of intervention. Drawing from extensive program observation, the following three chapters attempt to indicate how the program was carried out. Chapters 6 and 7 present the evaluative research accompanying the Essexfields project, and Chapter 8 summarizes comparative research on similar programs. The last chapter draws conclusions from the collective evidence of these researches.

Initially identified as guided group interaction, the development of this group-focused approach to corrections has involved a large number of people over a long period of time. The authors of this book cannot hope to acknowledge their indebtedness to each individual here. At best, we can mention some of those who supported and participated in the Essexfields research in the belief that they might stand as some representation of the extent of the full acknowledgment due.

The Ford Foundation supported the Essexfields project during its experimental phase and provided the funds for the accompanying research. During the course of research, the Public Health Service of the U. S. Department of Health, Education, and Welfare awarded a research grant for analysis of psychological data, and the Research Council of Rutgers, the State University of New Jersey, made a one year Faculty Fellowship available to the Principal Investigator. The New Jersey Department of Institutions and Agencies, through its program of student research internships, provided stipends for graduate students who assisted in research throughout the study. Among these former students, special mention should be made of Dr. John McGrath, presently Chairman of the Sociology Department at Virginia Commonwealth University.

The study was fortunate to have the full cooperation of the courts, correctional officials, and probation and parole authorities. Dr. Lloyd W. McCorkle, former Commissioner of Institutions and Agencies and the first director of Highfields, affirmed his recognition of the necessity of evaluative research by his guidance and support in the early stages of the research design. Mr. Albert Elias, a former director of Highfields and superintendent of the state Youth Reception and Correction Center, served as a Research Associate throughout the study. The Honorable Judges Harry W. Lindeman, Horace S. Bellfatto, Herbert J. Kenarik, and Neil G. Duffy of the Essex County Juvenile Court extended their complete cooperation. Mr. Manton E. Morris, former Chief, New Jersey Bureau of Parole, and Mr. Howard Forrest, in charge of the Newark parole office, were always helpful when it was necessary to seek their counsel.

Dr. Saul Pilnick, former director of Essexfields, and his Assistant, Mr. Neil Clapp, gave their unfailing cooperation and support. The Directors of the Group Centers, Messrs. Vincent Regan, Albert Axelrod, and Laurance Houston were most helpful in administering the psychological test given each boy as he left the Centers. Mr. Royale Eddy, former Superintendent of Annandale, and his successor, U. Samuel Vukcevich, gave their full cooperation. The Essex County Probation Department was always helpful during the course of the study, and the Sheriff's office of Essex County generously made possible a major source of the recidivism data. Mr. Horace Volz, former deputy Chief of the Essex County Probation Department, served as a wise consultant throughout the project, and Mr. George T. Donahue, Sheriff's Officer of the Juvenile and Domestic Relations Court, gave invaluable service in the collection of data.

To these and the many others, including the youths who participated in the program, we are very grateful. Convention should not obscure the importance of the customary acknowledgment that any shortcomings or deficiencies are those of the authors.

GROUP INTERACTION
AS THERAPY

1

The Group Basis of
Crime and Correction

The primary contention of sociological theories of crime causation is that the criminal or delinquent is the product of his social environment. He is not born a criminal; nor is he deviant because of some pathological emotional status which makes criminality inevitable. Instead, the law violator should be seen as one who has learned certain frequently practiced precepts, often acceptable in his particular environmental setting, which help him adapt to environmental adversities which may be defined as criminal by the larger society. The criminal or delinquent is a product of his social milieu, and the way in which he adjusts to it is different only in substance from the conventional or non-deviant method of adjustment.

This approach to understanding criminal behavior stands in contrast to those that seek explanations of crime causation in individual pathology or maladaptation. While it is recognized that some forms of criminality may be an expression of individual abnormality, this is viewed as the limited rather than the general case. Instead of looking for criminal traits in the individual, the criminal or delinquent is seen as one whose behavior is comprehensible once the specific social context within which he operates is known and understood. Within this social context, a young man may learn to become a criminal just as a young recruit learns to become a soldier within the social context of the military. Just as the military context is highly conducive to the development of attitudes and behaviors thought representative of a good soldier, so certain other social structures appear to support the development of criminal and delinquent behavior. This view is associated with theories of cultural transmission, and the social condition that fosters and sustains patterns of crime and delinquency is generally referred to as social disorganization.

SOCIAL DISORGANIZATION

The pioneer work of Shaw and McKay[1] stressed the role of social factors in explaining deviant behavior. Following the lead of Burgess, they divided the city of Chicago into five concentric zones based upon ecological characteristics. They discovered that the highest rates of crime and delinquency were for those areas included in, or adjacent to, the industrial and commercial zones (1 and 2). These areas of elevated crime were characterized by high mobility rates, great density of population, much family dependency, physical deterioration, a decreasing population, and high percentage of foreign and Negro population. In addition, there was an "absence of a basic social solidarity"[2] which did not allow the community to function as an effective means of social control.

> Children who grow up in these deteriorated and disorganized neighborhoods of the city are not subject to the same constructive and restraining influences that surround those in the more homogeneous residential communities farther removed from the industrial and commercial centers. These disorganized neighborhoods fail to provide a consistent set of cultural standards and a wholesome social life for the development of a stable and socially acceptable form of the behavior of the child.[3]

Shaw and McKay, then, saw disorganized neighborhoods as fertile ground for the growth of criminal and delinquent behavior. The poverty, the insufficient acculturation, and the marginality of the neighborhood residents caused whatever social organization was originally present to break down and cease to function effectively. Original group norms collapsed and were no longer adequate to control the behavior of the group member. At the same time, and largely for the same reasons, individuals were exposed to conflicting value systems and modes of behavior. While Shaw and McKay recognized the existence of conforming values in disorganized areas, they point out that youths are far more likely to encounter deviant values in the zone of transition than in the other zones.

In summary, then, social disorganization seems to be characterized by the following conditions: the emergence of subcultural groups based upon narrow and particularistic interests; availability of alternative means and goals; lack of consensus with regard to norms, values, and goals; ambiguity of social roles; inability of social pressures to induce conformity; conflicting requirements made on the individual with multi-group membership; ignorance of the social norms accepted by the larger society to guide behavior; and the availability of conflicting models of behavior, each clear and consistent, with no certain balance of support and control favoring conformity. Unfortunately, few empirical studies have attempted to measure these conditions in any systematic way, so it is not known how many must be present or to what degree in order to disorganize a social system. Disorganization theorists generally agree, though, that some combination of these conditions does tend to disrupt the functioning of the social system and may well result in deviant behavior on the individual level.

This focus on social disorganization has been modified by the idea that disorganization does not necessarily characterize areas of high delinquency and crime. Rather, these areas may be structured and organized, but tend to support values and behavior in conflict with more conventional society or with those in power and authority. With the exception of the small percentage of persons who deviate from the generally accepted social norms as a result of some emotional illness,[4] the traditional sociological frame of reference has seen the social deviate as a "normal" person who is pressured into deviancy by environmental conditions or learns deviance by direct exposure to it. This is true of the juvenile delinquent and adult criminal as well as for other types of deviates. The breakdown of social organization or the presence of organized deviance appear to enhance the possibilities of norm violation. Aside from Shaw and McKay's passing reference to differences in personality, family relationships and exposure to diverse elements,[5] this theoretical perspective does not tell us why structural disorganization or organized deviance results in *individual* norm violation. As a result of this deficiency, several theories have focused on the process by which criminal and delinquent behavior is derived from general environmental conditions. The most important explanations of this sort have been offered by Sutherland, Cohen, Miller, and Cloward and Ohlin.

DIFFERENTIAL ASSOCIATION

Edwin Sutherland conceived of criminality as participation in a cultural tradition resulting from association with representatives of that tradition.[6]

He believed that criminal behavior, just like any other type, is learned, and that it is learned through association and interaction with others who were already delinquent. The person becomes delinquent once he has internalized the criminal skills and attitudes he has been exposed to in intimate, primary associations with delinquents.

Sutherland used differential association to account for all types of crime regardless of the social class of the offender. Law violators were seen as reflecting the behavioral patterns of the groups with which they had prolonged and meaningful relations. If the behavioral patterns learned in association with others happen to be delinquent, then the individual is likely to become a delinquent. Of course, there is much more opportunity for the individual to have criminal associations in areas with high crime and delinquency rates. This helps explain the preponderance of lower-class or working-class boys among adjudicated delinquents. But, by seeing delinquency as merely imitative behavior, the theory of differential association does not attempt to suggest any provocations for this norm-violating behavior. It was left to others interested in the etiology of delinquency to turn their efforts in this direction.

DELINQUENT SUBCULTURES

It is the contention of Albert K. Cohen that delinquency is primarily a lower-class phenomenon and that certain working-class boys are carriers of a delinquent subculture resulting from their socialization in lower-class families and their inability to function successfully in middle class institutions.[7] The working-class boy's inability to function successfully in institutions dominated by middle-class values results in his experiencing great frustration. The middle-class value pattern which is strange and unacceptable to the working-class boy is alleged to emphasize ambition, individual responsibility, skill, deferred gratification, rationality, manners, control of physical aggression, wholesome use of leisure time, and respect for property. Even though the working-class boy learns very early to value middle-class status, he does not find these values exemplified in his family and in his lower-class neighborhood. Therefore, it is much more difficult for him to identify with them and to internalize them to the extent that they act as controls over his behavior.

Nevertheless, Cohen does recognize that there are alternative ways in which the working-class boy may adjust to his status. The most common type of adjustment to the requirements of a middle-class society is acceptance of lower-class life. The boy withdraws into a community of peers and manages to avoid delinquency. Another response may be an attempt to achieve middle-class status through education, the working-class boy's major legitimate vehicle of upward mobility. Following the lead of William F. Whyte,[8] Cohen refers to the boys who respond by accepting their life-style as "corner boys," and to those who respond by striving for middle-class status as "college boys."

However, some working-class boys have a delinquency response because they cannot make the adjustments of the "corner boy" or the "college boy." The delinquency response, which is best exemplified in lower-class gang behavior, lashes out and rejects middle-class norms and values. Middle-class standards are inverted by working-class delinquents simply because middle-class boys abide by them. These delinquents divorce themselves from middle-class norms and strike back at the source of their frustration by legitimizing aggressive and hostile behavior. Perhaps more importantly, though, the delinquent subculture provides criteria of success and status which the working-class delinquent can meet.

In summary, Cohen believes that lower-class boys gravitate toward delinquency because they feel that they cannot gain status in a middle-class society. They reject middle-class values and accept the values of the delinquent subculture which predominates in lower-class neighborhoods. Within the delinquent subculture, the working-class boy learns how to alleviate the status frustrations which motivate him. Those lower-class boys who do not become delinquent manage, somehow, to internalize non-deviant norms and to isolate themselves from the delinquent subculture.

Walter B. Miller, who has spent a great deal of time studying lower-class delinquent gangs, has also made a significant contribution to the subculture theory of delinquency.[9] Miller asserts that a society may contain several value systems of unequal dominance, and that adherence to a subordinate value system may evoke punishment from the agents of the dominant value system. In American society, the subordinate value system is that of the lower class. The lower class is seen as a distinct and separate subculture primarily because its family type (mother versus father centered), is different than the middle-class family type.

There are three main points in the Miller thesis:

1. The lower class is characterized by distinctive values;

2. These lower-class values are quite unlike middle-class values upon which our legal code is allegedly based; and

3. Conformity with the lower-class values may in some cases mean automatic violation of the law. As he puts it:

Engaging in certain cultural practices which comprise essential elements of the total life pattern of lower culture automatically violates certain legal norms. Examples of this may be seen in the use of profanity, in hanging around or loitering, and in the serial-mating pattern characteristic of many homes.[10]

The "focal concerns" or values of lower-class culture in Miller's schema are trouble, toughness, smartness, excitement, fate and autonomy. Trouble means generalized difficulty and involvement; toughness includes physical prowess, masculinity, and bravery; smartness involves the ability to outsmart or dupe others; excitement consists of the search for thrills and adventure, relief from monotony; fate is an acceptance of the philosophy of destiny or luck; and autonomy reflects the desire not to be bossed or controlled. Those who have internalized these values as a result of being socialized in the lower-class sub-culture are especially prone to delinquency, crime, or other types of deviant behavior. Such behavior is seen as a natural consequence of adherence to lower-class norms.

On the other hand, the "focal concerns" or values of the middle class are quite similar to those posited by Cohen. They consist of desire for achievement, willingness to accept deferred gratification, acceptance of less rigid child-rearing practices, accumulation of material property, education, participation in formal organizations, the practice of cleanliness, and devotion to getting ahead. Just as the acceptance of lower-class values makes one susceptible to crime and delinquency, the internalization of middle-class "focal concerns" protects one from it. The relatively rare middle-class delinquent is one who has failed to internalize the immunizing values of his culture.

Although the ideas of Miller and Cohen are similar, there are distinct and important differences. Perhaps the most important difference is that Miller does not believe, as Cohen does, that lower-class boys must be frustrated in their status ambitions before taking on the characteristics of the delinquent subculture. For Miller, delinquency is the expression of lower-class norms and the mere presence of boys in the lower-class subculture is enough to produce it. However, he does admit that most juveniles in lower-class society are not delinquents because their aspiration level is higher than that of the delinquents. Lower-class non-delinquency depends upon "a realistic desire for upward social movement" and "the extent to which such upward aspirations are actually feasible in light of the youngster's early family training and his resultant personality characteristics."[11]

Sykes and Matza also disagree with Cohen's thesis that gang delinquency is a reaction formation on the part of boys experiencing status frustration.[12] They assert that middle-class values are shared by lower-class delinquents who develop techniques to neutralize the guilt resulting from the violation of norms to which they are committed. These "techniques of neutralization" permit the delinquent to engage in behavior which he views as valid for him but which is seen as unlawful by the larger society. Such techniques include: denying responsibility for deviant action; denying that the behavior causes any great harm when no one is injured; denying the wrongfulness of injury to the victim in light of the circumstances; condemning those who condemn him, thereby shifting attention to the supposed deviancy of others; and appealing to higher loyalties in the peer group at the expense of society's demands. This last technique does not imply that the delinquent necessarily repudiates the values of the dominant system. Although he may accept conventional norms, the norms of the gang are more important in determining his behavior.

LIMITED OPPORTUNITY

A more recent theory of delinquency has been provided by Richard A. Cloward and Lloyd E. Ohlin, who explain it as a function of a limited opportunity system.[13] A basis for this view can be found in Durkheim, who contended that it was necessary to keep goals in modern society within the bounds of possible achievement.[14] Later, Merton, restating Durkheim, claimed that many groups in American society have similar aspirations, but for various reasons (class, race, ethnicity) there is great inequality in their ability to achieve their goals.[15] When there is a breakdown in the relationship of goals and legitimate avenues of access to them, a condition of *anomie* (in which regulative norms become ineffective) will result. Under such conditions, people will attempt to achieve their goals in whatever way possible. Thus, members of the lower-class, aware of limited opportunity to realize their aspirations, engage in crime and delinquency more often than those in middle-class society with greater success opportunities.

Specifically, Cloward and Ohlin contend that delinquency is one consequence of a search for solutions to adjustment problems. They believe that pressures toward the formation of a delinquency subculture originate in inconsistencies between aspirations and means for achieving them legitimately. Pressures for deviancy are produced by differential access to the means of attaining common goals. As they state:

Our hypothesis can be summarized as follows: The disparity between what lower-class youth are led to want and what is actually available to them is the source of a major problem of adjustment. Adolescents who form delinquent subcultures, we suggest, have internalized an emphasis upon conventional goals. Faced with limitations on legitimate avenues of access to these goals, and unable to revise their aspirations downward, they experience intense frustrations; the explorations of nonconformist alternatives may be the result.[16]

In American society, education is the main avenue to legitimate opportunity. However, different class groups have differential access to education. Many youths in high delinquency areas or in city slums are restricted in occupational choices because of their lack of education; hence, for them there is no escape from poverty, and, consequently, they resort to non-legitimate means of fulfilling their personal aspirations. In other words, lower-class boys growing up in transitional areas are in a situation of low legitimate opportunity but high illegitimate opportunity. They find legitimate means of achievement closed but illegitimate means open and readily available.

How the deprived youth deals with his problems of blocked opportunity and unfulfilled aspirations depends upon what is available in his particular social setting. In an area where there is organized and professional crime, where adult criminals may serve as role models, and where youths aspire to the criminal role, a "criminal subculture" may develop around stealing. In a disorganized area where there is no tradition of professional or organized crime and where there are few skilled criminals available for emulation, a "conflict subculture" may develop around violence and fighting. Lastly, individuals who can adopt neither of these behavioral patterns because of moral prohibitions, because the subcultures are not available to them, or because they have already failed in the delinquent role, may form a "retreatist subculture" which focuses on the use of drugs and alcohol. In short, Cloward and Ohlin believe that the type of delinquent subculture that will develop is dependent upon the opportunities available in the neighborhood.

Although many attempts to explain the etiology of delinquency appear to link it almost inextricably with economic deprivation, one must not assume that it is solely a lower-class form of adaptation. Indeed, several studies indicate that delinquency rates are not directly correlated with social class.[17] Middle-class delinquency bears witness to the fact that economic deprivation is not the only condition giving rise to delinquency. A more realistic view is to see it as one among many sources of a feeling of deprivation which is likely to give rise to a strain that may be "handled" by the individual in a socially deviant fashion. More specifically, when one believes he cannot achieve his legitimate goals or satisfactions within conventional structures for whatever reason, he is likely to become estranged from these structures, or at least uninvolved in them. Antipathy or ambivalence towards socially acceptable modes of achieving personal satisfactions may occur in any social class as youths differentially define their status and opportunities.

If one defines conventional opportunity structures as inoperative, a likely alternative is to turn to similar individuals to work out sources of satisfaction. Cutting himself adrift from conformist structures and developing new associations in which his perceptions of status and opportunity are shared and reinforced are very likely to lead the individual to deviant methods of problem solving. In many cases, these deviant behavior patterns are also likely to be defined by conformists as delinquent or criminal.

Once a youth becomes involved with a delinquent group, a process of labeling usually ensues.[18] That is, official and unofficial responses to his behavior tend to cut him off even further from conventional groups and force him to rely to a greater extent upon delinquent groups. This is especially true when official legal agencies label a youth as delinquent. Thereafter, he is clearly categorized in the minds of others and they now respond to him in terms of this new designation. Family members, neighbors, peers, teachers and certainly police and court personnel begin to react to him in a way that reinforces his initial attraction to delinquent behavior and groups. Not only is the community's reaction often an important factor in pushing one towards more extensive delinquency involvement, but it also serves to sustain delinquent groups and their culture. As Kitsuse and Dietrick have indicated, ". . . the delinquent subculture persists because, once established, it creates for those who participate in it, the very problems which were the bases for its emergence."[19]

The sociological theories of crime and delinquency which have been reviewed here emphasize the role of the social structure in the development of deviant behavior. Rather than stressing individual abnormality or faulty personality development, these theories have seen etiological factors lying outside the individual, in the social milieu which engulfs him. Environmental factors serve as pressures on the individual which he is not able to handle adequately. An illegal response is merely one way of adjusting to the structural

problems that impinge upon the person. This response, like all other responses, is learned. It is learned by interacting with others who are sophisticated in criminal techniques and who can pass their knowledge on to new-
comers.

Admittedly, these theories of juvenile delinquency and adult crime have
shortcomings. Among others, questions have been raised regarding the inability of such theoretical statements to account for the differential response of individuals to the problems of the social structure. Most sociological theories have failed to explain the lack of a one-to-one relationship
between structural disequilibrium and law-violating behavior. The ideas of
differential association, delinquent subculture, lack of legitimate opportunity, and others do not account for individuals who experience these pressures but do not become delinquent and criminal. Even in the worst slum
or the highest delinquency area, many—probably most—do not consistently
violate the law and do conform reasonably well to the social norms. There
are "good" boys in high delinquency areas, boys who do not associate with
delinquents, who may recognize the limitations of their social system but do
not invert conventional values and still have high aspirations.[20] Theories
that attempt to link the social structure to a particular type of behavioral
response cannot explain this phenomenon.

THE SELF FACTOR

In order to explain why some of those who experience adverse social conditions do not participate in norm violating behavior as well as why some do,
it appears necessary to introduce a variable that will permit linkage between
the social structure and individual behavior. This is the social psychological
factor of self-concept. Self-concept theory, in general, implies that primary
determinants of behavior are self and other concepts that the individual has
internalized. The individual's concept of himself is a feedback of the way significant others regard him. This interpretation of how others see him and
the resulting self-concept determine the person's reaction to life situations.

A number of research studies and general statements in criminology have
used a widely based self theory to explain delinquent and criminal behavior.[21] One of the most recent statements of self theory, however, has
been put forth by Walter C. Reckless.[22] Reckless' "containment theory"
specifies an inner control system and an outer control system. These systems
may work alone or together so that the individual either overcomes the forces

conducive to delinquency or falls victim to them. The outer control system refers to the individual's social world, the external social structure designed to guide his behavior in a socially approved manner. Inner controls, on the other hand, consist mainly of self components which provide an internal buffer protecting against deviation. These two control systems should form a solid, united front against the adversities and pressures of the environment.

In industrial societies, external containment resides primarily in the family and other groups in which the person participates. When the outer controls are adequate, they will contain the individual and prevent deviation. When they are inadequate, and structural supports cannot contain the individual, the inner control system must serve to hold the person in line. Its ability to do this is dependent upon the presence of either a good or poor self-concept.

> A good self-concept is assumed to represent a favorable internalization of presumably favorable life experiences, including an acceptance or incorporation of the proper concern which significant others have had for the person. It acts selectively on experience and holds the line against adversities (pressures), the subculture of delinquency, wrong-doing, and crime (pull), as well as discontent and frustrations (pushes). The poor self-concept is a residue of less favorable growth, the acceptance of less concern or a different concern (value-wise) of significant others. Because of unique experience and the uniqueness of individuals, it is possible for the person not to incorporate or internalize favorable exposures in the socialization process, and it is possible for the individual to reject unfavorable exposures and to incorporate better models of self. Both good and poor self-concept are normal products and are within normal range of childhood, adolescent, and adult development.[23]

According to Reckless, the direction of socialization and the resulting good or bad concept of self are the chief factors responsible for one's insulation against deviancy or his involvement in unlawful behavior. This is especially true in those areas characterized by great social disorganization. Here the outer controls on the person's behavior are weak, if they have not completely broken down, and the direction of his actions will be dependent upon his self image. But, as mentioned, the self-concept is a composite of interactive experience, so chances for developing a good self are much less in a bad environment than they would be in an adequate social environment. In spite of this, most lower-class boys socialized by lower-class parents in lower-class neighbor-hoods are able to develop a self-concept that is strong enough to protect them from norm violating behavior.[24]

The two containing systems (or lack of them) are not seen as causes of juvenile delinquency.[25] The "causes" or contributing factors may be delin-quent companions, status frustration, differential opportunity, exposure to the delinquent subculture or anything else that has been suggested. The con-taining systems serve as the individual's insulation or protection against those forces that might influence him towards delinquency. When they are weak, the person is vulnerable and might succumb. When they are strong, he is likely to remain law-abiding despite the environmental pressures.

In American society, and particularly among the urban lower class, the effectiveness of external social structural controls seems to be diminishing. Hence, greater responsibility is placed on internal or self controls as deter-minants of behavior. A good self-concept is usually strong enough to prevent delinquency even when external controls are weak. A poor self-concept cannot contain the individual under such circumstances. This is not to say that a poor self-concept is a gross lack of development of personal controls. Instead it should be seen as a normal lack of inner controls that has potential for posi-tive change if and when the individual favorably internalizes the right kind of experiences later in life.

For the most part, crime and delinquency result from the interplay be-tween environmental and personal factors. Certain environmental conditions, part of a syndrome of general disorganization, serve as strains and pressures upon the individuals who experience them. Some individuals are able to over-come these environmental pressures and identify with non-deviant norms and expectations. Others simply reconcile themselves to their status position and lead fairly law-abiding, but perhaps somewhat marginal, lives. Others, how-ever, are not able to identify with societal norms and expectations and are also not able to reconcile themselves to their status position. This group often turns to criminal or delinquent behavior as a legitimate alternative for handling environmentally induced strain. One's self-concept, the product of a wide variety of socialization experiences, differentiates these groups and determines how one will respond.

SMALL GROUP TREATMENT

Once the individual has made the criminal or delinquency commitment and becomes officially labelled, we refer to intervention attempts as "rehabilitation." Officially adjudicated criminals and delinquents are usually committed by a court to participate in some type of rehabilitative effort. Until recently, this has generally amounted to little more than incarceration. The traditional reformatory, irrespective of any therapeutic attempts within its walls, has failed to bring about the desired behavioral change. The mortification of the individual, stripping him of human dignity,[26] and the anti-administration and anti-rehabilitation attitudes that develop within the inmate subculture of total correctional institutions, severely inhibit rehabilitation and confine staff activity largely to security and custodial functions.[27] Hence, many alternatives to total incarceration have recently been developed.

One of the most significant alternatives to traditional incarceration has been the growth of small group programs, both in and out of the community. The use of the small group as a therapeutic tool is of uncertain origin, although most historians of this practice agree that its great proliferation and general acceptance have occurred rather recently.[28] Used initially in the early decades of the twentieth century with the physically and mentally ill, group techniques of rehabilitation and therapy were quickly adopted in other areas where behavioral change was desirable. Hence, at the present time, various forms of group interaction have been used in attempts to modify the behavior of mental patients, convicts, delinquents, probationers, discordant marriage partners, cigarette smokers, drug users, compulsive drinkers, unwed mothers, overeaters and alienated youth.

Known by various names (group therapy, group psychotherapy, encounter groups, guided group interaction), group treatment is a method in which patients or subjects are treated in small, homogeneous aggregates. Here, however, is where the similarity among the various forms of group treatment seems to end. Most of the approaches invoking the label "group" can be divided into two general categories: group psychotherapy and group therapy.[29] The former refers basically to individual therapy carried on in a group setting, where several persons can obtain psychotherapy at one time, and the group is regarded essentially as a convenient context of treatment. The latter category, on the other hand, implies that the group itself constitutes an important element in the therapeutic process, serving as both the means and the context of treatment. The group is generally composed of persons with similar problems who are not held to ordinary standards of interaction. The subject is encouraged to express himself freely and to share with the group his most intimate experiences, fears and anxieties while at the same time being protected from traditional authority. In addition, this form of therapeutic interaction helps eliminate the constraints imposed by fixed patterns of expected behavior.

The group therapy approach to inducing behavioral change is based largely upon a sociological explanation of deviancy. If deviant behavior is social in nature, it can be changed only when the deviate's relations with social groups are changed, since it was his group identifications which determined his attitudes, values, self-concept, and behavior. To a decisive degree, the group has been as responsible for determining the deviate's non-conformity as it has the non-deviate's conformity. Both behave as they do because of their group associations. Both share the attitudes and values of their reference groups.

Primarily because of this group orientation to the social processes involved in personality development, it is assumed that many of the deviate's socially unacceptable qualities can be modified or changed as a result of his participation in small groups designed to provide him with new learning experiences.[30] Thus, whether the social deviate changes or not will be greatly influenced by his group associations. He must disassociate himself from the deviancy-inducing groups and assume new groups with whom to identify, or the groups with whom he now identifies must be changed into conforming groups.

Cartwright feels that it is valuable to view the group process of change in at least three different ways.[31] (1) The group may be used as a "medium of change" if it acts to influence the member's behavior by offering him support for it or by blocking it. (2) The group may become the "target of change" by changing its very nature (standards, leadership, emotional atmosphere, stratification) and thereby changing the individual. (3) Groups may be seen as "agents of change" if they utilize organized efforts to bring about individual change.

Cressey, adapting the view of the group as a "medium of change" (statements one through five below) and as "a target of change" (statement six), has developed a set of principles underlying group therapy with criminals:[32]

1. If criminals are to be changed, they must be assimilated into groups which emphasize values conducive to law-abiding behavior and, concurrently, alienated from groups emphasizing values conducive to criminality. Since our experience has been that the majority of criminals experience great difficulty in securing intimate contacts in ordinary groups, special groups whose major common goal is the reformation of criminals must be created.

2. The more relevant the common purpose of the group to the reformation of criminals, the greater will be its influence on the criminal members' attitudes and values. Just as a labor union

exerts strong influence over its members' attitudes toward management but less influence on their attitudes toward say, Negroes, so a group organized for recreational or welfare purposes will have less success in influencing criminalistic attitudes and values than will one whose explicit purpose is to change criminals.

3. The more cohesive the group the greater the members' readiness to influence others and the more relevant the problem of conformity to group norms. The criminals who are to be reformed and the persons expected to effect the change must, then, have a strong sense of belonging to one group: between them there must be a genuine "we" feeling. The reformers, consequently, should not be identifiable as correctional workers, probation or parole officers, or social workers.

4. Both reformers and those to be reformed must achieve status within the group by exhibition of "pro-reform" or anticriminal values and behavior patterns. As a novitiate, the one to be reformed is likely to assign status according to social position outside the group, and part of the reformation process consists of influencing him both to assign and to achieve status on the basis of behavior patterns relevant to reformation. If he should assign status solely on the basis of social position in the community, he is likely to be influenced only slightly by the group. Even if he becomes better adjusted, socially and psychologically, by association with members having high status in the community, he is a therapeutic parasite and not actually a member until he accepts the group's own system for assigning status.

5. The most effective mechanism for exerting group pressure on members will be found in groups so organized that criminals are induced to join with non-criminals for the purpose of changing other criminals. A group in which criminal A joins with some noncriminals to change criminal B is probably most effective in changing criminal A, not B; in order to change criminal B, criminal A must necessarily share the values of the anticriminal members.

6. When an entire group is the target of change, as in prison or among delinquent gangs, strong pressure for change can be

achieved by convincing the members of the need for a change,
thus making the group itself the source of pressure for change.
Rather than inducing criminals to become members of pre-
established anticriminal groups, the problem here is to change
anti-reform and pro-criminal subcultures, so that group leaders
evolve from among those who show the most marked hospital-
ity to anticriminal values, attitudes, and behavior. . . . If the
subculture is not changed, the person to be reformed is likely
to exhibit two sets of attitudes and behaviors, one characteristic
of the agency or person trying to change him, the other of the
subculture.

These and similar principles[33] of rehabilitative change underlie group therapy techniques used with many types of deviates. Although these techniques
may not always be formally known as "group therapy," they share the common format of free and informal discussion among peers, where shared problems are analyzed and solutions evaluated.

GROUP TREATMENT IN CORRECTIONS

Group treatment was first used systematically in correctional settings
during World War II when the pressing need for allaying the problems of military offenders with a small therapeutic staff made this the only practicable
solution. However, rather than use the group as a therapeutic tool, group
therapists continued to practice psychotherapy with individuals in small aggregates. Abrahams and McCorkle[34] have described the rehabilitation programs
carried on at Fort Knox, Kentucky, perhaps the most serious early attempt to
use group treatment with adult criminal offenders.

At Fort Knox, the men were assigned to one of four large groups: (1)
aggressive; (2) depressed and withdrawn; (3) the normal; and (4) the introductory.[35] Each man was also assigned to one of twelve smaller subgroups in
order to facilitate greater interactive participation. The inmate met with one
of the two groups to which he belonged for one hour daily, on alternate days,
six days a week. In addition to participating in the group sessions, each inmate
engaged in activities comparable to the regular basic training course for new
recruits. While in the introductory phase of the program, or "pre-honor" company, the inmates spent half a day in hard labor as well.

All these activities were calculated to produce, insofar as was possible during
the war, an environment which would ". . . give the rehabilitee a 'total push'

toward maturation and reorientation."[36] Although principles of psychoanalysis were utilized in the group sessions, the program's focus was preparing the prisoners for restoration to Army life. This made it most expedient to try to utilize the force of the peer group to hasten the rehabilitation process. Using the peer group as a change agent, inmates were helped in handling real-life problems of adjustment and in functioning more appropriately in a social setting. This unique program, mixing individual therapy in a group context with utilization of the group as a means of change, helped launch a variety of group approaches in corrections.

Civilian therapists in correctional settings now began turning their efforts to group techniques. The composition and methods of the groups varied widely, but all seemed to be characterized to some extent by the influence of individual psychotherapy. Slavson has described a group of adolescent girls in a co-educational, residential training school.[37] After reporting the content of this group's first session, he "interprets" the actions and conversation of the girls and the therapist in a traditionally psychoanalytic manner. This interpretation begins with a diagnosis of each individual girl's problems, is followed by an analysis of each segment of their behavior in the group, and concludes with his placing these activities into the appropriate diagnostic framework. The following excerpt from this interpretation may serve to illustrate how the early use of group techniques in corrections was little more than individual psychotherapy in a group setting:

> If we analyzed further the girls' attitude toward the school we may find that the hostility is similar in every respect to the hostility that patients have toward their mothers. . . . Thus the school becomes the mother figure. . . . Rhoda gets what she wants. She acts out her Oedipal conflict in relation to the school. She sees her boyfriend despite the rules. Marian confirms our suspicion that her impersonal questions concerning girls who are not attractive but are chosen by boys are related to herself. Marian admits that she has no boyfriend. She again defends the staff because of her fear of aggression. When the worker very advisedly asks the meaning of their belligerancy, the girls come through with their nuclear problem, namely their relation to their fathers, but in this instance, the father substitute is the director of the school. He is seen by them as the father figure, as the school is the mother figure.[38]

In the period following World War II, the appeal of group techniques for inducing behavioral change began to spread and several reports described attempts at group treatment with different kinds of inmates in numerous correctional settings. Illing, for example, described an experimental group of adult, male, hardened criminals set in an "Honor Farm" in California.[39] The experiment was suggested by the meetings held by the chaplain which seemed to have a definite therapeutic value. Since this group met rather infrequently and for a relatively short period, little in the way of intensive therapy was accomplished, although Illing believed it had some positive effect on the subsequent criminal careers of the men involved.

Taylor has outlined a seemingly successful experiment with New Zealand prisoners.[40] The therapist had previously attempted to institute group treatment in the prison program with two separate groups. According to Taylor, these groups failed because they were artificially comprised rather than containing members of naturally evolved groupings in the institution.[41] The group he describes, however, consisted of eight security risks who had been transferred to the institution from other prisons just prior to the formation of the group and who had many characteristics in common. After passing through "aggressive" and "defensive" stages, the group members settled down to discussing their problems seriously. Only when a new member was introduced into the group or when a member of the group was in trouble with the institutional officials, did the members revert briefly to behavior typical of the earlier stages.

Although Taylor cites case material to support his contention that participants in the group were greatly improved, he does not provide any relevant systematic evidence of behavioral change. In like manner, he asserts that he has taken the social system and the values of the inmate population into consideration in structuring the treatment program, but he does not deal with these issues specifically, nor does he point out what effect such consideration had on the program.

Shellow, Ward and Rubenfeld have also discussed their problems in attempting group treatment with juvenile delinquents in the National Training School for Boys.[42] They suggest that, in an institution, group programs must be "tailor-made" to the problems related to setting up a therapy program in a custody oriented setting.[43] These problems and others implied in the literature[44] suggest that perhaps group treatment would enjoy greater efficacy if the institution in which it were being practiced were "tailor-made" to the needs of the therapy. In most reformatories for juvenile or adult offenders, as in the National Training School, the group programs have played only a minor role in the inmate's life in the institution.

Without question, the most systematic use of group techniques of rehabilitation in the area of corrections has been made by the state of New Jersey. Under the leadership of F. Lovell Bixley and Lloyd W. McCorkle, two of the early advocates of group therapy in the Fort Knox Rehabilitation Center, New Jersey, inaugurated group therapy programs in its correctional institutions in the late 1940s. The New Jersey Department of Institutions and Agencies decided to name its version of the group technique "guided group interaction" in order to "avoid confusion with the use of group psychotherapy as practiced by psychiatrists, and to avoid any implication that all inmates are mentally abnormal and unbalanced."[45] Guided group interaction has been defined as "using free discussion in a friendly, supportive atmosphere to reeducate the delinquent to accept the restrictions of society by finding greater personal satisfaction in conforming to social rules than by following delinquent patterns."[46] It is a form of group therapy in which the anti-criminal attitudes of the group are internalized by the delinquent as a result of the group's influence upon him. In guided group interaction, the major emphasis is on the group and its development as a rehabilitative agent. Since their early application in New Jersey, the principles of guided group interaction have spread to both residential and community correctional programs in the United States and abroad.[47]

In an attempt to make a clearer distinction between guided group interaction and other forms of group therapy, McCorkle distinguishes among the analytic, didactic, and repression-inspirational techniques of group treatment.[48] McCorkle claims that analytical therapists intuitively interpret material presented in the "free association" of the members of the group. The aim of this interpretation is to urge the patients to consciously recognize and analyze their repressed, asocial desires, and then find suitable outlets for the energy which had heretofore been bound in needless repression.

Didactic therapy refers to a situation in which the therapist lectures a group on the kinds of behavior which are defined as acceptable in the social world to which the patients will shortly return. This approach ideally leads to the patient's developing greater insight into his problems, at least on a superficial level. A good example of this technique in reformatories and prisons is the "parole class" given by the institutional parole officer to inmates who will be released within a short time. Such a situation is considered successful if the parolees are released with a good verbal understanding of the rules of parole and the kinds of behavior which constitute violations of these rules.

Both analytic and didactic therapy are examples of what Moreno has called "therapist centered methods."[49] In these situations, the therapist deals with the problems of individual patients in a group setting, but he does not utilize the members of the group to help one another. In contrast, repressive-inspirational techniques are strongly "group-centered methods." Each member of the group is a potential therapeutic agent for every other member by virtue of the incisive comments he makes in the context of spontaneous group discussion.

Repressive-inspirational types of group therapy use the emotionalism generated in a group with a "cause." This emotionally charged atmosphere is focused upon redirecting the inner tensions of the individual members of the group. The group member is urged to forget his worries and find an inspiration in some other aspect of life; frequently this inspiration takes the form of proselytizing others into the "miracle" group. Such an attitude reflects, as a matter of fact, an extremely important phase in the treatment process; it signifies the patient's acceptance of the group's values. Later, of course, the member must find a more conventional focus of attention in order to support himself. Another important source of inspiration may be the group's "heroes," those past or present group members who can be held up as examples worthy of emulation for the newest members of the group.

McCorkle claims that guided group interaction is a modification of analytic group therapy.[50] The modifications, however, are quite significant. In guided group interaction, the role of the therapist is considerably less important than in the analytical group, and the group member is urged to interpret material for himself. In addition, the group assumes an important new dimension by providing the member with new learning experiences and opportunities to acquire insight into shared problems. Individual members are expected to help others conform, because such help is regarded as an effective mechanism for inducing change in the member himself, as well as demonstrating the change he has already achieved. In many ways, guided group interaction seems to be a modification of the repressive-inspirational type of group therapy as well as the analytic type. A fundamental modification is based on the assumption that the participants in these programs are psychologically normal and that the search for the etiology of their deviance properly begins with an analysis of the social environment which supplied the context for this behavior.

GOALS OF GROUP PROGRAMS

The primary objective of any program of rehabilitation is to restore the individual to a presumed prior level of competence or well being. This is as true for social rehabilitation programs as for programs of physical and emotional rehabilitation. In the case of programs designed to rehabilitate criminals and delinquents, the primary goal is to bring about changes, internal or external to the individual, which will mitigate against future law-violating behavior. To achieve this ultimate objective, a rehabilitation program must first achieve certain instrumental objectives, which may be seen as the necessary hurdles to be overcome in order to deter criminal and delinquent behavior. When these objectives have been achieved, it is assumed that the ultimate goal of preventing future law-violating behavior among the program participants will have been achieved. At least two sets of instrumental objectives or goals have been postulated for programs of guided group interaction.

In their book *The Highfields Story,* McCorkle, Elias and Bixby equate deterring future delinquency among participants in the guided group interaction program with modifying the delinquent's self-concept.[51] In their estimation, the delinquent's behavioral problems stem largely from his conception of self as a hostile, aggressive, inadequate person. When this self-concept is modified, the boy is less likely to engage in non-conforming behavior. Therefore, the objectives of the program[52] must work towards such modification of the participant's self-concept.

1. The delinquent boy must be made to feel that he can work up to conforming and acceptable behavior, and that he is not expected to adopt new standards immediately. The total situation must be designed to make the individual boy feel that he can be accepted and understood as he is. He must feel that the program is designed to help him during a troubled period in his life. To expect immediate and sudden change in behavior, values and attitudes is to alienate the confused and bitter delinquent further.

2. Situations must be developed which give the boy an opportunity to choose among several alternative behaviors and then to discuss the choices he makes. Because the boy will have to choose between alternative actions once he returns to the community, the rehabilitation program should provide him with experience in making independent choices. However, the program must also provide him with an opportunity to discuss his choices with other program participants so that both criticism and reinforcement will come from his peers and not supervising adults.

3. The rehabilitative atmosphere must be flexible enough to permit individual development, and structured enough to be supportive. There must not be excessive rules and regulations, and those that do exist should not become fixed. The boys in the program should be permitted to work out their own rules and regulations that go beyond the simple maintenance of order. By

permitting such latitude, rules will be flexible enough to change as situations change, and those rules which do exist will have greater meaning.

4. The delinquent must be assisted in understanding that his problems are a result of his own motives, values and attitudes, and he must be encouraged to change these personal factors. In other words, the boy must come to understand that his problems lie within himself and not in the environment. He must stop projecting blame and be assisted in gaining insight into his problems and changing himself.

5. The program participant must have opportunities to learn and to test new modes of human interaction. The entire program should be structured so as to provide such opportunities. As new interactive patterns emerge and are found to be satisfactory and rewarding, they will replace the old patterns which led to delinquent behavior.

These instrumental objectives may also be seen as conditions of optimum program effectiveness. If a guided group interaction program is able to guarantee the full implementation of these conditions, the primary goal of deterring future delinquency will be achieved. Although McCorkle, Elias and Bixby do not always specify just how some of these program objectives or conditions will lead to individual reformation, Donald R. Cressey attempts to do just that by analyzing McCorkle's definition of guided group interaction.[53] Cressey points out that guided group interaction is assumed to bring about individual reformation by having the delinquent get beneath the surface of his problems, acquire insight, accept the general restrictions of society, and gain experience as a law-abiding person. Although Cressey specifically refers to these as "four principal expectations about the processes by which the group sessions contribute to individual reformation,"[54] they too can be viewed as instrumental objectives of the guided group interaction program.

"Getting beneath the surface."–Through the use of guided group interaction, it is expected that the group participant will be better able to delve into his problems and "face the facts" of his case. This process is necessary for any type of meaningful rehabilitation to prevent the offender's rationalizing his problems away and blaming extraneous elements for his predicament. He must reject his own superficial "justifications" for his criminal behavior and realize that the roots of his problems may well lie beneath the surface where he cannot recognize them. In the guided group interaction program, this goal is thought to be achieved because fellow inmates who have had similar experiences and hardships help the offender get beneath the surface.

"Acquiring insight."–According to Cressey's analysis of guided group interaction, the second expectation or objective of the program is for the inmate to acquire insight into his problems and behavior. To Cressey, this means that the inmate is able to identify his problems in the psychological terminology of the group therapist. If the opportunity to ventilate is provided along with this insight, the inmate will reform. Cressey states it this way:

> This is obviously in keeping with the hypothesis, based on the individualization principle, that if a delinquent or criminal becomes convinced that his criminality is due to such attitudes or conditions as "feelings of weakness," "resentment of authority," "feelings of guilt," or "frustration," and is then able, through ventilation to dissipate the "tensions" and "anxieties" arising from these undesirable atittudes, he will be reformed.[55]

"**Accepting general restrictions of society.**"–Thirdly, it is expected that by conforming to and accepting the rules and regulations of the inmate group, the offender will gain experience in accepting the restrictions of the larger society. The offender is primarily an ego-centered person who does not think in terms of the group or "society." However, this individualistic orientation is attacked and broken down by the therapists and fellow inmates in the group sessions. This, though, is not enough. Once the old crime-supporting values, motives and rationalizations have broken down, they must be replaced with new ones which support law-abiding behavior. It is the objective, then, of the guided group interaction program to acquaint the inmate with the attitudes and values of those social groups which conform to the law, and to help him integrate these new values and attitudes into his personality.

"**Gaining experience as a law-abiding person.**"–The fourth expectation of guided group interaction is to provide participants with an opportunity to practice and to gain experience with the new values, attitudes, and rationalizations they have incorporated into their personalities. According to Cressey, "It is expected that each participant in the group sessions gains experiences in the role of a law-abiding person and that this experience will carry over to the life outside the session. . . ."[56] This experience as a law-abiding person is gained not as a reformee but as a reformer. That is, the inmate gains this type of experience when he attempts to help his fellow inmates to reform, when he condemns their law-violating behavior, and when he identifies with anticriminal groups. The guided group interaction program, in providing for the inmate reformer role in its very structure, is thereby giving the group participant an opportunity to gain experience as a law-abiding person.

On the basis of an intensive study of the guided group interaction technique of rehabilitating delinquent boys, the authors have independently concluded that there are four instrumental goals or objectives that must be achieved in order to deter future law violation.[57] These instrumental goals contain elements of both McCorkle, Elias, and Bixby's objectives of guided group interaction and Cressey's expectations of guided group interaction, and represent an attempt to explicitly identify the goals toward which a group interaction program must work in order to rehabilitate the socialized delinquent. In other words, it is our contention that resocializing the criminal or delinquent in a group treatment setting will be enhanced if the program is able to achieve the following instrumental objectives: pierce and undermine the delinquent's defensive attitudes toward delinquency, change the delinquent's attitudes toward conventional behavior, change the delinquent's self-concept, and teach the delinquent to accept and practice alternative, conventional ways of behavior.

The first objective of the guided group interaction program must be to pierce and to undermine the delinquent's defensive attitudes toward delinquency. The delinquent is usually immune to rehabilitative efforts because he has insulated himself with attitudes and rationalizations that prevent his accepting new behavior patterns. These pro-criminal attitudes and rationalizations permit the delinquent to justify his behavior and make it personally acceptable. As Sykes and Matza have pointed out, ". . . much delinquency is based on what is essentially an unrecognized extension of defenses to crimes, in the form of justifications for deviance that are seen as valid by the delinquent but not by the legal system or society at large."[58]

Delinquents characteristically rationalize and attempt to justify their deviant behavior. They often construct an elaborate system of defenses that protects them from the castigation of conventional society. These defenses carry over into the delinquent's involvement in the guided group interaction treatment program and thereby constitute a barrier that must be overcome. Hence, it is necessary for any meaningful rehabilitation program to break through and to undermine this defense. Of course, there are certain conditions that make this goal easier to achieve, the most important of which is the delinquent's breaking his identity with delinquent groups and their culture. When this occurs, he is much more susceptible to having his defensive attitudes toward delinquency broken down. This in turn is facilitated by his developing an awareness of group pressures. Once he becomes aware of the new treatment group's depreciation of delinquent behavior and delinquent friends, the delinquent will begin to develop an ambivalence and anxiety about his past delinquent behavior. These feelings are a result of the social pressure of the new group. The delinquent is likely to reject his former delinquent reference group, and in its place accept the new conforming peer group. This, of course, facilitates the process of piercing and undermining defensive attitudes toward delinquency.

The second objective of the guided group interaction program must be to change the delinquent's attitudes towards conventional behavior. By the time the average delinquent enters a rehabilitation program, he has undergone many years of socialization into the delinquent subculture. This socialization process may well have started while he was in elementary school and was carried on by peers who were very significant in his young life. It probably resulted in his learning a set of attitudes and values quite contrary to the attitudes and values of the conforming society. One important aspect of this subculture is the disparagement of conventional behavior. This behavior is left for the "squares" and contrary behavior is prestigious and rewarding.

Perhaps this is the result of the delinquent's search for excitement and thrills. At least one observer has noted that this need for excitement is not easily satisfied by legitimate means.[59] Conventional activities are seen as dull and boring and do not satisfy the delinquent. On the other hand, breaking the law is viewed as exciting and appears to satisfy his desire for thrills and adventure. In addition to satisfying this apparent need, unlawful behavior may also be prestigious, proving to the peer group that the boy is courageous and has "heart." He enhances his image in their eyes, showing them that he is one of them and shares their values and attitudes. In addition, he may even get psychic satisfaction out of breaking the laws of a society in which he feels he has no place and to which he feels no commitment. The lower-class boy, cut off from legitimate opportunities and beset by status frustration, is very likely to regard conventional behavior as unrewarding. Meaningful resocialization presupposes the changing of this attitude and the boy's learning that conventional behavior can be just as rewarding as deviant behavior.

This goal, too, can be achieved only when certain other conditions are realized. When the delinquent breaks his identity with delinquent groups and their culture and develops ambivalence and anxiety regarding delinquency, changing his attitudes toward conventional behavior becomes a more realistic goal. But several other conditions must also be met before this goal can be achieved. It is necessary, for example, for the delinquent to broaden his perspective of others. That is to say, he must learn how his behavior is influenced by others and how his behavior influences others. He must learn to take into account the feelings, values, and motivations of other people. In addition, the delinquent must learn to inhibit his initial behavioral responses and extend his time perspective. He must learn to check immediate reactions and to postpone gratifications. When the guided group interaction program has brought about these necessary conditions, the goal of changing the delinquent's attitudes toward conventional behavior can be realized.

The third goal of the guided group interaction program is to change the delinquent's self-concept. The delinquent usually conceives of himself in a negative and self-defeating way. He sees himself as an inadequate, hostile, aggressive person who has had little success in his family relationships, in school, or in the conventional community. Not only does he have a negative image of himself, but he is certain that others see him in the same way. Some believe that the delinquent has grave doubts about his sex identity and therefore attempts to prove his masculinity by being "tough" and engaging in aggressive behavior.[60] In addition, he sees himself as being "smart," or able to dupe or outwit others. Other people outside of his own immediate peer group are seen by the delinquent as "wise-guys" or "suckers" who are to be taken advantage of and exploited whenever possible.

Such a self-image permits the boy to engage in delinquent behavior without questioning his own action. As a result of faulty socialization, the delinquent sees himself as a "bad" boy and has no qualms about acting like one. When doing so, he is merely conforming to his own conception of self and the conception of himself which he believes others have. If the self-concept is positively changed so that the individual has new expectations of himself, he will question and assess his potential behavior in light of these new self-expectations and his new self-concept. A new, positive self-concept will act as an internalized policeman, sanctioning some behavior but, more importantly, forbidding other behavior.

Many of the conditions which are necessary to achieve the first two goals are also necessary to achieve this goal. For example, the delinquent's broadening his perspective of others, developing ambivalence and anxiety regarding delinquency, extending his time perspective, and breaking his identity with delinquent groups and their culture will all greatly facilitate his changing his self-concept. But, in addition, and perhaps more importantly, it is necessary for him to develop a sense of self-awareness, self-confidence, or self-reliance. For the delinquent who feels basically inadequate and attempts to cover this over with a facade of bravado, this appears to be absolutely necessary. However, this condition also involves the delinquent's becoming aware of the concept of self-determination or rational autonomy. To achieve the goal of a changed self-concept, the delinquent must first believe that his life events are not predetermined and that he is, to a large extent, the master of his own destiny.

The last instrumental objective or goal of the guided group interaction program must be to acquaint the delinquent with alternative conventional ways of behaving. In other words, he has to learn how to stay out of trouble. This is necessary because the delinquent has lived a good part of his life in an isolated setting where he has not had an opportunity to learn and practice conventional behavior. His delinquency has alienated him from such socializing structures as family, school, and work where socially accepted behavior is learned and practiced. Instead, his most meaningful interaction has taken place in the delinquent peer group where he has had little or no opportunity to learn socially accepted responses to many behavioral situations. Hence, the delinquent has not been acquainted with many conventional responses to recurring incidents in his life. Not only is it necessary, then, to change the boy's whole general attitude toward conventional behavior, but it is also imperative that conventional alternative responses be made known to him.

Again, certain conditions appear to be necessary in order to achieve this goal. The delinquent's learning to inhibit his initial behavioral responses, developing ambivalence and anxiety about delinquency, and extending his time perspective will facilitate the achievement of this goal as well as the others. However, along with acquainting the delinquent with alternative ways of behaving, it is also necessary to make the consequences of these alternatives known to him. It is not enough for him to know that alternatives exist. He must learn that there are potential ramifications and consequences of each alternative he is considering. When he possesses this knowledge, it is assumed that he will be in a better position to choose the conventional alternative.[61]

When the juvenile offender who is being resocialized internalizes law-abiding norms, values, and attitudes, learns conventional behavioral patterns, and develops a non-deviant self-image, changes in the personality have taken place which will function as internal controls over his behavior. However, these are not easy goals to achieve. Because the delinquent's personality, like everyone else's, is developed early in life, his ways of thinking and acting are deeply embedded. They can be unlearned, changed, modified, or altered only if the right techniques are discovered and implemented. Nevertheless, such change is the objective of most programs of rehabilitation.

In the chapters to follow, one unique group treatment program for delinquent boys, Essexfields, is analyzed in detail. The purpose of this analysis is to understand more fully the dynamics of a treatment program based upon group interaction and to demonstrate how such programs attempt to achieve the instrumental goals discussed above. From understanding this program, we shall better understand precisely how group interaction serves to influence behavioral change.

NOTES

1. Clifford R. Shaw and Henry D. McKay, *Juvenile Delinquency and Urban Areas* (Chicago: University of Chicago Press, 1942).

2. Clifford R. Shaw and Henry D. McKay, "Report on Social Factors in Juvenile Delinquency," *Report on the Causes of Crime,* Report No. 13, Volume II (Washington: Government Printing Office, 1937), p. 110.

3. Shaw and McKay, "Report on Social Factors."

4. Estimates of the size of the group of emotionally disturbed norm violators have varied greatly, but we are inclined to agree with Walter B. Miller that this group does not make up more than 25 per cent of the delinquent population. See: William C. Kvaraceus and Walter B. Miller, *Delinquent Behavior: Culture and the Individual* (Washington, D.C.: National Education Association, 1959), p. 54. Furthermore, it is clear that emotional disturbance exists among non-delinquents and that such a condition is not inevitably expressed in behavior that is officially labeled delinquent.

5. Shaw and McKay, *Juvenile Delinquency and Urban Areas,* p. 441.

6. Edwin H. Sutherland and Donald R. Cressey, *Criminology,* 8th ed. (Philadelphia: J. B. Lippincott Company, 1970), Chapter 4, "A Sociological Theory of Criminal Behavior."

7. Albert K. Cohen, *Delinquent Boys: The Culture of the Gang* (Glencoe: The Free Press, 1955).

8. William F. Whyte, *Street Corner Society: The Social Structure of an Italian Slum,* Enl. Ed. (Chicago: The University of Chicago Press, 1955).

9. Walter B. Miller, "Lower Class Culture as a Generating Milieu of Gang Delinquency," *Journal of Social Issues* 14 (1958): 5-19; and Kvaraceus and Miller, *Delinquent Behavior,* pp. 68-69.

10. Kvaraceus and Miller, *Delinquent Behavior,* pp. 68-69.

11. Kvaraceus and Miller, *Delinquent Behavior,* p. 72.

12. Gresham M. Sykes and David Matza, "Techniques of Neutralization: A Theory of Delinquency," *American Sociological Review* 22 (December 1957): 664-670.

13. Richard A. Cloward and Lloyd E. Ohlin, *Delinquency and Opportunity* (Glencoe: The Free Press, 1960).

14. Emile Durkheim, *Suicide,* trans. by John A. Spaulding and George Simpson (Glencoe: The Free Press, 1951), pp. 255-256.

15. Robert K. Merton, *Social Theory and Social Structure,* Rev. and Enl. ed. (Glencoe: The Free Press, 1957), Chapter 4.

16. Cloward and Ohlin, *Delinquency and Opportunity,* p. 86.

17. F. Ivan Nye, James F. Short and Virgil J. Olson, "Socioeconomic Status and Delinquent Behavior," *American Journal of Sociology* 63 (January 1958): 381-89; John P. Clark and Eugene Wenninger, "Socioeconomic Class and Area as Correlates of Illegal Behavior among Juveniles," *American Sociological Review* 27 (December 1962): 826-34.

18. Relevant works in the area of labeling process include: Frank Tannenbaum, *Crime and the Community* (New York: Columbia University Press, 1938); Edwin M. Lemert, *Social Pathology* (New York: McGraw-Hill Inc. 1951); Howard S. Becker, *Outsiders: Studies in the Sociology of Deviance* (New York: The Free Press, 1963); John I. Kitsuse, "Societal Reaction to Deviant Behavior: Problems of Theory and Method," in Howard S. Becker, ed., *The Other Side: Perspectives on Deviance* (New York: The Free Press, 1964), pp. 87-102; Earl Rubington and Martin S. Weinberg, editors, *Deviance: The Interactionist Perspective* (New York: The Macmillan Co., 1968); Irving Piliavin and Scott Briar, "Police Encounters with Juveniles," *American Journal of Sociology* 69 (September 1964): 206-14; and Edwin M. Shur, *Labeling Deviant Behavior* (New York: Harper and Row, 1971).

19. John I. Kitsuse and David C. Dietrick, "Delinquent Boys: A Critique," *American Sociological Review* 24 (April 1959): 215. For a detailed analysis of the consequences of labeling, see Edwin M. Lemert, *Human Deviance, Social Problems and Social Control* (Englewood Cliffs, N. J.: Prentice-Hall, Inc., 1967), Chapter 3, "The Concept of Secondary Deviation." Also see Lemert, second edition (1972), Chapter 1, for a critical evaluation of labeling theory.

20. The interesting study of the "good" boy in a high delinquency area made by Reckless and his associates indicates that certain boys in slum areas are able to "insulate" themselves from delinquency by identifying with middle-class culture and developing a non-delinquent self-concept. In fact, recent evidence indicates that lower-class delinquents may even accept conventional values and have high aspirations despite their social status and delinquent activity. See: Walter C. Reckless, Simon Dinitz, and Ellen Murray, "Self Concept as an Insulator Against Delinquency," *American Sociological Review* 21 (December 1956): 744-46; Robert A. Gordon, James F. Short, Jr., Desmond S. Cartwright, and Fred L. Strodtbeck, "Values and Gang Delinquency: A Study of Street-Corner Groups," *American Journal of Sociology* 69 (September 1963): 109-28; Martin Gold, *Status Forces in Delinquent Boys* (Ann Arbor: Institute for Social Research, University of Michigan, 1963).

21. See, for example, J. P. Shalloo, "Trends in Criminological Research," *Federal Probation* 6 (October–November 1942): 22; Daniel Glaser, "Criminality Theories and Behavioral Images," *American Journal of Sociology* (March 1956): 433-44; Donald R. Cressey, "The Differential Association Theory and Compulsive Crime," *Journal of Criminal Law, Criminology and Police Science* 45 (May-June 1954): 27-40; Albert J. Reiss, Jr., "Delinquency as the Failure of Personal and Social Controls," *American Sociological Review* 16 (April 1951): 196-207.

22. Walter C. Reckless, *The Crime Problem* (New York: Appleton-Century-Crofts, Inc., 1961), Chapter 18. Also, see Travis Hirshi, *Causes of Delinquency* (Berkeley: University of California Press, 1972) for an analysis of control theories of delinquency and a research designed to investigate this theoretical position.

23. Reckless, *The Crime Problem,* pp. 351-52.

24. Evidence supporting this contention can be found in the following: Reckless, Dinitz, and Murray, "Self Concept as an Insulator"; Frank R. Scarpitti, Ellen Murray, Simon Dinitz, and Walter C. Reckless, "The 'Good' Boy in a High Delinquency Area: Four Years Later," *American Sociological Review* 27 (August 1962): 515-17; Jon E. Simpson, Simon Dinitz, Barbara Kay, and Walter C. Reckless, "Delinquency Potential of Pre-

Adolescents in High-Delinquency Areas," *The British Journal of Delinquency* 10 (January 1960): 211-15.

25. Reckless sees his theory as a middle range explanation not applicable to delinquency at the extremes. At one extreme, it cannot explain those delinquencies committed due to an abnormally strong internal push resulting from an extreme neurosis or psychosis. At the other extreme, the containment theory cannot explain norm violating behavior that is a way of life or widely practiced activity. In between these two extremes there is a large middle range of delinquency where the violator is seen as a psychologically normal individual who deviates from socially accepted standards of behavior.

26. Erving Goffman, *Asylums* (New York: Doubleday and Co., 1961).

27. Donald Clemmer, *The Prison Community* (New York: Rinehart and Co., 1958); Donald R. Cressey (ed.), *The Prison: Studies in Institutional Organization and Change* (New York: Holt, Rinehart and Winston, 1961); Richard A. Cloward, *et al., Theoretical Studies in Social Organization of the Prison* (New York: Social Science Research Council, Pamphlet 15, 1960).

28. For a concise statement of the early history of group techniques, including an excellent bibliography, see Hugh Mullan and Max Rosenbaum *Group Psychotherapy: Theory and Practice* (New York: The Free Press, 1962), Chapter 1. The following are also of interest: Joseph H. Pratt, "The Clan Method of Treating Consumption in the Homes of the Poor," *Journal of the American Medical Association* 49 (August 31, 1907): 755-59; L. C. Marsh, "Group Therapy and the Psychiatric Clinic," *Journal of Nervous and Mental Disease* 82 (October 1935): 381-92; T. L. Burrow, *The Social Basis of Consciousness* (New York: Harcourt, Brace and World, 1927); J. L. Moreno and E. S. Whitin, *Application of the Group Method of Classification* (New York: National Commission on Prisons and Prison Labor, 1932); Samuel Slavson, *An Introduction to Group Therapy* (New York: Commonwealth Fund, 1943); Rudolf Dreikurs, "Early Experiments in Group Psychotherapy: A Historical Review," *American Journal of Psychotherapy* 13 (October 1959): 882-91.

29. Don C. Gibbons, *Changing the Lawbreaker* (Englewood Cliffs, N. J.: Prentice-Hall, Inc., 1965), pp. 143-88.

30. Dorwin Cartwright, "Achieving Change in People: Applications of Group Dynamics Theory," *Human Relations* 4 (1951): 381-92; Donald R. Cressey, "Contradictory Theories in Correctional Group Therapy Programs," *Federal Probation* 18 (June 1954): 20-26; Donald R. Cressey, "Changing Criminals: The Application of the Theory of Differential Association," *American Journal of Sociology* 61 (September 1955): 116-20.

31. Cartwright, "Achieving Change in People," p. 387.

32. Cressey, "Changing Criminals," pp. 118-19.

33. Cressey's six principles are based upon a set of eight principles of group therapy which are much more general in nature: see Cartwright, "Achieving Change in People," pp. 388-91.

34. J. Abrahams and L. W. McCorkle, "Group Psychotherapy of Military Offenders," *American Journal of Sociology* 51 (March 1946): 455-64.

35. Abrahams and McCorkle, "Military Offenders," p. 456.

36. Abrahams and McCorkle, "Military Offenders," p. 455.

37. S. R. Slavson, *Analytic Group Psychotherapy with Children, Adolescents and Adults* (New York: Columbia University Press, 1950).

38. Slavson, *Analytic Group Psychotherapy*, pp. 221-22.

39. Hans A. Illing, "The Prisoner in His Group," *International Journal of Group Psychotherapy* 1 (1951): 264-77.

40. A. J. W. Taylor, "A Therapeutic Group in Prison," *International Journal of Group Psychotherapy* 11 (1961): 180-87.

41. Taylor, "Therapeutic Group," p. 181.

42. Robert S. Shellow, Jack L. Ward and Seymour Rubenfeld, "A Group Therapy and the Institutionalized Delinquent," *International Journal of Group Psychotherapy* 8 (1958): 265-75.

43. Shellow, Ward, Rubenfeld, "Group Therapy and the Institutionalized Delinquent," p. 265.

44. See, for example, Charles Gersten, "An Experimental Evaluation of Group Therapy with Juvenile Delinquents," *International Journal of Group Psychotherapy* 1 (1951): 311-18; Kenneth Wollan, "Application of Group Therapy Principles to Institutional Treatment of Adolescents," *International Journal of Group Psychotherapy* 1 (1951): 356-64; Arthur I. Kassoff, "Advantages of Multiple Therapists in a Group of Severely Acting-Out Adolescent Boys," *International Journal of Group Psychotherapy* 8 (1958): 70-75.

45. Lloyd W. McCorkle, "Group Therapy" in Paul W. Tappan (ed.) *Contemporary Corrections* (New York: McGraw-Hill Book Co., 1951), p. 214.

46. Lloyd W. McCorkle, "Group Therapy in the Treatment of Offenders," *Federal Probation* 16 (December 1952): 23.

47. Donald D. Akman, Andre Normandau, and Marvin E. Wolfgang, "The Group Treatment Literature in Correctional Institutions: An International Bibliography, 1945-1967," *The Journal of Criminal Law, Criminology and Police Science*, 59 (1968): 41-56, gives vivid testimony to the use of various forms of group treatment in a variety of correctional programs.

48. McCorkle, "Group Therapy," pp. 211-12.

49. J. L. Moreno, "Scientific Foundation of Group Psychotherapy," *Sociometry* 8 (1945): 319.

50. McCorkle, "Group Therapy in the Treatment of Offenders," p. 23.

51. Lloyd W. McCorkle, Albert Elias and F. Lovell Bixby, *The Highfields Story* (New York: Henry Holt and Co., 1958), pp. 68-96.

52. McCorkle, Elias and Bixby, *Highfields Story*, pp. 70-72.

53. Cressey, "Contradictory Theories," pp. 22-23.

54. Cressey, "Contradictory Theories," p. 23.

55. Cressey, "Contradictory Theories."

56. Cressey, "Contradictory Theories," p. 24.

57. Frank R. Scarpitti and Richard M. Stephenson, "The Use of the Small Group in the Rehabilitation of Delinquents," *Federal Probation* 30 (September 1966): 45-50.

58. Sykes and Matza, "Techniques of Neutralization," p. 666.

59. Walter B. Miller, "Lower Class Culture as a Generating Milieu," pp. 10-11.

60. For example, see Miller, "Lower Class Culture," p. 9.

61. For a discussion of similar objectives and principles in a program designed to implement them see LaMar T. Empey and Jerome Rabow, "The Provo Experiment in Delinquency Rehabilitation," *The American Sociological Review*, 26 (October 1961): 679-695.

2

Essexfields: A Guided
Group Interaction Program

In 1951 the Highfields Group Rehabilitation Center in Hopewell, New Jersey, became the first civilian correctional institution specifically designed to include guided group interaction as a major part of its rehabilitative program.[1] Twenty sixteen and seventeen year old adjudicated male delinquents were brought together in a residential setting to live with the program director and his family, a sociological intern, and a set of cottage parents. During each week day, the boys worked at the New Jersey Neuro-Psychiatric Institute under the guidance of a work supervisor. Each evening, with the exception of Thursday and Saturday, the program participants attended one of two ninety-minute guided group interaction sessions led by the director or his assistant.

From the beginning, the innovative nature of Highfields led to program modifications not ordinarily found in traditional facilities for delinquents. Each boy, for example, was granted at least two furloughs of three to five days during his stay in the program regardless of his adjustment. He also received furloughs over the Christmas and Easter holidays if they occurred while he was at Highfields. He could have visitors from noon until seven on Sunday and was free to leave the grounds with them during that time. In an attempt to maintain community contacts, evening visits to the local community for recreation were permitted twice a week. Tradition was broken in many other ways, and a new format for inducing behavioral change was established.

The apparent success of the Highfields program[2] convinced New Jersey officials of its efficacy, and in the years that followed additional guided group interaction centers were created for both male and female delinquents. Like Highfields, they accommodated delinquents from around the state and were placed in rural settings away from the urban centers. By the end of the decade, however, the growing national popularity of various group methods of rehabilitation was joined by a new interest in community-based programs for the juvenile delinquent. The long-range rehabilitative consequences of allowing youngsters to remain in their home communities during treatment began to be discussed.

This new approach appeared to have many theoretical merits. If juvenile delinquency is an attempt to cope with environmental and group pressures and strains, the individual should learn how to handle these problems in a conformist manner in his natural setting, where they exist. Removing him from his community and placing him in a temporary institutional environment creates an artificial setting where his real-life situation can only be simulated at best. Participating in an intensive rehabilitation program while remaining in his real world should permit him to test his new learning immediately where it counts, and to seek ongoing assistance from the program as he confronts strain-producing problems. In addition, removing a youth from his home and family, even under the best of conditions, tends to alienate him from his parents, friends and community, and makes his eventual reintegration into these groups and institutions difficult. Stripping him of these interpersonal supports at a time of crisis in the young person's life may further his withdrawal from conventional activities. Finally, removal from the community and institutionalization has a profoundly negative impact upon the youth's definition of self and upon other's perceptions of him. Long after release, he is stigmatized in his own eyes as well as in the eyes of others. This condition cannot help but be a detriment to effective corrections.

These considerations, and perhaps implicitly an economic one, influenced the State of New Jersey to establish a group rehabilitation center in the heart of Newark, the state's largest city, in 1961. Patterned after Highfields and other group center programs, Essexfields (a name derived from the fact that it was located in Essex County and that it owed its programmatic origins to Highfields) differed from Highfields in one important respect: it was nonresidential. Boys committed to Essexfields returned to their homes every night and lived at home during the weekends.[3]

Albert Elias, long-time director of Highfields, and Saul Pilnick, director of Essexfields, tell how the program was started:

> In planning the Essexfields project, several important decisions
> were implemented. It was felt that a crucial and severe test of the

new program should be made. Therefore, the highest delinquency area in the state was selected as the site for the project.

Secondly, there appeared to be a need to utilize the services of a well-established juvenile court and probation department that had experience, over a period of time, with Highfields boys. Essex County was asked to participate as a result.

Thirdly, meetings and consultations were held with public officials, elected and appointed, in the county, to acquaint them with the project. About the same time, an advisory board of representative and prominent local citizens was appointed to secure broad-based community support.

In addition, arrangements were made for the boys in the program to work under the supervision of the County Shade Tree Commission which was based on the grounds of the County Mental Hospital. Moreover, two meals each day were to be provided by the hospital authorities.

Also, it was decided to initiate the project by selecting as the first admissions a small group of Highfields boys who had been sent there by the Essex County Juvenile Court. In this way, an attempt was made to insure the transmission of the Highfields culture to Essexfields. This procedure had been employed previously in establishing other residential group centers in the state. Moreover, the first director of Essexfields was selected and sent to Highfields for a short period of training. Finally, in April, 1961, the first boys were transported to Essexfields to get the program underway. Subsequently, no more transfers were made, and cases were admitted which were sent by the Juvenile Court directly.[4]

The Essexfields program was located in an old private residence in a relatively high delinquency area in Newark. At various times, several members of the staff and their families maintained apartments on the second and third floors of the building. The first floor, composed of four rooms and a lavatory, was used for office space and the group meetings. A large basement and one room on the first floor were used for recreational purposes and informal meetings. A small back yard was also available for recreation.

RESIDENTS AND STAFF

Only twenty boys, ages 16 and 17, participated in the Essexfields program at one time. Each boy had been referred by a single juvenile court (Essex

County) and participated as a condition of his probation. At his court hearing, the delinquent was told by the judge that he was being placed on probation with the condition that he attend and participate fully in the Essexfields program. He was not given much choice, since his failure to agree to these conditions would usually mean that he would be sent to a state reformatory. In addition, criteria for admission excluded the severely emotionally disturbed or retarded, overt homosexuals, and those who had previous institutional experience. Essexfields also attempted to restrict admission to those boys who have come to be known in the sociological and psychological literature as "socialized" or "adaptive" delinquents.[5] It was thought that the boy whose participation in delinquent activities is usually accompanied by peer group affiliations and who is responding in a typical sub-cultural way is a better candidate for group treatment than is the "lone-wolf," whose deviance may well be symptomatic of a psychological compulsion. Although the length of participation in the program was indeterminate, most boys were released within four to five months.

The Essexfields staff consisted of the executive director and his assistant (both group therapists), a secretary, and a work supervisor. The relatively small number of boys and staff members allowed everyone connected with the Essexfields program to engage in intimate, interpersonal relationships thought to be essential for effective group therapy.

THE PROGRAM

The Essexfields rehabilitation program was divided into two major parts—work and group meetings. All boys assigned to Essexfields participated in the formally structured work program five days a week, for which they were paid a small wage. After reporting in at 7:30 a.m., the boys were driven by the work supervisor in a bus to a county mental hospital where they worked until 4:30 p.m. The work program and use of leisure time will be discussed in detail in Chapter 5.

The second major part of the program consisted of two ninety-minute guided group interaction meetings held every weekday evening. The two meetings consisted of an average of ten boys, and an attempt was made to keep these groups intact so that they could develop a distinct identity. The meetings are discussed in Chapter 4.

A DAY AT ESSEXFIELDS

Perhaps the principal features of the program can best be understood by reviewing a typical day at Essexfields. Each morning the boys in the program rode in the Essexfields bus to the grounds of the hospital where they worked. Job responsibilities were assigned by the work supervisor. Before the morning work program began, he designated two boys to serve as group leaders for the day. These were usually the two boys with the longest tenure in the group.

A group leader functioned in the role of a foreman and was responsible to the work supervisor for the smooth operation of the day's work. The jobs performed by the boys consisted of chopping wood, weeding, cutting hedges, trimming and edging grass, helping in the plant nursery, and working at snow removal in the winter. When the weather was bad, the boys were assigned to chop and saw wood under cover.

The boys ate their lunch from 11:15 to 12:00 noon in the hospital employee's dining room. From noon until 12:30 they played ball or participated in some other form of recreation. After returning to work at 12:30, they worked until 3:45 when they ate their dinner in the same dining room. At approximately 4:30, they began their return trip to Essexfields, arriving at 5:30 p.m. Throughout the day, the boys were expected to interact with other boys working nearby. This informal interaction, during which the boys were expected to discuss their problems, was especially emphasized during the bus trip to and from work, during the noon and evening meals, and during the period after lunch when the boys were relaxing. In other words, there was no time throughout the day when the boys were not expected to be actively engaged in the group process.

After arriving back at Essexfields, the informal interaction continued. The boys discussed their individual problems or anything else that was pertinent to the group during the hour and a half preceding the first meeting. The first meeting began at 7:00 p.m. and lasted until 8:30. The second meeting began when the first ended and concluded at 10:00 p.m. Prior to the first meeting, the boys who participated in that group got together informally, usually in the basement of the building, and decided which boy should "get the meeting" that night and have his problems discussed by the whole group. The same thing was done by the boys in the second group prior to their 8:30 meeting. After the second meeting, the boys left the center and went home, in most cases by public transportation.

This schedule of work and group meetings was followed every day except Saturday, when the boys reported to Essexfields in the morning from 7:30 until 11:30 a.m. At that time, housekeeping tasks were assigned to the boys by the staff members. Again a group leader was selected, and he was placed in charge of supervising the other boys' work. When a staff member felt that any work was unsatisfactory, he communicated this to the group leader who in turn passed it on to the boy or boys in charge of that particular job. They were then expected to do it over until it was done to the satisfaction of the staff member. At the end of the Saturday morning clean-up routine the boys were paid their week's wages. Each boy received a dollar for each weekday and fifty cents for Saturday morning. A boy who had been deprived of any part of his pay, as a penalty or fine for program violations during the week, had it deducted at that time. Any amount that the boys had borrowed against their week's wages was also withheld. After receiving their pay, the boys were free for the weekend and returned to the program Monday morning.

PROGRAM INNOVATIONS

Since its inception in 1961, several innovations were made in the Essexfields program in response to experience with it. It soon was apparent that the program could not operate independently of important elements in the boy's life outside the program. Like many others involved in rehabilitating the delinquent, the staff realized that a boy's family and home situation influenced his progress in the program. Boys were more likely to receive support and encouragement at home when their parents understood the program's purpose and objectives. Parents who did not understand the program's methods and goals were likely to undermine it when their son was with them.

In order to assure that the boy's parents would be acquainted with the program, they were interviewed by a staff member immediately after their son entered Essexfields. All aspects of the program were explained to them at this time, questions were answered, and they were encouraged to support their son's efforts in rehabilitation. The staff felt that this program innovation enhanced their rehabilitative efforts, making parents more supportive and cooperative. It was not unusual for the mother or father or even the brothers and sisters of a boy to inform the staff if they thought he was seeing delinquent friends, staying out late at night, or risking his Essexfields status in some other way.

These parental interviews made increased home visits necessary. The initial contact with the family was continued so that there was an ongoing liaison between the family members and the professional Essexfields staff. Needless to say, this continuing contact contributed greatly to family-staff rapport and cooperation and aided the boy in his efforts to overcome the problems which led to his delinquency.

The staff also maintained contact with the juvenile court and probation department. Initial support for Essexfields was obtained by close cooperation with these agencies before the program was instituted. This support and co-operation was maintained by continually working with them. Efforts were made to help advise the court on selection of boys most suitable for group treatment. The program was explained to new personnel in the probation department and individual cases were discussed with them. Visits to Essexfields by officials of these agencies and other interested persons were welcomed and encouraged. When appropriate, police and school officials were kept informed of the program, and it was discussed with interested clubs and service organizations. In such ways as these, the staff maintained good working relationships with the community and its official agencies.

The inability of the boys to find employment after leaving Essexfields was another problem that confronted the project. Corrections workers often feel that the gains made by their programs are quickly dissolved when the ex-delinquent is released and attempts to find a job. Although some boys were able to find employment or return to school, many were not so fortunate due to the poor local employment situation and their own personal deficiencies.

As a result of this situation, some boys were permitted to seek employment during the day while remaining in the program. These selected boys were expected to attend the group meeting in the evening. This was particularly helpful for the boy who was shy and withdrawn and fearful of seeking a job. In such cases, the timid applicant could receive group support while seeking employment. In addition, an Employment Opportunity Committee made up of members of the Essexfields Advisory Board was created to help boys find jobs after they had successfully completed the program. These men served as contacts with the business world and attempted to persuade employers to hire Essexfields graduates.

In certain instances, boys were permitted to return to school while remaining in the program. These boys reported to Essexfields immediately after their last class period and attended the evening group meetings. Between arrival and the first group meeting, they were expected to concentrate on homework.

A unique innovation was the provision made for graduates to return on Saturday mornings to participate in an alumni group. When the first group of boys began to leave the program after completing it successfully, it was found that some would pay informal visits to Essexfields on Saturday mornings. The purpose of their visits varied: some sought specific help such as information about enlisting in the Armed Services, some had personal problems that they wanted to talk over with the staff members, and some returned to show the boys and the staff that they were "making it on the outside." However, Elias and Pilnick believe that the majority of the graduates returned because of some attachment to the program.[6] The staff decided it would be useful for the boys and the program to arrange regular Saturday morning meetings for graduates who voluntarily wished to have them. A meeting place was provided and the staff was available for consultation. Boys continued to meet periodically in this way as long as the program was in progress.

Essexfields graduates also were periodically paid to act as consultants to a group meeting. This was done only when the boys in the group requested such services. The graduate who functioned as a consultant was expected to advise, criticize, and make suggestions to the group as to how the group meeting might be made more effective. The graduate-consultant had to be subtle and diplomatic so as not to antagonize the group members who might be hostile to criticism. This was one of several ways (e.g., hiring former Essexfields boys as summer employees) in which the Essexfields staff attempted to utilize the experience of its graduates. Such innovations not only provided mutual opportunities for the graduates and the program, but they also allowed successful alumni to serve as role models for present program members.

PROGRAM FEASIBILITY

Although this brief description of Essexfields may serve as a general orientation to the program, a moment of reflection will indicate that it raises more questions than it answers. What holds the boys to the program, how do they become involved in it, how are the delinquent pressures in the community combatted, how is behavior in the group controlled, how are the boys and the staff integrated into a working group, why do boys reveal themselves to others in the meetings, what prevents sophisticated delinquents from dominating the program, what are the available rewards and sanctions and why do the boys respond to them, how are program goals instrumented, and how does a program work that places the primary responsibility for control and rehabilitation on the delinquent boys themselves? These are but a few of the questions that are raised by this short discussion of a program calculated to rehabilitate delinquents by using a group of delinquents. We shall attempt to answer these questions in the following pages.

Such questions as these have to do with the *feasibility* of the program, quite apart from the question of its *effectiveness* in preventing further delinquency. Essexfields was based on the previous experience of Highfields, which had demonstrated that the operation of a group centered program was possible. As Ernest W. Burgess commented in his Foreword to Weeks' study:

> Experience demonstrated the practicability of organizing and operating this new type of treatment center for delinquent boys. It was administered successfully on a non-custodial basis. It did not develop institutional features but, instead, established and maintained free and informal relations between the small staff of the Center and the boys. Above all it was able to make rehabilitation the actual objective of the boys as well as of the superintendent.[7]

Essexfields, however, presented additional problems. It was located in the center of a large city rather than in the relative isolation of a rural estate near a small town. Furthermore, boys were on their own at night and on weekends. Nevertheless, Essexfields proved to be quite as feasible as Highfields. Indeed, Essexfields' rate of in-program failures was somewhat lower than Highfields and other residential group centers in the State, and they compared favorably with those of probation.[8]

PROGRAM OBSERVATION

In order to try to determine how the program worked, a series of intensive and periodic observations and interviews were conducted over a year and a half as part of a larger evaluative study of Essexfields. Thirty consecutive evening meetings, some sixty group sessions, were attended by the authors. Observation notes were taken independently on each meeting and compared and integrated after each session. During the course of these observations, two group interviews of the boys in each of the two evening sessions were held to clarify any questions that arose as a consequence of observation. In addition, over a period of six months, fifteen boys were individually interviewed and their answers to a long series of open-ended questions were tape-recorded.

Further observation was made of the work program and the Saturday morning clean-up of the Essexfields center building. Five days of work program observation were made over a period of a month. The observer left with the boys on the work bus at 7:30 each morning, observed and discussed the program with the boys and the work supervisor during the day, ate lunch and dinner with them, and returned to Essexfields by bus for the evening meetings.

Each day's observations were written up in detail immediately after the termination of the trip. The same procedure was followed for the Saturday morning clean-up. In addition, the director and his assistant were each interviewed independently. These interviews were based on a formal, detailed outline of the structure of the Essexfields program that was developed from extensive program observation. Interviews were tape-recorded and totaled approximately six hours each. The authors were also in frequent contact with the program and its personnel throughout the course of the three-year evaluative research and had numerous occasions for less formal observation and interrogation of the boys and the staff.

THE "CULTURE" OF ESSEXFIELDS

One of the first objectives of these observations and interviews was to determine the general outlines of the structure of Essexfields *as perceived by the boys themselves.* This involved an attempt to discover how the boys viewed the program and what they thought their rights and responsibilities were in carrying it out. During the course of the investigation it soon became apparent that the boys had a fairly clear and generally shared conception of the dimensions of the program and its spatial and temporal aspects.

The total structure and process of Essexfields was known to the boys as "the program," and whatever took place during the program hours was "in the program."[9] Non-residential activities were "outside the meetings" but "in the program." Thus, what a boy said inside the meeting should be manifested in behavior outside the meetings. Similarly, how a boy behaved outside the program should reflect his behavior inside the program. The experience at the county hospital grounds was simply known as "work," and leisure time activities were variously identified, such as, "having recreation" or "having store" (as when a boy was sent to buy soda and candy at the local store after the boys returned to Essexfields from work). Time prior to admission to the program was known as "before Essexfields"; delinquent activity was identified as "outside," "street," or "delinquent ways"; and prior delinquent associates were called "undesirables." Boys who completed the program were said to be "on their own on the outside" and, if they "made it on their own," they were "helped boys." Boys in the program were either "new" or "old" boys depending on their length of stay, and might be identified variously by a number of argot terms that indicated their status relative to program objectives.

Each of these areas of activity, statuses, and time and space dimensions had characteristic patterns of their own, yet running through all of them were common patterns of expectations. These may be thought of as constituting the general culture of Essexfields. This culture changed over time in terms of what was emphasized, the current argot used to identify it, and as innovations were introduced by the boys. Yet observations of the day-to-day operation of the program revealed a relatively clear and consistent set of concepts that helped define the culture, a series of expectations and means for realizing them, and a number of formal and informal rules or "norms" of conduct accompanied by methods of enforcement and a system of sanctions.

INDIVIDUAL RESPONSIBILITIES

Boys defined the goals or the purpose of Essexfields in the following terms: to "help boys," to get boys to "give up their delinquent ways," to learn how to avoid "getting busted" (that is, to stay out of trouble), to "change boys," and to "help boys with their problems." In order for a boy to benefit from the program, he must "want to be helped," he must "find out about himself," and "face up to the truth about himself," and he must learn to "think for himself" and to "think about the consequences of his behavior."

As these remarks indicate, the boys did not express the goals of Essexfields in precise detail, although there was common agreement that Essexfields was there to help them. However, they were considerably more articulate in indicating what they expected of each other and their own responsibilities in carrying out the program.

It was the first responsibility of each new boy in the program to "find out about the program." This meant that he must learn what was expected of him and how the program operated *from the other boys*. He could not expect the staff to tell him, nor would he find any convenient written or verbal summary of the program at Essexfields. This meant he must "put effort" into the program. A boy could not simply "do time" or "play it cool." He had to participate actively and contribute to the activities and processes of the program. Boys who were not participating sufficiently were defined as "lacking effort."

To put effort into the program meant, among other things, that a boy must learn to "talk up" and express his "opinions" and "impressions." The expression of opinions and impressions was necessary to "help boys," and "helping others" was a primary norm at Essexfields. Therefore, a boy had to learn to participate in the meetings, to take the initiative, and to verbalize his feelings concerning himself, others, and the program in all discussions in and outside the meetings.

To talk up meaningfully, a boy must "make other boys understand him." This meant that he must learn how to communicate with others so that they could understand what he was saying. This may be one explanation for the existence of a special Essexfields argot,[10] and for the relatively short time it took a new boy to pick it up. The term "confused" was sometimes applied to boys who failed to communicate accurately. In this context it meant that a boy "will say one thing, but thinks he has said something else." In other words, the boy failed to communicate what he wished to.

A boy not only had to learn to express his opinions and impressions clearly, but he had to be able to give "reasons" for them. Thus, when a boy expressed an opinion, he had to be prepared to defend and explain it in detail. Simple repetition of another boy's opinions was not acceptable. Impressions should be his own and should be clearly thought out and based on a reality and rationale acceptable or understandable to the group.

To "be helped," a boy must be willing to "get help from the other boys." He must take their opinions, impressions, advice, and counsel seriously and without resentment. He must not only "want to be helped," but he must be willing to receive that help from his peers in terms defined by the group. In order to get help from them, he must "tell the other boys what's on his mind." Therefore, a boy should not withhold from the group anything that they would consider important. He should not try to hide his troubles and problems from other boys, nor should he suppress his "true feelings" about the boys or the program. One form of "cliquing" (pronounced "clicking"), which was a general term for deviance in the program, was "cliquing with yourself," and meant a boy "is not telling the group what he is thinking about."

To tell the other boys what's on your mind was to "level with the group" and "show your true self." A boy was expected at all times to be honest and straightforward with the other boys and the staff. By leveling, a boy "showed himself"; that is, he showed his true feelings and what he "really is." "Not revealing your true self" was "playing a role," and the most forbidden type of role playing was pretending to be reformed without really changing. A boy might be guilty of "bull-shitting," not giving straight answers or "covering up"; or "cliquing in the program," withholding from the group anything that could help oneself or the other boys; or "impressing," giving the group or staff a false impression of yourself; or being "sneaky," not being straight with the boys. All were examples of a failure to level and show your true self.

In order to be accepted by the group, a boy must "gain the confidence" of the group and staff. If boys showed that they were willing to level, show their true selves, and put effort into the program, they gained the confidence of the group and the staff. When a boy initially came into the program, he was "on trial," which was defined by the boys as a kind of probationary period prior to their acceptance of him based on his gaining the confidence of the group. Once he had gained the group's confidence, he was no longer in an "on trial" status and was eligible for help and support.

If a boy was to be helped at Essexfields, he must "find out what his problems are." Although it was the boy's responsibility to locate his own problems, the whole interaction process was designed to reveal them to him and the other boys. Once he had "found out about his problems," he was expected to learn how to "handle" them. The learning process was known as "working on your problems," and each boy was expected, with the help of the group, to "work on" or "help with" his problems during his stay at Essexfields. Working on problems consisted of attempting, both verbally and in action, to understand and cope with problems sufficiently so that they no longer were a source of serious difficulty or a basis for getting into trouble.

One reason each boy was required to put effort into the program, "to talk up" and "give reasons," was to help him gain confidence in himself. As a consequence of this experience in the program, it was expected that a boy learn to think and act for himself. To gain confidence in yourself was, furthermore, to "believe you can be helped." And although Essexfields was viewed as a means to help, it was recognized that the ultimate responsibility for being helped lay with the boy himself. Therefore, a boy must "rely on himself to be helped."

If a boy was to be helped by other boys, he had to learn to abide by group decisions. Although boys had the right and responsibility to participate in group decisions, they also were expected to recognize the legitimacy of the group and conform to its expectations. A boy was said to be "defying" the group when he refused to conform to legitimate decisions made by it. Similarly, when other boys "get on" him, he should define it as "help," since this was part of the process of getting help from the group. "Getting on" a boy consisted of verbal probing, cross-examination, testing, and discussion in order to "find out" about a boy and help him with his problems. He should not be "easily aggravated" by this activity and should accept it in the name of getting help from the other boys. At various times, "getting on" a boy was known as "applying pressure," "ball busting," and "hiking," or "hiking on," a boy. Sometimes these terms were used to indicate an illegitimate use of pressure, such as getting on a boy but not really wanting to help him, "staying on" a boy constantly, or being "on his back" too much. This behavior was taboo since it was viewed simply as a means of "getting back at a boy because he got on you." It was one form of "taking out revenge," which identified any illegitimate means for attempting to "get even" with another boy or the group.

During the course of a boy's "progress" at Essexfields, he was expected to learn to "check himself." To "check yourself" was to inhibit initial response and learn to respond to others and to situations in a manner that was acceptable to the group. A new boy might first encounter this concept when he was told by the other boys to "check yourself" as he was about to violate a group expectation. However, he was expected to learn to check himself, in conformity with the norm that a boy should learn to want to help himself and rely upon himself to do so.

GROUP RESPONSIBILITIES

Such individual responsibilities as these were supported by group responsibilities, for the complement of individual effort was group effort and the expectations to which each boy was held reflected the normative pattern of the group as a whole. It was the first and primary responsibility of all the boys to be responsible for the program. Just as a boy must help himself, the group must make the program work. If the meetings were not working effectively, or a boy was not progressing, it was up to the group to do something about it. Difficulties and problems that arose should be handled by the group. The boys could not turn to formulated rules and regulations to guide them, nor could they expect the staff to solve their problems for them. Stalemates, failures, abuses of privilege, and the like were defined as group problems, to be solved by the group itself.

When a new boy entered a group, it was the responsibility of its members to find out about him and learn what his problems were. They should get on him when necessary, and check him until he learned to check himself. If he failed to report program deviances, group members should "confess on him." If they lacked confidence in him, they should explain to him their reasons for it. If they felt that he was not being helped, they should explain precisely how he displayed this shortcoming and what he might do to overcome it. Group decisions must be acceptable to all members, and boys must continue discussion until unanimity was assured. In sum, the group had to learn to "run a meeting" and to develop an integrated and cohesive unit that would make it possible to "help boys help themselves."

The foregoing discussion by no means exhausts all of the normative expectations held at Essexfields nor the variety of ways they were articulated, but it does serve to indicate what the boys expected of themselves and each other and what they should be doing in the program. But how might these expectations be realized in practice, and how was the program designed to integrate the activities and objectives of the staff with those of the boys? Beginning with the problem of staff-inmate integration, the following three chapters will examine major dimensions of the Essexfields program in a search for answers to the elusive question: Why and how does the program work?

NOTES

1. A complete description of the Highfields program can be found in Lloyd W. McCorkle, Albert Elias and F. Lovell Bixby, *The Highfields Story* (New York: Holt and Co., 1957).

2. H. Ashley Weeks, *Youthful Offenders at Highfields* (Ann Arbor: University of Michigan Press, 1958).

3. This discussion is based upon the authors' extensive observations of the Essexfields program and their interviews with the staff and boys who participated in the program over a period of a year and a half. In addition, some material was derived from an article by Albert Elias and Saul Pilnick, "The Essexfields Group Rehabilitation Project for Youthful Offenders," *Correction in the Community: Alternatives to Incarceration,* Monograph No. 4, Board of Corrections, State of California (June 1964): 51-57.

4. Elias and Pilnick, "The Essexfields Group Rehabilitation Project," p. 52.

5. Richard Jenkins, "Adaptive and Maladaptive Delinquency," *The Nervous Child* 2 (October 1955): 9-11.

6. Elias and Pilnick, "The Essexfields Group Rehabilitation Project," p. 56.

7. Weeks, *Youthful Offenders at Highfields,* p. ix.

8. This conclusion is based upon data presented and discussed in Chapter 7.

9. The conceptions the boys had of the program and their roles in it were frequently communicated through an argot that was brought from Highfields by the first boys in the program or that developed at Essexfields later (see Appendix A for a glossary of argot terms). In the following discussion and throughout the text, terms and phrases particular to Essexfields are placed within quotation marks to indicate this special usage.

10. Some of the therapeutic functions of Essexfields argot are discussed in Richard M. Stephenson and Frank R. Scarpitti, "Argot in a Therapeutic Correctional Milieu," *Social Problems* 15 (Winter 1968): 384-395.

3

Program Integration[1]

Each particular program of corrections has its own problems and difficulties, but there are two obstacles that confront any organized effort aimed at the rehabilitation or treatment of offenders. The first of these is concerned with the relationship of the inmates to the administrative staff. The second is concerned with involvement of the inmate in the correctional program. Both may be viewed essentially as problems of integration.

Donald Clemmer was among the first to analyze in detail the divisive organization that frequently exists in the prison community.[2] He observed that the prison is organized into two systems, an informal inmate system and a formally structured administrative system. Because the norms and values of the inmate system are in a large part anti-social and anti-administration, and since intimate, day-to-day associations and basic controls and sanctions operate within the inmate community, prisoners tend to be isolated and insulated from whatever rehabilitative measures the administrative staff may have organized. In varying degree, prisoners are assimilated into the inmate culture in a process of "prisonization" that is likely to broaden and deepen criminality and anti-social conduct.

Further research and analysis have modified and extended Clemmer's observations. Focusing on the functions of the inmate system, McCorkle and Korn have contended that the system develops from and is sustained by a need on the part of the inmates to avoid social rejections. The anti-social and anti-administrative norms of the system permit inmates to defend themselves against self-rejection by "rejecting their rejectors."[3] Sykes' study of a maximum security prison led him to conclude that the movement towards group cohesion and solidarity in the inmate population inhibits a "war of all against all" and protects inmates from a multitude of deprivations and pains of prison life.[4] Studies focusing on prisonization have emphasized the variable effects of this process in different types of institutions or on different types of inmates, and suggest that the extent of prisonization may be mitigated by adaptive and compliant conformity to the inmate system that does not necessarily involve commitment to it.[5] None of these studies has substantially reduced the significance of the potentiality of the problem posed by Clemmer. To the extent that the inmate community fails to reflect, reinforce, and support in some substantial measure the administration's program of rehabilitation, or if the formal structure of the staff is not organized to inhibit, penetrate, and overcome resistance from the inmate system, the lack of integration of the inmate and staff communities presents a major barrier to treatment or therapy.

Involving the inmate in the process of rehabilitation is a closely related and overlapping problem. Irrespective of the status of the inmate system, there is the matter of the nature of the motivation, orientation, and characteristic patterns of adaptation that the individual brings with him to the institution. Independent of the inmate system, there is the question of the extent of structural support, both outside and inside the institution, for involvement of the individual in treatment.

Whether the term be "treatment," "correction," "rehabilitation," or "therapy," there are certain implicit assumptions concerning it. In the first place, it is assumed that the individual is in some state or condition that needs to be treated, corrected, or rehabilitated. It is assumed further that ordinarily the individual needs some help beyond his own resources to effect treatment, that he has a right to it (or in the case of confinement he *should* have it), that the condition to be treated is undesirable, and that the individual is obliged to cooperate in the treatment process in exchange for the desired end results.[6] Furthermore, it is assumed that some effective means for treatment or rehabilitation are available. Finally, in our society, the initiative to contact and involve oneself in treatment usually rests with the person who has a perceived need for it.

Assuming that there is some specification of the condition to be treated and some means of effecting treatment, the problem of involving the delinquent in treatment arises because there is so little structure in support of it.[7] Most structure actually works in the opposite direction, supporting avoidance of contact with treating facilities and personnel, minimal commitment to the treatment program once contacted, and eager determination to terminate therapy as soon as possible. Unless some means are developed, largely within a treating agency, to integrate the individual into the treatment process, another major barrier to rehabilitation is raised.

INMATE-STAFF INTEGRATION

Research and speculation concerning the development and maintenance of an anti-therapeutic inmate system have suggested a number of interrelated conditions in support of it. The following represent some of the major aspects of the correctional setting that are believed to affect the inmate system:[8]

1. Large size. Large institutions give rise to bureaucratic organization and accompanying problems of social control, increased social distance, communication between inmates and administration and among the administrative staff, formal organization of relationship, and the like. Problems of security and maintenance of internal order are likely to overshadow those of rehabilitation and treatment, and the integration of diverse subgroups within both the inmate and staff communities and day-to-day administrative difficulties become of central concern.

2. Deprivations of confinement. Stripped of most of the physical and symbolic facilities of ordinary social life, deprived of normal heterosexual relations, and exposed to a criminal community of potential threat and danger, prisoners are motivated to organize and maintain in good working order an informal system to reduce the physical and psychological deprivations of prison life. This system is said to control potential sources of inmate aggression, facilitate orderly exchange among inmates, provide a meaningful reference group, and create a climate within which the individual may secure a measure of self-esteem.

3. Custodial emphasis. Where the primary function of the institution is the maintenance of internal order and security, resources are devoted to elaboration of staff controls. Formal relations between staff and inmates and formal regulations governing the inmate community give rise to informal arrangements between inmates and guards and the subsequent undermining of administrative authority.

4. Duration of confinement. The presence of a substantial number of inmates who are confined for long periods of time encourages a stable inmate system controlled and perpetuated by those most likely to benefit from it and least likely to be oriented towards rehabilitative measures.

5. Effects of confinement on inmate self-conception. The status of the prisoner and the organization of prison life reflect a rejection of the criminal

and his characteristic patterns of behavior. Particularly for those relatively committed to criminality, the deviant inmate community supports prior self-concepts and permits a rejection of the staff and administrative programs.

6. Communication and accommodation between officials and inmates. The extent to which the inmate system may be manipulated in support of administrative policy may depend upon the control of communication within the prison and the types of accommodation that take place between correctional officers and inmates. Administrative awareness, combined with the development of new channels of communication between staff and inmates, cuts off the visibility and power of the more aggressive and deviantly committed, probably inhibiting the obstructive impact of the inmate system.

7. Divergent administrative policies. Failure to integrate and coordinate the activities of security and treatment personnel may result in their operating at cross-purposes. Security and therapeutic officials may have little understanding of each other's problems, and the inmates may play one group off against the other.

8. Staff and inmate perceptual distortion. Both staff and inmates may share a perceptual distortion of their respective roles that greatly exaggerates differences and supports traditional views of staff-inmate conflict. Mutual expectations of behavior may be developed that have a vicious circle effect in the perpetuation of hostility and aggression.

9. Discrepancies between rehabilitation anticipated and achieved. Increasingly, institutions have been assigned rehabilitative functions beyond confinement and punishment. Frequently, however, they are without substantial resources to carry out a treatment program, or the larger society may be unwilling or unable to reintegrate the rehabilitated inmate into conventional life. Inmates who desire help may become cynical and hostile. Others, less therapeutically oriented, may insulate themselves from treatment and then castigate the administration for not having helped them.

10. Saliency of the inmate society. The development and influence of the inmate system may be affected by the extent to which conventional reference groups are available to inmates. In turn, this is dependent upon both the previous orientation of inmates and what is available during the period of confinement. Men who have had less experience with criminal groups and culture, who are able to maintain communication with conventional individuals and groups outside the prison during confinement, and who can become engaged in meaningful activities of administration-sponsored groups, presumably are less likely to seek out and become involved in the inmate system.

Although most studies of inmate-staff relationships have taken place in adult institutions, there is little reason to believe that juvenile facilities are not faced with similar problems.[9] It is probable that juveniles are less likely to have relatively stable or fixed criminal orientations. On the other hand, it is also probable that they are more susceptible to peer group influences. By the time a youth is institutionalized as a delinquent, he usually has had a relatively extended history of delinquency and considerable experience with police and courts, which are unlikely to dispose him favorably to administrative controls and sanctions. Furthermore, it may be expected that he has had some involvement in the culture of delinquency and considerable interaction with other delinquents. In the absence of contrary structure, these conditions are likely to dispose him to seek support for prior orientations and to be susceptible to the development and maintenance of an essentially anti-social and anti-administration inmate culture. Partly in recognition of these conditions and partly as a consequence of program development over time, Essexfields possessed a number of structural characteristics that were aimed at inhibiting divisive inmate-staff relationships and fostering integration within the program.

Small Size

Ordinarily there were no more than twenty boys in the program at any given time, and the staff consisted of but four adults. This size offered the potentiality of primary group relations. No member of the community could easily avoid social relations with all the others, and there was likely to be a maximal and even exposure to the treatment program. This reduced differentiation within the group and inhibited the social isolation of individuals or the formation of cliques. Informal means of social control were possible, and formal rules and regulations accompanied by elaborate systems of enforcement were less necessary. Communication among people was direct and immediate: among the boys, among staff members, and between boys and the staff. The activities of each individual were highly visible to all, and physical proximity and informal relations offered readily available channels for interaction between staff and boys.

Under these conditions, problems that ordinarily accompany bureaucratic organization were substantially reduced or eliminated. It should not be assumed, however, that small size automatically produced integration or had a therapeutic effect. Many characteristics of the small group are favorable to a divisive inmate system, and, in the absence of other conditions, are very likely to foster it.

Staggered Entrances and Exits

The flow of boys through Essexfields was controlled by the system of release from the program and the maintenance of a maximum capacity of about twenty. Since the length of residence always varied within the group, and date of release was governed by progress made rather than a fixed period of time, boys usually left Essexfields one at a time and at intervals of several days or weeks. This resulted in the presence of a significant number of boys who were familiar with the program and who were able to maintain the group culture. At the same time, boys were taken into the program at approximately the same rate as they left. Thus, the group was not faced with problems of assimilating a relatively large number of new boys. Also, new boys were in such a minority as to make it difficult for them to function as a clique or subgroup. This system of staggered entrances and exits inhibited the intrusion of too many boys who might bring with them an anti-therapeutic and anti-administration orientation and prevented the loss of too many boys already inducted into the group processes and culture of Essexfields.

Reduced Custodial Functions

The staff was largely relieved of usual custodial duties, since there were few formal security measures. A major deterrent to breaching security was the fact that a boy might be returned to the court for further disposition, and one alternative was a reformatory sentence. It should be noted, however, that professional and practical consideration strongly challenged the staff to involve boys in the program. Relief from traditional custodial functions permitted the staff to devote time and energy to treatment, integrated staff functions, and eliminated the potential of division between security and professional personnel. It also created an atmosphere within the program in support of staff-inmate integration. Deprivations accompanying measures of strict security were relatively absent. At the same time, boys were relieved of the associated activities of bucking authority and playing the game of outwitting constraints. Under these conditions, getting helped by means of the program could be defined as the effective way of getting out of Essexfields.

Reduced Deprivations

Many of the deprivations ordinarily associated with confinement were absent in the Essexfields program. Boys were permitted a considerable amount of freedom and autonomy within the program, and they spent evenings and weekends at home. Group definitions of boys were such that they were not rejected by either the staff or the group. The process of induction of new boys, to be discussed below, was structured to permit a boy to change his self-conception from a delinquent to a boy with problems who needs help. Major deprivations in the program were structured around the process of treatment and worked in the direction of therapy. A boy was able to achieve and maintain self-esteem and the esteem of his peers as he progressed towards the status of a boy who has been helped by the program. When a boy experienced rejection, it was in terms of specific behavior and attitude and, most importantly, it came from his peers. In this situation, many of the motives for "rejecting the rejecters" were absent. Rather, the program was structured to foster rejection of self-conceptions and conceptions of others held by boys prior to entering Essexfields.

Maintenance of Community Contacts
The fact that Essexfields was non-residential permitted boys to continue certain of their relationships in the community. In addition, helped boys could be relieved of work assignments in the program to seek employment and, where successful, to work outside the program or attend school. This decreased the impact of complete institutionalization, maintained whatever favorable relationships a boy had established outside, and supported associations that might be instrumental to community reintegration after treatment.

Homogeneity
Generally speaking, Essexfields boys were in the sixteen and seventeen-year-old age group, possessed normal intelligence, were free from the more obvious psychopathologies, had experienced no previous institutionalization, had reasonably similar delinquency histories, and came from somewhat similar socio-economic backgrounds. At the same time, they were all exposed to a relatively homogeneous program environment, since they all worked in the same work program, attended group meetings, and experienced similar group controls and sanctions that operated in all aspects of the program. In addition, the term of stay at Essexfields was ordinarily about four months for most boys. This homogeneity offered the possibility of avoiding subgroup development and the splintering, divisive effects of a heterogeneous population which creates a fragmentary, intermittent, and uneven program of treatment.

Cross-cutting Statuses
Although a small, homogeneous population presents some potential for staff-inmate integration, it also may support a divergent inmate culture in the absence of controlling structures. One such control at Essexfields was the presence of a number of statuses that restrained a tendency for boys to close

ranks against the staff and perpetuate previous orientations. These statuses were so arranged that they were likely to divide the group on the basis of progress in treatment rather than unite it in opposition to the program. Boys who entered Essexfields or had been in the program for only a matter of weeks were known as "new boys"; those who were there longer were "old boys." Boys who had just entered the program had an "on trial" status and were not accepted by the group until they conformed to its norms. Boys participated in two consecutive evening meetings in groups known as the "new group" and the "old group." Both groups were composed of both old and new members, but the ratio of new to old in each group determined its status. Regardless of length of residence, boys who were successful in the program were known as "helped boys." Helped boys were usually old boys, but old boys were not necessarily helped boys. Boys who appeared to be adapting to the program but not changing were role players or, in the argot of the group, "playing a role."

Old boys were expected to have an intimate knowledge of the program's operation and to help new boys when they entered it. They were also expected to make "progress," and length of residence served as a bench mark against which to measure it. Progress was defined as moving towards the status of a helped boy in terms of achieving the major objectives of the program. The old group was expected to have achieved more progress than the new group. However, since there were both old and new boys in each group, there was a basis for comparison of progress among individuals in each group. At the same time, boys in the new group were anxious to measure up to the standards of the old group, since it conferred more prestige and was the group nearest completion of treatment. Role playing was a major deviant status in both groups, and individual and group effort was continually exerted to reveal boys who were playing a role. (This effort was known as "busting a role.")

In the work situation, in the evening group sessions, and in their informal relations, boys were continually probing and discussing their problems, how they were working on them, and the progress they were making. Old boys were expected to "get on" new boys; that is, find out what their problems were and help them. Helped boys, especially, were expected to get on boys who weren't helped or who "don't want to be helped," since helping others was one indicant of being helped. New boys and boys who were having difficulty in the program were, in turn, in a position to challenge old boys for not being helped. Since there was a constant feedback between what was said in the meetings and what took place in the rest of the program, what a boy *did* either confirmed or denied what he *said* and became a source for group evaluation and discussion. Every boy was subject to group evaluation and probing when he "had the meeting," and each was evaluated by both the group and the staff when his "monthly report" (the Director's evaluation sent to the Court) was read at the meeting.

In this status structure, with this system of interaction, the program had the potential of operating on the basis of divide and conquer. The division was both horizontal (length of residence indicated by new and old boy roles and the new and old boy groups) and vertical (not making progress, role playing, not fulfilling the expectations of an old boy at any given time). Status differences were geared to treatment objectives, integration into the group was linked to staff norms, and interaction was structured to reveal deviance and to define it as a legitimate subject of discussion and a basis for needing and getting help.

Sharing Administrative Authority

As a group, the boys at Essexfields were in a position to exercise a considerable amount of autonomy. There were few formal rules laid down by the staff, and their veto power was exercised sparingly. Individual and group problems and difficulties were subjects for group discussion and action rather than for fixed and predictable response from administrative authority. Boys were in a position to have a genuine sense of participation in carrying out, modifying, and altering the program. The group decided who was to have a meeting and who was responsible for carrying out discussions. Boys participated in the monthly staff evaluations, discussed decisions concerning relief from work to seek employment or release from the program, and summarized the meetings. Staff participation in the meetings was largely non-directive and limited primarily to guiding the meetings in the direction of the therapeutic process. Should the boys decide the meetings were not going well, they might call a "meeting's meeting," which would be devoted to discussing what was wrong with the meetings and devising ways to improve them. Meeting's meetings also could be used for general discussion of the program when it was felt that the group was failing to carry out program objectives. Innovation and experimentation were encouraged by the staff, but were always subject to their review. In the same way, boys were given considerable latitude in reporting, discussing, and determining deviance within the program and in deciding what to do about it. Although there was a work supervisor, the old boys acted as group leaders in carrying out routine work assignments. In these ways, boys

had a genuine sense of participating in decisions and actions that were important to them. The fact that the staff and the boys operated as a unit presented
a structured potentiality for lowering traditional barriers between them and
diminishing a sense of separation, distrust, and hostility.

Mediating Adult Authority

Youths of the age of the boys at Essexfields are likely to present a double
problem in relating to authority and authority figures. There is the general
problem of staff authority and inmate response commented upon above, and
there is the further problem of adolescent-adult conflict. This is compounded
in the case of delinquents, because their relations with adult authority figures
are likely to have been negative in character. Furthermore, the nature of their
delinquency and the support they may seek from age peers tend to isolate
them from conventional adults and from the adult world in general. Some are
alienated from their immediate families or have not developed strong identities
with their parents, particularly their fathers. Others are school drop-outs who
have not established firm relations within the world of work. These conditions
are inclined to have a vicious circle effect that progressively isolates and alien-
ates them from conventional adults who might serve as models for identification. In this situation, they are likely to be trapped in the constricted role of
delinquency which separates them from conventional male adults, while at
the same time they are struggling to achieve adult, masculine identities. These
factors work together to present a strong potential barrier to staff-inmate
interaction and inhibit whatever therapeutic role the staff may play.

The Essexfields program offered a number of opportunities to mediate
adult authority and overcome traditional barriers between the boys and adults
in official authority. Because of the small size of the group and regularity of
contact between staff and boys, interaction was frequent and informal. Since
the major part of the boys' day-to-day activities was governed by informal
norms they developed and maintained themselves, the staff was not so likely
to be regarded as a symbol of regulatory authority. Furthermore, both the de-
tection and public revelation of violations of staff rules and group norms
were a primary function of the boys as individuals and as a group. In addition,
punitive action against violators was mediated by the peer group, since deviance was always subject to group discussion, and punitive measures were
enforced by the group. Finally, it should be noted that moral condemnation
of delinquency and the rationale for convention emanated from the boys
themselves. They were expected, and expected each other, not only to know
or learn what is wrong, but to understand why it is wrong.

Under these conditions the staff could be defined in terms of help and guidance rather than as an isolated source of authority, punishment, and condemnation. It was possible for boys to legitimate adult authority and to view it as supportive and entitled to acceptance. For its part, the staff maintained a calculated flexibility in its response to the boys. Violations were handled on an individual basis, without reference to precedent or formalized rule and regulation. The onus of evaluating behavior and making decisions concerning it rested directly on the boy and his group. Thus, it was difficult for the boys to stereotype the staff or to link it to preconceived images of official, adult authority. In addition, the absence of a predictable response from the staff was likely to create anxiety on the part of the boys and encourage them to seek relief by means of the program.

Depreciation of Prior Identity

To the extent that boys coming to Essexfields perceived themselves as delinquents and identified with the culture of delinquency, both the program and the existing group culture were threatened. Such boys were likely to be constrained to maintain their prior identities and seek support for them from Essexfields boys. The various arrangements already mentioned were calculated to work in the direction of inhibiting this tendency. However, there were more positive elements of the program that were inhospitable to the extension of orientations that boys might bring with them. There developed among the boys at least a verbal recognition of time and space dimensions that supported the concept of change and the definition of the Essexfields program as the instrument for changing.

In the argot of the group, both a spatial and temporal distinction was made by the term "outside" or the phrase "outside the program." "The outside" referred to space and time beyond the physical and programmatic dimensions of Essexfields. For example, a boy might discuss his delinquency in terms of how he behaved "on the outside," or boys would castigate a role player by asserting that he did not act on the "outside" as he did "inside the program." Outside ways were also called "street ways" or "delinquent ways" and denoted ways of behaving that violated Essexfields norms. Hence, a boy should learn to "give up his outside ways." Delinquent associates on the outside world were termed "undesirables," and the relationship was called "consorting with undesirables." Thus, a boy might be accused of "consorting with undesirables" while in the program, or the group might point out to the boy that he had an "easily influenced problem" that was aggravated by consorting with undesirables. Within the program, a further distinction was made between what took place in the meetings (what a boy said) and what took place in the other aspects of the program (what a boy did). What a boy said "inside the meeting" should be manifested in behavior "outside the meeting."

The temporal element implicit in "the outside" was sharpened further by the phrase "before Essexfields." This term carried a negative connotation and referred to attitudes and actions prior to the Essexfields experience. For example, in an interview, when asked to express attitudes or describe characteristic modes of adaptation, an old boy would frequently ask, "Before Essexfields or after?" What he wanted to convey by this question was the distinction between his attitudes and behavior before coming to Essexfields and those he avowed after becoming a "helped boy" by means of the Essexfields program.

In summary, the Essexfields program was structured to encourage the integration of staff and inmates into a single system oriented to treatment objectives. The interaction of the boys as a group was a primary means for the attainment of this end, with a view to encouraging group solidarity but reversing traditional inmate system orientations. No attempt was made to isolate the boys from each other spatially or structurally, or to regulate and control behavior by means of an elaborate system of formal rules and close administrative supervision. The traditional group relations of these delinquent boys was used as a natural vehicle for control and supervision as well as a means of resocialization. The aspects of the program mentioned above provided an opportunity for eliminating or reducing many of the usual barriers to staff-inmate integration. To the extent that such integration was accomplished, a setting was provided within which therapeutic processes might take place.

INDIVIDUAL-GROUP INTEGRATION

Eligibility or need for treatment implies a limited and controlled legitimation of the condition to be treated; that is, the "patient" or "client" has some right to treatment or help because he may not be entirely responsible for his condition, and "cure" ordinarily cannot be effected without the aid of qualified others. In exchange, the person to be treated is expected to cooperate in the process, recognize the undesirability of his condition, and legitimate the therapists in some measure.

In the case of the delinquent, several problems immediately arise. There is the unresolved question of the delinquent's responsibility for his behavior and for the role he plays in his delinquent acts. By assigning him a "sick" role or ascribing his delinquency to "society," there is the danger that he will abrogate any sense of responsibility for behavior or for involvement in or commitment to treatment. This stance may elaborate into a defensive posture in support of deviance and become a basis for attack on legitimate authority for not getting "helped" or "cured." Beyond this, the delinquent who is relatively committed to the culture of delinquency or a captive of it is unlikely to define his deviance as undesirable or to embrace conventionality as legitimate *for him.* More positively, there are aspects of the delinquent life that are gratifying, especially immediately, and there is little in delinquent activity that develops a perception of a need for treatment or motivates contact and engagement in it. This is compounded by the fact that the "therapists" are linked to the very machinery of the law that is to be avoided, and the treatment involves a surrender of ordinary privileges and rights (as in any treatment process) that may not be viewed as a fair exchange for "cure." In addition, the delinquent ordinarily is not likely to see any meaningful linkage between his behavior and the treatment proffered, and visible indicants of his progress during the process of rehabilitation are likely to be absent. Under these conditions, the sequence of treatment is likely to be one of "contact" by police and courts, "involvement" by incarceration, and "cure" by release to the community.

The nature of the Essexfields program of rehabilitation required the full involvement of the boys in it. Since the peer group was a central treatment medium, it was essential that new boys be integrated into it. Both by initial design and through informal innovation, the Essexfields program contained a number of mechanisms promoting involvement in the treatment and in the group processes.

Informal Structure

Unlike many others in treatment situations, delinquents establish contact with treatment facilities on a non-voluntary basis *after* what they perceive to be a negative experience of apprehension, detention, and court disposition. There then follows a period of relatively intense orientation to the correctional facility, which usually is governed by a rather elaborate and rigid set of regulations and routines enforced by watchful supervision. It seems unlikely that this is an effective setting for involving the delinquent in treatment processes. It was precisely at this point of induction, however, that the structure of involvement at Essexfields began. Paradoxically, it began with a minimum of structure or, at least, formal structure.

When a court disposition to Essexfields was made, the boy was brought to Essexfields, usually in the morning, and reported to the director or his assistant. He was officially checked in, but no lengthy orientation or stipulation of rules or regulations was given. Should he ask questions about the program, they were answered briefly or he was told that he would find out about Essexfields from the other boys. After the boy had checked in, he usually left immediately for the work program. There he was placed in contact with the other boys performing their work assignments, ate his lunch and dinner at the hospital, and returned for his group session or "meeting." From this point on, it was largely the boy's responsibility, with the help of the group, to learn the nature of the program and to help himself in his rehabilitation or treatment.

This informal and loose structure had several advantages in motivating a new boy to involve himself in the group and its processes. In the first place, ignorance of the structure inhibited a stance calculated to "beat the system." Boys who had developed a "con" reaction to figures and organizations representing convention or authority found themselves unable to adapt characteristically because they were not sure what they were "up against." Although sympathetic and supportive, the staff did not fill them in. They had to find out for themselves from other boys, who defined the situation in a phrase that became virtually a slogan, "There are no rules at Essexfields." There were, of course, an intricate web of informal "rules" (norms), and even some that were formal; but in order to learn them, a boy had to involve himself with the other boys.

Furthermore, in order to act at all in the program, a new boy simply had to find out what was going on. This, in itself, provided a strong motive for involvement, reinforced by the anxiety the situation produced in him. In the argot of the old boys, a new boy was "on trial" with the group, which meant he was not accepted until he "leveled" with the boys, participated on their terms, and "revealed his true self."

Cultural Transmission
A new boy was aided in his orientation and involvement in a number of ways. Probably the most general descriptive concept of the role group members played in integrating new boys was the phrase "helping others." The idea of helping others was involved in the total process of group therapy, but in terms of new boys it carried the expectation that boys already in the program, and particularly old boys, be the instruments of cultural transmission. This is an expectation they did not take lightly, since the group judged their progress in the program partially in terms of helping others. Furthermore, to the group, helping others was one index of helping yourself and, hence, making

progress towards release from the program. The work situation, riding the bus to and from work, waiting for a meeting, the lunch and dinner periods, or any other occasion were opportunities for initiating and assimilating new boys.

During the course of the program, the boys also developed more structured occasions for assimilation of new boys. For example, a meeting might be used specifically to instruct new boys who were not "catching on" in the operation of the program. Similarly, a boy who seemed to be having particular difficulty might be given an "easy day" in the work program, where he would be relieved from work in order to discuss his problems with other boys who were working. The impact of this experience was likely to be effective, since the new boy was learning from his peers. While he might reject or mitigate adult authority or insulate himself from conventional others, it was difficult to respond this way to boys who were like him, with whom he ordinarily identified, and who knew the culture of delinquency so well.

Initial Involvement

A new boy's participation in the meeting was another occasion for involvement. The group decided who was to "have the meeting" at each session. This discussion usually took place informally before the meeting, but frequently continued into the beginning of the meeting as well. The norm for who got the meeting was "the boy who needs it most." A boy who wanted the meeting had to defend his need for it, as did those who supported his candidacy. Since one function of meetings was to locate and work on problems, most boys were eager to state and defend their need for the meeting. The loud, heated, and apparently disordered discussion as to who got the meeting was an occasion for the new boy to become involved, if only superficially, in a setting familiar to him—one in which street language, loud and disorderly argument, taunting and baiting were not taboo.

Deeper Involvement

Deeper involvement began when a new boy "told his story." Each boy had to discuss with the group what brought him to Essexfields. This involved a lengthy unfolding of his delinquency history and might take several meetings. Telling your story appeared to perform several functions for involvement. For some boys it might serve as an initial catharsis, since they may not have had an opportunity to express themselves in such a free and open environment before. They learned that other boys like them have similar problems, fears, and anxieties, and they did not need (indeed, were not permitted by the group) to rationalize, defend, and express sentiment in support of delinquency.

The fact that a boy's debut at the meetings focused upon himself was likely to encourage ego involvement. The further fact that he was under constant cross-examination when he told his story provided a strong motive for involvement in order to explain, defend, or reveal his "true self" to his peers. Nor did this pressure terminate with telling his story, since the group might decide later that it was necessary to "go deep into the boy's story." This involved further probing, but under conditions where the group knew more about the boy and how he acted *in the program.*

Changing Identity

One purpose of telling your story was to locate "problems." Problems were things that get boys into trouble, and there was virtually an endless list of them. They ranged from "lightfingered," "drinking," and "duking" (fighting) problems through "family," "going along with the boys," and "easily discouraged" problems to "loud mouthing," "easily aggravated," and "inconsiderate of others" problems. They were continually identified, discussed, and "worked on" by the boys in all aspects of the program. Once problems were located and a new boy accepted them as his, the possibility emerged for him to change his identity from a "delinquent boy" to a "boy with problems." This new or altered identity was fostered and maintained by the group, which also identified him as a boy with problems rather than a delinquent. This identity in no way relieved him of responsibility for his behavior, but it permitted him to see himself in a new light and to begin to respond to a new set of expectations while interacting with others who were significant to him.

Specification of Treatment Objectives and Means

By their own admission, many boys who came to Essexfields defined the situation as one in which they would simply "do time" and get out. They were likely to discover soon, however, that working on or "helping" their problems was expected and demanded by the group. To the extent that a boy attempted to understand and tried to solve his problems, he was eligible for help from the group. Since the group defined its controls and sanctions as "help," the boy was able to accept strong group pressures that otherwise might be perceived as severely punitive. As he began to make progress in terms of group norms, he was accepted by, and received the support of, his peers. This was rewarding in itself, but a further source of potential reward lay in making progress towards the status of a "helped boy." Since a boy's progress was continually evaluated in the meetings and tested in behavior throughout the program, a boy was able to experience success in working towards and achieving a goal that was acceptable to him, his peers, and conventional society. It also was possible for him to establish a linkage between his delinquency and the rehabilitative treatment designed to overcome it. At the same time, verbal and behavioral evidence of progress (or lack of it) in treatment was visible to both the boy and the group.

Group Consensus

It has been noted that there was a considerable amount of group autonomy in the Essexfields program. The boys as a group were permitted to make collective decisions about things important to them. However, these decisions had to be unanimous, a rule which appeared to have several consequences for integration into the group and involvement in treatment. Because there must be shared agreement, no single boy could be easily isolated from the group, and it was difficult for two or three dissidents to form a clique against the others. Furthermore, every boy had an equal right (and, indeed, a responsibility) to express his "opinions" and "impressions," irrespective of his status or behavior prior to entering the program.[10] Every boy was considered an important element in the program and was expected to play a role in it. Thus, old boys could not entirely dominate the group, and a new boy had the opportunity to be part of the structure of power, control, and sanction. At the same time, each boy could develop an interest, concern, and psychological investment in what was taking place in the program. Group norms demanded that a boy be convinced of his opinions and impressions and any alteration or change he might make in them. No boy could simply "drop his opinion" because of group pressure, and it was each boy's responsibility to convince the group of the sincerity of his acceptance of others' decisions.[11]

Program Flexibility

It should be noted that the structure of the program at Essexfields was not only informal, but flexible as well. Informal norms and techniques for carrying out program objectives changed over time. This was encouraged by the staff, both in their response to the boys' behavior and in sharing administrative authority. As indicated earlier, the staff avoided fixed and categorical responses to individual or group behavior, particularly deviant behavior. At the same time, a good deal of responsibility was given to the individual and the group in carrying out the program. This resulted in a situation in which innovation and experimentation could be brought to bear on difficulties and problems as they arose in the program.

This program flexibility could function to motivate involvement in two

ways. On the one hand, it was likely to inhibit a tendency to "beat the system," since the system was always subject to change. There were few fixed
rules or routines to beat, and these few might be changed by the time a boy
had developed techniques to circumvent them. On the other hand, a boy need
not feel that he faced an immutable structure that had been arbitrarily organized and fixed for all time. Rather, he could have a feeling of genuine creative
participation in the program and a sense that Essexfields was designed to help
him help himself.

Roles for Deviants

Given the kind of structure that has been described, there are two obvious
types of boys who could present special problems of involvement. One was
the very weak boy who could not stand up against the kinds of pressure and
rough give-and-take that were commonplace in the program. Such a boy was
likely to fall far short of the model of the street boy or sophisticated delinquent. The other type of problem boy was the essence of that model. Each
was recognized in group argot by the terms "weak boy" and "role player."

The "weak boy" was one of many more or less institutionalized roles at
Essexfields. The term was not necessarily derogatory, but implied that the
group should "go easy" on the boy. This did not mean that he was relieved
of responsibility in the program, but old boys were expected to be more supportive of him—not "ride him too hard," not expect him to "speak up" at
the meetings as frequently as others, and the like. This held in both the more
formal aspects of the program, such as work and meetings, and in the informal
relations that took place among the boys. Old boys were expected to make a
special effort to acquaint such boys with the program and help to integrate
them into the group. Although much of this was done informally, there were
at least two more highly structured avenues for accomplishing such supportive
instruction. Although applicable to any new boy, a weak boy who was having
difficulty could be given an "easy day," one version of which consisted of free-
ing the boy from the work program for a day so that he might be assigned to
an old boy who would talk over problems and the program with him. Similarly, a meeting could be devoted to such special help and instruction.

In contrast, role players were not to be tolerated, and "playing a role"
was definitely taboo. A boy was playing a role when he attempted to make
others think he was helped, while remaining unchanged. This was accomplished
by careful and calculated outward conformity to the norms of the program
without any inner commitment to them. The techniques developed to reveal

role players were called "busting a role." They consisted of a variety of measures designed to get a boy to "reveal his true self" to the group and to himself.

The interplay between the individual boy and the rest of the program constituted a major barrier to role playing. What a boy professed verbally in a meeting had to be demonstrated in action in the work situation, at meals, in informal relationships within the group, and on the "outside" when a boy was in the community. Conversely, what a boy did "outside the meetings" was subject for discussion in the meetings. In this way, a boy who said he was being helped and was changing had to demonstrate it in his actions with the group. It was possible, of course, for a boy to match his words with behavior and still not be sincere. For such a boy, a number of means could be employed to "bust his role" and induce him to reveal his true self.

Within the meetings, a boy could not simply profess to be helped. He had to explain to the satisfaction of the others *how* he was being helped. This involved, among other things, a clear understanding of what his problems were and how he proposed to "help his problems." Furthermore, a boy could not simply say that he would relinquish his delinquent ways; he had to explain *why* he should. Similarly, boys should not only know what was wrong, but why it was wrong. A boy's opinions and impressions were always subject to deep probing by the group. He could not easily "dodge criticism" or "go along with the boys."

The norm for the boy who had the meeting was that the group questioned and the boy answered. He was not permitted to turn the table on his questioners by answering a question with a question. Nor, in order to relieve "pressure," could he accuse other boys of the same behavior about which they were questioning him. This was called "comparing," and was not permitted in the meeting. Probing cross-examination might be accompanied by hypothetical questions calculated to see how a boy had learned to handle his problems and stay out of trouble. Contrite and easy answers received the scorn of the group. Nor could a boy hope to escape by merely not taking a meeting, since the group could elect "to give" a boy a meeting whenever it decided that he needed it.

Outside the meetings each boy's behavior was subject to continual scrutiny and testing by other boys. Boys were expected to report their own deviances or those of others so that they could be properly discussed at group meetings. This reporting procedure was known as "confessing on yourself" and "confessing on others" and was defined as a means of helping. This definition appeared to mitigate in some real measure the more usual conception of such behavior as "ratting" or playing the "stool pigeon." The rationale was that a boy could not be in a position to be helped unless he knew what was wrong, why he did what was wrong, and how he might improve his behavior. His revealed deviances provided an opportunity to learn, and group discussion of these deviances offered an opportunity for help. To the extent that this definition was accepted, confessing was legitimated.

In severe instances of suspected role playing, boys might resort to what they called "psyching." Psyching consisted of tempting a boy to deviate in order to test him. Boys "psyched" in order to get other boys to confess on themselves, which was considered far better than having others confess on them. This was "good" psyching; "bad" psyching was simply trying to get a boy into trouble. In the latter case, the boy who perpetuated the bad psyching would become the focus of group discussion.

A parallel, but less severe, type of testing took the form of "aggravating." Boys recognized that many of them acted on impulse and characteristically responded physically to aggravation. This was known as an "easily aggravated" problem. In order to learn to inhibit initial response and to test out role players, boys would engage one another in baiting, taunting, and teasing. This type of behavior is similar to the "sounding" or probing and insulting that takes place frequently among delinquents on the outside. The difference lies in the response to aggravation, for a boy was supposed to learn to rely upon self-evaluation and to control his responses. If he failed to do so, the extent to which he was helped or really wanted to be helped was questioned and discussed.

It should be understood that according to group norms none of these measures of control and testing should be used out of spite or malice. Boys subjected to them, as all boys were sometime in the program, had the right to be heard in the group and to defend and explain their behavior. Illegitimate use of these methods was frequently referred to as "taking out revenge," which was defined as getting on other boys simply because they got on you, or attempting to get even with other boys. A boy who engaged in the spurious use of these means for "helping" might, himself, be revealed by the group as a role player. Furthermore, boys recognized that role playing could be more unconscious than deliberate. This was called "playing a role with yourself," and probing and testing by the group was one means by which a boy could determine if he had really been helped and was changing.

Program Integration and Continuity

Although various aspects of the program have been taken up separately in the foregoing discussion, it is important to understand that they constituted an integrated whole. Any one aspect of the program was supported by the others. If a boy was involved in one, he was likely to be involved in them all. This integration was sustained over time by the staggered system of admissions and dispositions, by the gradual sequence from new to old boy, by progression from the new to the old group in the evening meetings, and by the careful guidance of a permanent staff. The integration and continuity of the program made it difficult for a boy to involve himself selectively or simply adapt instrumentally to those aspects of the program for which he had a special talent. Rather, the very omnipresence of the program was such that it involved a boy in spite of himself.

In summary, such structures as have been described above presented an opportunity for involving boys in the treatment program. The therapeutic group provided limited legitimation of the role that brought the boy to Essexfields. An essential feature of this role, as defined at Essexfields, was the public recognition by members of the Essexfields community that the boy needed and was eligible for help. He found himself in a milieu where he could define himself and was defined by others not as a delinquent boy, but as a boy with problems. At the same time, the role was defined as "undesirable" and one to be "worked on;" that is, one that required help and demanded involvement in treatment. This definition relieved him of a need to defend his delinquent behavior or self-concept, but required that he make every effort to change it. It was held by a "public" that was significant to the boy (his cultural and age peers) and was reinforced by the legitimate adult authority of the staff. The boy, in turn, was in a position to legitimate the treatment and the agents of treatment, since controls and sanctions were defined as help and were initiated primarily by peers. In addition, the boy himself was in a position to play an active role in the structures of power, sanction, and control.

Because a boy had to take active initiative in learning the program, and since he could not act in it or interact meaningfully with peers without learning something about the program, he had to involve himself in it. The loose and flexible structure inhibited instrumental adaptation; a boy could not simply "play it cool" and "do his time." Overcoming problems provided concrete goals in the treatment process, and progress in treatment was clearly visible in the interaction between group evaluation and action in the program.

Success models were available in helped boys, and acceptable conventional, adult authority figures were present in the staff. Finally, rewards were forthcoming for making progress, attaining the status of a helped boy, and helping others, which constituted criteria for success and release from the program.

COMMENTS

The characteristics of the Essexfields program discussed in this chapter provided the basis for the staff-inmate and group integration necessary for the operation of a group oriented program of corrections. Whatever Essexfields' impact on those involved in it, the program required the initiation and maintenance of a structure that motivated members to participate and developed a sense of group identity. However, if change was to take place, the nature of the group and the processes taking place within it had to be conducive to change.

As indicated in the first chapter, Cressey and others have stipulated various conditions necessary for change, where the group is both the means and the target of change. Among these conditions are assimilation of the delinquent into a group whose values are conducive to law-abiding behavior, and alienation from groups supporting law-violating behavior; relevance of the common purpose of the group to reformation and change; cohesion of the group and integration of effort to the common purpose of reform; assignment of status in the group on the basis of change; active participation of the delinquent in joint effort with reformed delinquents or non-delinquents to change other delinquents; and creation of a pro-reform culture within the group that expresses a need for change so that the group is the source of pressure for change.

Many of the program characteristics discussed in this chapter appear to meet these needs. The process of induction into the program offered a structure for the assimilation of new boys, and those most active in this process presented at least a declared commitment to pro-reform and anti-delinquent values. The program's explicit purpose was to change delinquents, and relationships were structured so that interaction was relevant to this end. Since all of the boys were expected to play an active role in the staff-supported process of change, there was a potential group cohesion that inhibited the separation of the reformers from those to be reformed. Status gained on the outside by delinquent attitudes and behavior could be deflated by downgrading prior identities and transformed by assignment of status in the program on the basis of helping and being helped. The expectation that each boy should help others while being helped by them provided an opportunity for a new boy to work actively with helped boys and the staff for the purpose of changing other delinquents and, in the process, inducing change in him. Finally, the autonomy granted boys in carrying out the program and the emphasis upon both individual and group responsibility for its success offered the potential of united effort through group pressure to bring about change.

The extent to which these potentials and opportunities were realized at Essexfields may best be explored by examining the context in which they took place. Although the integration and continuity of the program has been emphasized, activities may be described generally in terms of the meetings, the work program, and recreation and leisure time within the program and at home. The next two chapters will be devoted to these activities.

NOTES

1. Parts of this chapter have appeared in condensed form in Richard M. Stephenson and Frank R. Scarpitti, "Establishing a Therapeutic Milieu in a Noninstitutional Setting for Delinquent Boys," *Corrective Psychiatry and Journal of Social Therapy* 14:1 (Spring 1968): 10-23.

2. Donald Clemmer, *The Prison Community* (New York: Holt, Rinehart and Winston, 1958, first published in 1940).

3. Lloyd W. McCorkle and Richard Korn, "Resocialization within Walls," *The Annals of the American Academy of Political and Social Science,* 293 (May 1954): 88-98.

4. Gresham Sykes and Sheldon L. Messinger, "Inmate Social System," in Richard A. Cloward, *et al., Theoretical Studies in the Social Organization of the Prison* (New York: Social Science Research Council Pamphlet #15, 1960): 5-19. Also see Gresham M. Sykes, *The Society of Captives* (Princeton, N. J.: Princeton University Press, 1958).

5. A number of such studies and observations are discussed in Donald R. Cressey, ed., *The Prison: Studies in Institutional Organization and Change* (New York: Holt, Rinehart and Winston, Inc., 1961); also Cloward, *Theoretical Studies.* Also see Norman S. Hayner, "Washington State Correctional Institutions as Communities," *Social Forces* 21 (March 1943): 316-322; David Street, "The Inmate Group in Custodial and Treatment Settings," *American Sociological Review* 30 (February 1965): 40-45; Bernard S. Berk, "Organizational Goals and Inmate Organization," *American Journal of Sociology* 71 (March 1966): 522-534; and Stanton Wheeler, "Socialization in Correctional Communities," *American Sociological Review* 26 (October 1961): 699-712.

6. Talcott Parsons has systematically analyzed the therapeutic relationship involved in the patient-doctor roles and discussed its relevance to deviance and social control in *The Social System* (New York: The Free Press of Glencoe, 1951), Chapter X; also, see his *Social Structure and Personality,* same publisher, 1964, Part III. This discussion has drawn upon these sources.

7. The assumption of conditions and means is frequently made too easily. Correctional programs are sometimes carried on without any clear specification of what is to

be corrected or how the treatment will correct it. Chapter I has attempted to indicate conditions to be treated and the following chapters will attempt to indicate the treatment process.

8. Although there is an extended bibliography of material on the subject, two summary presentations previously cited (Cressey, *The Prison* and Cloward, *Theoretical Studies*) conveniently discuss a wide range of contemporary research and previously published material. For studies of inmate systems in correctional institutions for women, see David A. Ward and Gene S. Kassebaum, *Women's Prison* (New York: Wiley, 1965) and Rose Giallombardo, *Society of Women, A Study of a Women's Prison* (New York: Wiley, 1966).

9. Howard W. Polsky's *Cottage Six: The Social System of Delinquent Boys in Residential Treatment* (New York: Wiley Science Editions, 1965) presents a vivid account of how the culture and informal interactions of delinquent boys inhibit effective therapy by the professional staff and support and maintain a pattern of deviant values and activities.

10. The terms "opinion" and "impression" were sometimes used synonymously, but generally the former referred to individual statements boys made during the process of arriving at group decisions, and the latter to individual feelings boys had about one another.

11. The group could elect to "drop" a boy's opinion (that is, refuse to accept it as legitimate) only if they unanimously agreed that a boy was being "bull-headed," "bull-shitting," or in other ways not being sincere with the group. A boy could "drop" his own opinion, but had to give the group a legitimate reason for doing so. This was required in order to inhibit "going along with the boys."

4

The Meetings

The Essexfields program did not consist only of guided group interaction meetings; nor would the meetings be sufficient without the rest of the program. However, they provided a useful focus for understanding the dynamics of the day-to-day operation of Essexfields because most of what took place in the rest of the program ultimately came up for discussion at the meetings, and many of the characteristics of the meetings were reflected in the relationships that took place outside them.

THE OLD GROUP AND THE NEW GROUP

It has been indicated earlier that there were two consecutive meetings each evening of approximately ten boys each, which divided the Essexfields population into the "new group" and the "old group." It will be recalled that the staggered system of admissions and discharges resulted in a situation in which each boy, while progressing in status from a new to an old boy in the program, also retained membership in a group that changed in status from a new to an old group. Since the boys were anxious to get on with the meeting after their return from work, rather than wait in the "back room," the first meeting was considered the more desirable of the two. As a matter of seniority and in recognition of their advanced standing in the program, it was given to the old group.

GETTING THE MEETING

When the boys returned from work after their evening meal, they had about an hour and a half for leisure and recreation before the first group meeting. This constituted part of the free time activity, but it was significant to the meetings because it was here that boys began to decide who "has the meeting." Competition for the meeting was the established pattern, although at one time a group decided to simply rotate it. This proved to be unsatisfactory since it inhibited spontaneity, failed to assure that the boy who had the meeting "needed it most," and did not readily permit discussion of important experiences and problems a particular boy may have encountered during the day or over the weekend.

Who got the meeting was seldom decided prior to the meeting proper, so that the discussion usually was carried on into the meeting and became the first order of business. Promptly at 7:00 the boys in the old group filed into the large room that also served as the staff office. The director or his assistant was usually seated at his desk, and the boys sat in a number of chairs arranged in a rough circle nearby. An opening ritual that was practiced earlier at Essexfields consisted of turning a small electric clock face down. This was done in order to inhibit "clock watching," but was later discarded when the boys agreed that they needed to budget their time during the meeting. This is a minor but characteristic example of the flexibility and innovation that the boys maintained in the program.

There was no formal pattern to the seating arrangements. Old boys sometimes exercised priority in selection of chairs, and during a meeting—particularly the process of getting the meeting—there might be a good deal of moving and milling about. Also, old boys could elect to sit next to a new boy in order to help explain the meeting or lend moral support, and frequently a boy would move his chair close to the one who had the meeting for more intense questioning and discussion. When a meeting was relatively quiet, boys would tend to pull their chairs into a small circle, and in a loud meeting they would tend to spread out. Sometimes a boy would choose to sit with his back towards the director or would pull his chair towards the fringe of the group. Beyond these random variations, there was no clear or consistent pattern to the seating arrangements.

Getting the meeting was often a heated and excited process which to the outside observer appeared to be completely chaotic. Loud, face-to-face debate took place, or the group might break into several clusters for heated argument accompanied by invective shouting and cursing. Actual physical violence was avoided by the unwritten rule that "you can't touch another boy," which was literally and rigidly enforced by the group. After such a period of debate, the pandemonium would suddenly cease as if by a prearranged signal, and the boys would indicate who had the meeting.

In the later history of Essexfields, boys sometimes entered the room and simply declared who had the meeting that night, since a decision had been reached prior to the meeting. On some occasions, a decision would be made to have a "split meeting," shared by two boys. If three or more boys shared a meeting, it was called a "meeting's meeting." A meeting's meeting could also be called when the group felt that it was failing to function effectively. Observation indicated that essentially the same process took place whenever the decision was made concerning who got the meeting. Variations were determined by what may have taken place "outside the meeting" that day, the nature of the group making the decision, the urgency of a particular boy's problems, and—since the later pattern was to shorten the debate period—the course of development of Essexfields itself. By whichever means the selection was made, one rule governed the final choice: it must be unanimous.

Sometimes getting the meeting consumed a good portion of the hour and a half available. However, it appeared to play an important role in support of program goals and objectives. The part it played in bringing new boys into the program has been indicated in the preceding chapter. However, it was equally useful for boys who had been in the program for some time. Since the group as a whole should be deeply involved at all times in every meeting, it seems likely that this initial contest fostered considerable psychological investment on the part of group members in what followed, and created a demand that the boy who got the meeting make the most of it. If he failed to do so, he would be accused of wasting the group's time and depriving another boy of help.

Getting the meeting also required that the boys be familiar with each other's activities and feelings outside the meeting, since needing a meeting might be based on an incident at work or at home or even a boy's feelings during the day. The disorder and confusion that accompanied getting the meeting served a group purpose as well, since it was one way boys learned how to run a meeting. Particularly with new groups, getting the meeting might leave little time for the more pressing business of helping boys. The boys soon learned that it was up to them to carry out an effective meeting and would begin to improvise more efficient ways of doing it. As a group became older, who had the meeting was more likely to have been decided prior to the meeting itself.

The fact that getting and having the meeting was often a difficult and even traumatic experience raises the question as to why boys would ask for it at all. Indeed, some boys would not ask for the meeting even when other boys felt they needed it. In such a case, it was the right of the group to "give a boy the meeting." When a boy was given the meeting, he was subject to the same proceedings as if he had asked for it. Actually, most boys eagerly sought to get the meeting, and strong motivation to do so was provided in several ways.

Release from Essexfields was geared to working on problems and making progress, and failure to do so could jeopardize early release or even result in return to the court. Each boy knew precisely where he stood and how he was doing in the program through his interaction with other boys. In addition, he was subject to a "monthly report," written and sent to the juvenile court by the staff director of his meeting. Before the report was written, part of a meeting would normally be devoted to the boys' expressing their opinions as to his adjustments at Essexfields. Time allotted for discussing a boy's monthly report was at the discretion of the boy who had the meeting, but time was usually granted. Ten or twenty minutes might be devoted to expressing opinions as to the boy's progress. Sometimes only the two oldest boys were called upon to express their opinions; other times, any boy who wished to could do so. However a particular case was handled by the group, each boy was subject to a monthly review by his peers. It was up to the boy who had the meeting to see to it that opinion was carried out effectively and with dispatch, for he would be accused of trying to avoid the meeting or "not caring" if he failed to do so.

These inducements to getting the meeting, taking the initiative, and running the meeting efficiently were supported by the sense of urgency inherent in the time budget presented by the old and new boy and the old and new group statuses. Ask a boy at Essexfields how long he had been there, and he could tell you precisely to the month, week, and day. In group discussions, and when boys got on each other outside the meetings, the length of time a boy had been in the program served as a measuring rod of expected progress. Each boy's time position was indicated by comparing him with the boys in his meeting and those in the total program. Thus, every boy had a unique time position. The last boy to have entered the old meeting would be a relatively new boy in that meeting, but an old boy in the program; the oldest boy in the new group would be a relatively new boy in the program. An old boy in the meeting or program who had not measured up to group expectations received scathing criticism from the others and would be told he must shape up and put greater effort into the program. He might be told that he did not deserve to be at Essexfields, and that he was taking up a spot that could be filled by a boy who really wanted to be helped. Dire predictions were made that if he failed to help himself, he would end up at the state reformatory.

Most boys found it difficult to resist such criticism and comment since it came from their peers. They could not escape it because it could be carried on in every aspect of the day's activities. The same kind of group pressure that may have been instrumental in getting them into trouble on the outside was brought to bear to try to make them conform to the program. Since taking a meeting was one means for getting help and some evidence of willingness to put effort into the program, most boys were constrained to take a meeting even though they would rather have avoided it.

A positive acceptance of the meeting was supported by the fact that a number of rewards and privileges afforded boys in the program could only be fully achieved by getting the meeting. This included the approbation boys gave to those who had been helped, and some privileges, such as attending school or seeking employment while at Essexfields, which required group discussion and agreement before they were granted. Certainly many boys, and probably eventually most boys, wanted to get the meeting, which is to say that the Essexfields program motivated boys to want to be helped and recognize the need for it. The fact that there was never a dearth of candidates for the meeting, that they put great effort into getting it, and that other boys in the group were highly involved in the process strongly suggests this. Furthermore, the distinction between voluntary and forced participation implicit in getting a meeting rather than being given it by the group indicated the boys' recognition of the desirability of a positive orientation towards getting the meeting.

"TELLING YOUR STORY"

A new boy participated in a number of meetings before he was called upon to "tell his story." By this time, he had gained some familiarity with the mechanics of the meeting and may even have heard some other boy tell his story. He usually began by relating events that led up to his entrance into Essexfields. Boys carefully cross-examined and probed his story, and, using leads provided by it, they attempted to get a complete and detailed account of his delinquency history.

Telling your story played a vital role in the program for both the boy and the group. When a boy told his story, he was able, perhaps for the first time, to discuss his delinquency free from the shared misunderstandings that were likely to have supported his deviance when he was with other delinquents on the outside. His previous interactions were unlikely to have resulted in serious questioning and discussion of his behavior, even though subjectively he might have had feelings of guilt and doubt concerning his own actions. Rather, the delinquent group was likely to have provided ready-made rationalizations of delinquency and mutual support for it, so that the weight of influence was in favor of the delinquent rather than the conforming side of his ambivalence.[1] Similarly, his experience with adult authority figures may have served largely to sharpen and perfect his defenses and to widen the distance between conventional and delinquent attitudes.

In the meetings, it was difficult for even the most sophisticated delinquent to avoid at least some introspective examination of his behavior, and the opportunity to discuss it freely and openly with other delinquents where he was neither a "chicken" nor a "squealer" was a new experience for most of the boys. There were two rules at Essexfields that encouraged this "leveling" with the group. Whatever was said in the meetings was viewed as confidential information, and no boy could be penalized by the group for what he said there. Under these conditions, it was not unusual for boys to reveal serious past delinquencies that had never been brought to the attention of the police or courts, or to relate program violations that otherwise would have been unknown to the group. Enthusiastic invention of a story was discouraged, however, by careful cross-examination or accusations of trying to "impress" the group.

For the group, a boy's story was one means by which they "found out what kind of a boy he was." To find out about a boy was to get him to level with the group and to reveal his true self. Not only what a boy said, but how he said it, was important, because the way a boy related his story often revealed impressing, role playing, bogarding, going along with the boys, or being sneaky. In addition, a boy's story gave a basis for understanding why a boy acted as he did in the program. Knowing a boy's background provided the group with information that could be reflected upon when the boy came up later for discussion concerning his behavior at Essexfields. Thus, finding out about a boy was defined as necessary to helping him; and to help a boy, both the boy and the group must find out about his problems.

PROBLEMS

Telling your story was the traditional source of finding problems, since the group got some insight into a boy's home life, his association with other boys, his school or work experience, his delinquency history, and the like.

Problems also might be discovered through interaction within the program, and sometimes groups sought to get at problems by means of discussion of a new boy's behavior at Essexfields. When the group felt that the roots of a problem in the program might be found in a boy's previous experiences, such discussions would lead to a boy's story.

The argot of Essexfields identified a wide variety of problems that were recognized by the boys and associated with them. Problems were initially identified by means of a boy's story, but they were elaborated and new ones arose throughout the duration of a boy's tenure in the program. The following can only suggest a few of the kinds of problems boys discussed in the meetings:

Easily influenced—failure to think for oneself; going along with the boys; allowing others to determine your action.

Inconsiderate of others—acting without thinking of consequences; failure to take others into account; thinking only of oneself. A boy may also be "inconsiderate of himself" when he does things that get him into trouble and are harmful to him, or when he fails to do things that will help him.

Easily aggravated—hasty and inappropriate response to others; aggressive or violent retort without justification.

Family problem—inability to get along with parents or family members; if viewed as boy's fault, he should try to learn how to handle it; if viewed as family's fault, he should try to develop sympathetic understanding of their problems and learn to live with it or perhaps get away from it.

Drugs or drinking—getting into trouble because of drinking too much; using barbiturates, sniffing glue or other intoxicants or depressants, using heavy drugs; this is "being inconsiderate of yourself."

Impressing—getting into trouble because a boy is trying to impress others; trying to be a big shot; getting the attention of others.

Easily discouraged—not exerting sufficient effort or trying hard; letting little things get a boy down; getting into trouble because a boy is fed up with things.

Denying—a boy won't tell the truth; habitually seeks to cover up his deviances; won't be straight with the boys or others.

While identifying problems was viewed as one step towards getting help, the process of locating and working on them appeared to perform a number of related functions. For some of the boys, leveling with the group and revealing your true self seemed to have a genuine cathartic effect. Some boys appeared to eagerly seek to unburden themselves; others held back for weeks and suddenly opened up and poured out their innermost thoughts and feelings.

This was reinforced by the fact that boys soon learned that others had the same problems too.

For both the individual and the group, problems provided a focus for rehabilitation that is not present in most programs of correction. As indicated earlier, the treatment concept implies the presence of something to be treated and a program of treatment, and neither may be very apparent to a delinquent, even in a treatment oriented facility. At Essexfields, a delinquent was defined as one who needs help (that is, treatment). The perceived sources of his difficulties were made apparent to him in his problems. It was his responsibility and that of the group to work on these problems; that is, to change his attitudes and behavior. What had to be changed was continually made apparent in the group meetings and in interaction in the rest of the program. Evidence of failure to change (that is, to "work on" problems) was immediately apparent in the response of other boys to what was said and done in the program. Attitudes were continually appraised in the meetings, and their expression in behavior was constantly tested in outside interaction. In this structure, each boy knew what he was expected to do in order to be helped, whether or not he was making progress toward being helped, and when some evidence of help was expected. Since he was engaged in the "treatment" of others while undergoing "treatment" himself, there could be little question as to what was being treated or what was expected in the process.

WORKING ON PROBLEMS

After a boy had told his story and located his problems, he assumed the double role of a boy working on his problems and helping others to work on theirs. His activities in the program outside the meetings became a testing ground and formed the basis for evaluation of his progress towards learning to handle his problems. He might be required to keep a list of his problems, and could be called upon in and outside the meeting to enumerate them. Progress in problem-handling was evaluated by the group, and indications of new problems that might arise were discussed in the meetings by several alternative means.

A boy could simply ask for a meeting in order to get help with his problems or get the other boys' opinions and impressions as to how he was progressing. The group would frankly discuss their impressions of him. He might be told that he was not taking the program seriously, that he was playing a role, that boys had to confess on him because he did not confess on himself, that he was not helping new boys, that he was letting the other boys down and giving Essexfields a bad name, that he would not talk up because he was afraid of the other boys' impressions of him, that he did not want to be helped, or any other of the vast variety of indications of failure to be helped. His time position in the program would be pointed out to him, both in terms of the meeting and the program. For example, he might be told that "he was the second oldest boy in the meeting and the fourth oldest boy in the program," and that as such he had not made sufficient progress. Specific instances of his failures would be discussed in detail, and boys would give their impressions as to why these failures occurred. The boy would be questioned as to alternative ways he might have handled his problems, and the group would discuss these alternatives with him and suggest others. If a boy said he was being helped but the group did not think so, they would show him "where he is not being helped" and indicate what he needed to do in order to get helped. If the boy told the group that he would try to change, they would demand to know *how* he would change. The group would explain why a boy's behavior was wrong and why he ought to act in another way, and they would tell him it was "up to him to convince the group that he is being helped." They would also tell him where they thought he was making progress and how they believed he was "helping his problems."

Sometimes a boy would ask for a meeting to see if he was "playing a role with himself," which meant that a boy sincerely believed he was helped, but was not certain of it. Although certain he was not playing a role with the group, he feared that he might be simply fooling himself. This rather subtle insight and uncertainty offered another opportunity for group appraisal and indicated the group belief that a boy must "convince himself" as well as the group that he was helped.

When a boy believed he was "ready" to seek employment or go to school while at Essexfields, he asked for a meeting in order to get the group's opinion. The boy would then present his case, stating why he believed he should have this privilege. Boys might interrupt to ask questions or challenge statements and it was up to the boy requesting permission to "convince the group" that he was "ready." After some discussion, each boy would state his opinion concerning the request. If the group did not arrive at a unanimous decision, they would debate until some consensus was reached.

Every boy had a meeting before his monthly report was made by the director and submitted to the court. It was here that a boy had an opportunity to receive the opinions and impressions of the group concerning his progress in a more formal structure. The discussion that followed offered another occasion for group evaluation and for a boy to learn his strengths and weaknesses and how he might more effectively work on his problems and make progress towards release. At the same time, the group was constrained to self-evaluation, since the progress made reflected on the effectiveness of the meetings and the group as a whole.

GROUP CONTROLS

When a boy had the meeting, he was likely to encounter sharp questioning by the other boys and to experience severe castigation, deep probing, and even verbal abuse. During the course of his story, he would be challenged as to the truth of what he had to say and demands would be made for full and frank disclosure. He would be asked to explain why he got into trouble, and familiar and easy rationalizations would be ruthlessly exposed. Understandably, it was not easy for a boy to endure what appeared to be such hostility and abuse. However, there were a number of reasons why he did so.

The unwritten, but frequently verbalized, rule of the meeting was that "the group questions and the boy answers." This meant that a boy could not "dodge criticism" when he had the meeting by turning the table of his questioners and accusing them of past or present misdeeds or demanding that they explain themselves. On the other hand, he was quite at liberty to do so and was expected to when he did not have the meeting. Furthermore, boys who abused their rights in the meeting were accused of "taking out revenge," and the group protected the boy who had the meeting from illegitimate badgering. Sometimes older and more experienced boys in the program might band together to get on a boy and be accused of forming a "revenge squad." This deviance would be subjected to group discussion, and such boys would be told to shape up and stop interfering with helping a boy. In addition, the previously mentioned "weak boy" role provided protection and support for a boy who was not particularly verbal or who found difficulty in relating readily and easily with other boys. Also, when the group expressed its impressions of the boy who had the meeting, he was usually referred to as "the boy," rather than by his name or the second or third person. When asked why this was done, the boys explained that they did not want a boy to "get conceited" or "big headed" or to think he is "too important." It seems likely, as well, that the term served to depersonalize the impact of the source of the impressions and to objectify the content of the remarks for the boy to whom they were directed.

More positively, a boy was likely to accept the group's response to him because it came from his peers and was given in the name of helping him. Boys pointed out that they were willing to listen to what other boys had to say, because they had had the same experiences as the boy who had the meeting and understood his situation. They said that "the boys don't just tell you something is wrong, they tell you why it is wrong" and that this is "not like the outside" where people simply "tell you" without explaining or trying to understand. The boys reasoned that just as it was necessary to get on boys in order to help them, it was necessary for boys to get on you in order to be helped. Also, the boy who had been your severe critic in the meeting was likely to be the same boy who took the bus home with you afterwards, helped you on the job the next day, and played ball with you during the rest period. Furthermore, a meeting involved both give and take. The boy who had the meeting not only had the right to defend and explain himself, he was expected to do so. Other boys could also defend him or help him to understand what the group was attempting to convey. Observation indicated that, because they could hardly avoid the group pressure exerted upon them, most new boys complied readily to the demands of the group. They appeared to quickly recognize the legitimacy of these demands, and gradually began to define them as necessary and helping.

A number of informal rules governed the meetings and were exercised to maintain order and keep the group focused on the task at hand. The following forms of behavior were unacceptable in the meetings and in the program generally:

Clowning—failing to take the meeting seriously; inappropriate laughter and joking; "fooling around" in the meeting.

Dodging criticism—defensive maneuvers to avoid or fend off group criticism; avoiding boys' getting on you; not admitting faults.

Bogarding—boisterous monopoly of the meeting; trying to get your own way by loud and threatening behavior.

Loud—being too noisy in the meeting; being boisterous without purpose pertinent to the meeting.

Bull shitting—not giving straight answers; covering up.

Cliquing with self—failing to confess on self; not telling boys what you are thinking about.

Cliquing in the program—not confessing on boys; holding back anything that could help yourself or the other boys.

Cliquing together—boys getting together to stick up for one another; covering each other's cliquing.

Defying—not doing what the boys tell you to do.

Easily discouraged—giving up; not trying; backing down; dropping opinion without good reason.

Easily influenced—going along with the boys; not giving good reasons for opinions and impressions; not thinking for yourself.

Hiding behind the program—taking advantage of group norms in order to pursue your own ends; for example, aggravating other boys knowing that the rule is that they should not hit you.

Impressing—giving the group a false image of yourself; trying to "look good" without changing or improving.

Inconsiderate of others—not helping other boys; doing things that violate program norms; interfering with getting helped or helping others.

Monopolizing—taking too much of the meeting's time; verbal dexterity, without bogarding, that does not permit other boys to enter the discussion.

Lacking effort—not participating sufficiently in the meetings or program.

Taking out revenge—getting on a boy simply because he got on you.

Mocking—making fun of a boy in the meeting or program.

Meeting playing a role—loud and active discussion just to impress new boys or the staff; trying to look good; lots of talking up just to avoid getting on each other.

Sneaky—not being straight with the boys; being underhanded.

Sponging—currying favor with staff or other boys; trying to get in good with them.

Sulking—sitting back and not participating in the meeting.

As these and other such terms suggest, boys made subtle distinctions between legitimate and illegitimate action in the meetings. For example, being loud was all right if it contributed to the meeting or helped a boy. If it seemed to have no purpose or led to general confusion, someone in the meeting would simply shout "hold it down," which was the signal to resume discussion in a more normal tone of voice. On the other hand, bogarding was a more serious offense because a boy was trying to get his way illegitimately. Similarly, while a boy must not defy the group, he also must not be easily influenced; he must not hide behind the program, but he must get on other boys; or he must get on other boys, but must not take out revenge. To a new boy, these rules were confusing and perhaps even appeared contradictory. As one boy put it, "Whatever you do at Essexfields is wrong." The key to comprehension of these group-created rules, however, is to understand that they were defined as a means for helping boys; to get program participants to under-

stand why boys behave as they do, to weigh alternatives, analyze consequences, think before they act, and to make their own decisions.

These rules were enforced during the meetings by a variety of controls
that were brought to bear on an individual boy or the group as a whole. Probably the most effective control was exercised by group disapproval, which
was immediate and vocal when a boy got out of line. Protests that he was not
helping or that he was wasting the meeting's time would be made. Frequent
repeaters would be identified by group argot and their deviance might be
assigned as a problem to be worked on. Occasionally, penalties would be
meted out by the group, although the form they took and the extent of their
use varied over time. Boys might be told to "get off the rug," which meant
they must stand outside the rug that covered the floor area where the chairs
were placed. Boys also might be told to stand or kneel during the meeting,
and 'for serious offenses, they could be ejected from the meeting. More
frequently, however, the group would elect to drop a boy's opinion. This was
perceived to be a rather severe sanction, since it meant the boys considered
his opinions worthless. In order to give everyone his fair share of the meeting,
a particularly verbose boy might be given a time limit for expressing his opinions
and impressions. This could be extended if necessary, but boys were usually
held to it.

Sometimes the boys as a group would decide that they were getting nowhere with the meeting, or that the meeting was playing a role. On such an
occasion, the group might elect to hold a "meeting's meeting," which is the
term that was also applied to a meeting that was shared by more than two
boys. The purpose of a meeting's meeting was to discuss what was wrong with
the meeting and to formulate ways for improving it. This was one source of
innovation in the program, since boys might agree upon entirely new procedures. A member of the old group might be called in for consultation, but
usually after discussion among themselves the boys would decide to "settle
down" and put more effort into the meeting.

Another important control on the meeting was the meeting summary. At
the end of each meeting, the director would call upon one or more boys to
"summarize the meeting." In a summary, a boy was expected to give both a
substantive account of what had happened and indicate what had been learned
from it. Attention would be directed to what the group had learned about a
boy and what the group may have learned about itself. Because summarizing
the meeting required a good deal of knowledge about the program and considerable experience in it, the older boys in the meeting were usually called

upon. Since any one or more of them might be asked to summarize, they had to pay sharp attention throughout the meeting. Furthermore, this was one way to see how a boy was learning the program and gaining insight into it. At the same time, it helped to teach new boys what to look for in a meeting.

CLIQUING AND CONFESSING

Although the general rule for getting the meeting was that it should be given to the "boy who needs it most," sometimes the boys would put this basic formula in terms of "the boy who needs it most *that day*." This usually referred to some specific incident that required immediate group discussion. Primary among such immediate candidates was a boy who had been cliquing. Cliquing, pronounced "clicking" by the boys, was a general argot term used to identify violation of program rules and group norms. Cliquing could come up for group discussion as a consequence of a boy's confessing on himself or being confessed on. If the cliquing involved a serious violation of group rules, the boy would be given the meeting immediately without long debate, since usually there had been informal discussion concerning the cliquing prior to the meeting.

Attitudes towards cliquing varied depending upon the seriousness of the deviance, the length of time a boy had been in the program, and how the cliquing had been revealed. The group responded to a new boy's minor infractions, such as getting a coke from the machine when he was not supposed to, by simply telling him not to do it again and explaining that it was not fair for him to do something the other boys could not. However, the same act by a boy who had been in the program for three or four months was regarded as a serious offense, since an old boy was expected to know and observe the rules. Such deviance was taken seriously by the boys because it symbolized a flaunting of group norms and a breach in group solidarity. Thus, a minor infraction by an old boy might be viewed as a major offense, since it represented a threat to group integrity and authority and evidence of group failure to handle one of its members effectively. Such deviances as failing to appear for work in the morning, drinking, staying out all night, or getting into trouble on the outside were considered serious offenses regardless of program exposure, although the new-old boy distinction might temper group response.

If a boy confessed on himself in the meeting, his cliquing was viewed differently than if he were confessed on. Confession in the meeting was taken as indicating some commitment to the program and to the norm of seeking help.

If a boy had to be confessed on, he was not leveling with the boys and not seeking help, hence, the group would take a more severe attitude towards him. Since whatever was said in the meeting was held to be "sacred" by the boys in order to encourage free discussion, no formal sanctions were given to a boy who confessed in a meeting. His violation would be discussed, boys would "get on" him, and severe "pressure" might be applied. However, he could not be given extra hours of work or other penalties for this evidence of a desire to be his true self and to level with the group. The norm that confessions in the meeting were inviolate not only fostered open discussion, but supported self-reporting. And because the group could not help a boy who hid his true self and played a role, confessing could be perceived as a means of "helping yourself with your problems."

Although there is little reason to believe that all or even the majority of deviances, particularly minor ones, were reported, it was remarkable that confessing became so thoroughly institutionalized at Essexfields. Largely because confession was defined as a necessary means of getting help and helping others, reporting of program deviance was a relatively frequent occurrence. Reporting could be defined as not only necessary but helpful because the violation was discussed with peers in terms of its relationship to problem solving and changing. In the meetings, violations were related to the boy's problems and progress, reasons for the violation were sought, explanations as to why the violation was wrong were given, and alternative solutions were argued. Furthermore, it was generally recognized that the cliquing would take place, and that the boy who did not engage in some cliquing was not only the exception, but the impossibility. Therefore, if a boy did not confess on himself or group members on others, there was clear evidence that both the individual and the group as a whole were failing to help themselves and others. Although there was ample evidence that new boys were reluctant to report others and regarded self-reporting as embarrassing and even foolish or silly, observation clearly indicated that old boys took confessing as a matter of course and reported themselves and others apparently without the severe inhibition or constraint usually associated with this activity on the outside.

Cliquing, which is to say deviance, played a vital role in the total program of Essexfields. Unlike most programs of correction, particularly in custodial and security oriented institutions, there was ample opportunity for deviance. Although this placed a heavy burden on the program and its directors in terms of containing deviance in reasonable proportion, it provided a basis for realistic socialization to more conventional behavior patterns. Thus, the phenomenon of deviance was as much a part of the program as was conformity. This seeming paradox is resolved if it is recognized that deviance may be functional for learning to conform.

Discussion of deviance played an important role in linking a boy's problems and progress to his daily activities while in the program. Particularly in the later history of Essexfields, failure to meet program expectations became a means for discovering a boy's problems. In such cases, group discussion uncovered sources of the deviance and linked them to broader patterns of behavior that were defined as "problems." Thus, a particular instance of fighting, stealing, or drinking would be viewed in terms of more general problems, such as "easily influenced," "family problem," or "impressing." Such problems were then discussed in terms of what the group knew about a boy from his story, going deeper into his story and, most importantly, what the group had learned from daily and intimate interaction with him. In this fashion, deviance in the program could provide a major source for realistic discussion of problems and their manifestations. Past delinquencies, hypothetical cases, and broad generalizations gave way to discussion of real events that were of significance to the individual and the group.

HELPED BOY

When any boy believed that he was ready to leave Essexfields, he asked for a meeting to discuss the matter. Again, a boy had to "convince the group," both by what he said in the meeting and by his behavior in and outside the program. "To convince the group" was to assure the boys that one was "ready to leave Essexfields," which meant that one was a "helped boy." A helped boy was one who understood what his problems were, had developed effective and acceptable ways of coping with them, rejected delinquency as a characteristic mode of adaptation, and was ready to assume a conventional role in the community.

To be a helped boy was to acquire a recognized status at Essexfields. Helped boys were usually old boys, but old boys were not necessarily helped boys. This status had to be conferred by the group. Since only a few boys in the Essexfields program at any given time achieved this status, and because it was awarded by a boy's peers and embodied the major objectives of the group, a helped boy had prestige in the eyes of the other boys. For the boy who achieved it, the helped boy status was the ultimate reward the group could grant him and the termination of a successful struggle to "help his problems" and "make progress" during his experience at Essexfields. For the other boys, the helped boy served as a model to emulate and a realistic example of the objectives of the program.

Although a helped boy might be so recognized before his requested meeting to discuss leaving Essexfields, this meeting represented a kind of summary examination and assessment of him. Because of the importance of the helped boy status and release from the program, group decisions in the matter were never taken lightly. From previous meetings and by means of the group discussions of his monthly reports, a boy would usually have some assurance from the group that he had made progress and was changing. However, in this crucial meeting, the boys would subject him to searching questions and cross-examination focused on his readiness to assume conventional roles in the community. The boy would be asked to explain how he thought the program had helped him, why he believed he could cope with his problems, what he had learned from his Essexfields experience, and how he intended to stay out of trouble in the future. One technique used during this period of discussion was the hypothetical question. Such probing took the form of "What would you do if . . .?" and centered around those aspects of the boy's behavior that the group knew to be his problems. Throughout the discussion the group continued to probe for reasons, explanations, and rational judgments in an attempt to assure that the boy was not playing a role with the group or with himself.

After a period of intensive questioning and discussion, each member of the group would give his opinion concerning the boy's readiness for release. Frequently, the group would decide that the boy was not ready and would then explain why and what he had to do to convince the group. Occasionally, they would decide that the boy did not want to be helped and that Essexfields had done all it could for him. In this case, it would be recommended that the boy be released anyway, so that a new boy who wanted help and was willing to put in effort could take his place. Such a recommended release was known as being "sent home on a humble" and meant that a boy did not earn his way out of Essexfields. This expression was an adaptation of the term "humble" as it was used on the outside, which meant "getting arrested for something you didn't do." If the group decision favored release of a helped boy, the meeting would terminate and the recommendation would be taken into consideration by the group director who made the ultimate decision.

By the time a boy was ready for a meeting to discuss his release, there was generally consensus between the staff and the boys. They all had observed him over a period of months and participated in probing discussion and exchange with him in intimate, daily relationships. Sometimes, however, the group would take a hard line with a particular boy or at some period of time might react negatively to any boy seeking release. If the director did not share the group's opinions and impressions, he would seek to convince them differently. This might be an occasion for pointing out that they were responsible for helping the boy, had not exerted sufficient effort, and should find out why they had failed. This could result in a "meeting's meeting" to consider the matter and sometimes was viewed as a major crisis for the group as a whole. At other times, the group might be too eager or hasty in its decision for release. This again became an occasion for group self-examination and evaluation.

GROUP PROGRESS

The foregoing discussion has focused primarily on the interaction of the boys in the meetings. It is important to indicate, however, that just as a boy might change and develop in the course of the meetings, the group as a whole moved through a sequence from a rather loosely structured, uninvolved, and confused collection of young men to a relatively cohesive, concerned, and knowledgeable group. This sequence was implicit in the distinction between the old and new groups and the expectation that the former could carry out an effective meeting and help other boys.[2]

Some structure was available to a new group because of the presence of a few old boys and the fact that the staggered system of entrance and exit filtered new boys into the group over a period of time. Furthermore, the program director or his assistant was present in the meetings. However, experienced old boys were in the minority, and it was believed that neither they nor the staff should dominate the meetings or be the only or principal participants. This engendered the need to involve new boys, to get them to learn how to run a meeting, develop self-confidence and reliance in running it, and learn related norms and attitudes of the current Essexfields culture. Moreover, the staff had to exercise a certain interested neutrality at this time in order to avoid an image of authoritarianism, hostility, or favoritism and gain the confidence and acceptance of the boys.

During the early history of a new group, there was a good deal of random "sounding" and testing, expression of aggression or hostility, bravado from "tough guys," silent skepticism on the part of "weak boys," scapegoating, covering up and defending of self, and the like. Much of the interaction was given to seeking some knowledge about one another. At this point, however, the members were far from understanding the Essexfields norm of "finding out about a boy" so he can be helped. Rather, they seemed to be motivated by curiosity about each other, the situation they found themselves in, and the desire common to street groups and gangs to establish a pecking order. At the same time, they began to form small cliques, partly for support in a milieu that was new or threatening and partly in defense against the impact of the program.

During this period, boys would begin to pick up the current Essexfields argot and pay lip service to the norms and standards of the older boys. Outside the meetings, old boys would check and get on them, explain the program, and initiate them to work routines. Shortly, the meeting would begin to develop some homogeneity in a leveling process calculated to "bust" outside roles, bring in boys who held back, and break down defenses of boys who defied the group. The staff would guide the meetings primarily through the summary. Here, they could give new boys some insight into what the meetings involved by probing questions and summary statements about what went on in the meeting each evening.

Although the early stage of the meetings played a positive role in acquainting the boys with the program and facilitating their interaction, several potential barriers to effective assimilation and treatment were still present. Outside roles (tough guy, punk, baddie, hipster, etc.) had to be altered in order to assume constructive roles in the program. Role playing in the program had to be exchanged for involvement in roles that helped oneself and other boys. Cliquing together had to give way to concern for all boys in and outside the meetings. The strain towards a pecking order and the aggression and hostility that accompanied it had to move towards trust, equality, and democratic participation in the group.

After boys had told their story and begun to identify problems, the meetings started to take on a new character and moved into the second phase of development. Role players in the meetings began to reveal their true selves during work and in the informal interactions of recreation and leisure. Cliquing assumed more serious implications as new boys observed old boys confessing and getting on each other for program violations. Cliquing together became less important as new boys started to develop some solidarity and identity in the new group and recognized and exercised their shared power in the program. As problems were identified and discussed, boys were drawn into participation in the meetings, and some awareness of themselves and others began to develop.

With greater involvement in what was taking place in the meetings and more awareness of each other outside them, there was less random discussion and restless behavior. Some individual anxiety and introspection was likely to take place as boys were exposed to group pressure and questioned about their attitudes and behavior.

The group as a whole would be in some tension at this point, since it was about midway through the program and preparing to move from the new to the old group status. This transition was accompanied by some ceremony, since it was assumed that the new group had made progress and the boys in it were ready to assume more responsibility. The few remaining old boys in the old group would congratulate the new group, and the new group would ceremoniously assume old group status by having their meeting first rather than waiting until the old group (now a new group composed mostly of new boys) had theirs.

This introspection and anxiety increased with continued involvement in the program. At the meetings, boys probed deeper into a boy's story, his problems, or his behavior. At the same time, each was more active in questioning others and getting on, checking, psyching, or confessing on them. This dual effect of acting on others while being acted upon himself by his peers placed a boy in an uneasy equilibrium and provided the foundation for the group to assume a third phase in its development.

For many boys, this period appeared to be one of personal crisis in which they must somehow resolve the distinction between what they were or are and what they at least outwardly urge themselves and others to become. If a boy was given responsibility and therefore the trust and confidence of his peers, charged with helping them as well as himself, received their concern and support, shared authority, and participated on equal terms, could he remain unchanged?

At this time, the boys were thoroughly familiar with the norms and expectations of the program and the mechanics of running a meeting. However, they were unlikely to have internalized the norms or used the meetings as an instrument for genuine help. In response to the heightened anxiety, the meetings might become turbulent. Most boys had abandoned outside roles and were seeking and testing new ones; the meeting discussed and probed them in search of patterns acceptable to both the boy and the group. Renewed efforts would be given to penetrating defenses and busting roles, interpersonal attacks and counter-attacks, demanding explanations, and expressing opinions and impressions. At the same time, there was greater elaboration in "explaining things," "giving reasons," and telling a boy where and why he was wrong and what he could do about it. This was accompanied by insistence that a boy convince the meeting that he wanted help and trying to convince him he should and could change.

The process of "convincing" was likely to have a circular effect, since in attempting to convince others to change, a boy might well convince himself. If the group was to convince a boy that his attitudes and behavior were wrong, members had to be effective in penetrating his defenses and giving reasons for change. They were likely to be relatively adept, since they knew the characteristic defenses as a result of their own past experiences. And if they were to convince a boy to change, they must have thoroughly thought through "good reasons" (ones that the boy and the group would accept) for it. Similarly, if a boy was to convince the group that he wanted their help and trust, he could not readily "con" them, since he was subject to constant and searching cross-examination and had to demonstrate his sincerity by his behavior. This situation presented a period of deep crisis for many of the boys in which they struggled with themselves and the group for rejection or acceptance of the goals of the program.

To the extent that the group successfully resolved this struggle in favor of the program, mutual identification and solidarity was heightened and it became an integrated, smoothly functioning unit. In this transition, the group moved into the fourth and terminal stage of development. Personal hostility and aggression were minimal. Major effort was directed to the problems of each boy, and as they were resolved or handled, a boy's self-confidence and that of the group were expressed in constructive helpfulness in the meetings and the rest of the program. Opinions and impressions were freely exchanged in a joint effort to understand the complexities and difficulties of a boy's past life. The content of past meetings and the variety of experiences in the program were drawn upon for insight, and advice was sought and given as to how to meet difficulties to be faced after release. The oldest boy in the group would ask for the meeting to discuss his readiness for release from the program. At this time, new boys would be introduced to the group as old boys left, and preparation would be made to assume the status of a new group.

While all groups experienced a relatively similar sequence of development and growth, each group also had a character of its own. This uniqueness was a consequence of the program flexibility, the kind of boys that made up the group, and the general state of the culture that prevailed at Essexfields at any given time. Some groups developed a remarkable capacity to function in the meetings while others were slow to learn. A sudden influx of new boys might make it difficult to create the solidarity and group identity that supported effective meetings. Too many old boys, occasioned by group reluctance to certify release, might result in flagging efforts. Periods of crisis might give vigor and vitality to a particular group. If a boy had been returned to court, for example, the group might call a meeting's meeting to discuss how they failed and ways of improving, returning the following evening with a new consciousness and self-awareness. A group that had a particularly resistant or defiant boy might rapidly develop solidarity as it closed ranks in a joint effort to help him. Having been helped himself, the same boy might spur on the group to renewed effort in helping other boys and making progress.

Because the boys were given ultimate responsibility for carrying out the program, shared authority and power in decisions important to them, and permission to question procedures and innovate new ones, the meetings could be adaptable to the particular group of boys who ran them. Under the helpful guidance of the staff, the meetings provided a flexible instrument for helping each boy, as together they learned, put into practice, and, hopefully, accepted the status of a helped boy.

COMMENTS

While many of the characteristics and processes discussed in this and the preceding chapter were evident in all aspects of the program, the meetings tended to bring them into sharp focus and involved a group of boys in concentrated discussion, confrontation, and exploration of their problems and ways of handling them. Although it must be recognized that the activities outside the meeting—to be discussed in the following chapter—were an integral part of the total program, the meetings afforded a kind of forum in which group effort could be brought to bear on the rehabilitation objectives discussed as program goals in the first chapter.

According to analysts of group centered corrections, an initial objective for change involves examination by the delinquent of his behavior and attitudes. Most pre-Essexfields relationships offered the boys little opportunity for mutual examination of behavior, and tended to support collective ignorance and shared avoidance of individual introspection. For many of the boys, it seems apparent that the meetings were a unique experience, since they were able to discuss their delinquency free from peer group constraints or defensive postures in response to adult authority. Perhaps for the first time, a boy was confronted by other delinquents who, rather than extending verbal support for delinquency, set about penetrating his defenses by scathing denunciation of familiar rationalizations. Because of this concerted effort to pierce and undermine delinquent attitudes and values, it was possible to activate latent ambivalence where present, or to create it where absent.

At the same time, effort was made to get beneath the surface of justifications and to develop insight into basic reasons for a boy's delinquency. Some ambivalence about behavior would seem to be a necessary condition for changing it, but diffuse anxiety does not offer the basis for a course of action leading to change. What is needed is some understanding of why a boy makes a decision for delinquency and what he can do about it. The meetings provided an occasion to examine problems that were linked to delinquent acts, giving a boy the basis for a course of action. Because criticism of delinquent roles and associations came from boys like himself, and since analysis of his problems and ways of handling them were defined as necessary help in which he ultimately was expected to play an active role, it was possible for a boy to accept and interact with the group. Although group acceptance was based on conformity to a new set of expectations, the meetings allowed a gradual introduction to them and provided ample opportunity to examine and debate alternatives and search for new roles. The focus on problems underscored the idea that a boy's delinquency was a consequence of his own motives, attitudes and values, that he could play an active role in changing them, and that ultimately it was his responsibility to do so.

A second objective of the group-centered approach to corrections involves changing the delinquent's attitudes towards conventional behavior and accepting or adapting to the general restrictions of group living. This involves both a broadening of one's perspectives of others and awareness of how group pressures influence behavior. The consequences of a boy's behavior for himself and others was a constant theme in the meetings. In the boys' terminology, behavior detrimental to others or oneself would be labeled as "inconsiderate of others" or "inconsiderate of yourself," and effort was directed toward revealing the nature of a boy's problem and why he acted in this way. A boy not only had to recognize when behavior violated group expectations, but to understand why it was felt the behavior was wrong. Since responsibility for conducting the meetings and participating in program activities rested directly on the group, boys had to learn to live together in a setting where each boy's behavior had direct and immediate consequence for the others. If a boy failed to check himself or acted in ways detrimental to others, his conduct was subject to detailed discussion in the meetings. Developing awareness of group influence on behavior paralleled this broadening of perspectives on others. When a boy stated his opinions and impressions, he had to be prepared to explain and defend them so as to convince the meeting that they were his own. Going along with the boys, being easily influenced, role playing, or dropping an opinion because of group pressure were subject to probing criticism. If a boy was to convince the group, he must first assure the meeting that he had convinced himself.

A third general objective of the group approach is to change the delinquent's conception of himself. His prior experience is unlikely to have developed much self-awareness, sense of self-worth, or a feeling of self-confidence and reliance, especially in conventional societal roles. Downgrading prior delinquent roles and associates, and defining a boy as a person with problems to be handled rather than a delinquent, set the stage for developing a new self-concept. Getting a boy to reveal and recognize his true self in exchange for group support and acceptance could help to sustain him in his search for a new identity without demanding immediate change that might either alienate him from the group or result in role playing conformity. In the meetings, a boy could learn that his opinions and impressions were important and respected by others. His dual role of helping others while being helped gave him a chance to assume responsibility for others important to him. The group assignment of self help and responsibility and the group support for change provided a structure in which a boy could gain confidence in his ability to have some control over his own destiny as well as to effect the lives of others. The kind of play-back of the day's activities or of events in the past that took place in the meetings allowed a boy to reflect on his self and to become aware of his motives and attitudes and their role in this difficult period of his life. At the same time, program flexibility and the help and support of others provided a setting in which he could search for and test new roles as he gained confidence in himself and his ability to change in a direction supported by the group. For the first time in perhaps many years, a boy could experience success and accomplishment in conventional roles and be rewarded for it by those significant to him.

A final objective of group programs is to acquaint boys with alternatives to delinquent solutions to problems, to learn and test new modes of behavior, and to gain experience as a law-abiding person. Discussion in the meetings frequently revealed that boys had given little thought to alternative ways of handling their problems. Customary modes of deviant adaptation, practiced and supported by associates, were readily available and served immediate needs. Innovation or search for alternatives was likely to take place in the company of other delinquents and to result in elaboration or exacerbation of the delinquent solution.

Once the barriers to collective introspection into delinquency had been pierced and problems identified, boys were in a position to consider ways of handling their difficulties. The same group processes that had tended to support and elaborate delinquent ways could be brought to bear on a search for alternatives. In the meetings, boys could sound out each other's ideas for action and arrive at collective solutions that transcended the limits of isolated individuals. Because each boy had the right and obligation to express his opinions and impressions without fear of punishment or ridicule, the range of inquiry was limited only by the imagination and creative capacity of the group. Unrealistic or unacceptable alternatives were controlled by the fact that boys had to be able to explain and defend them to the satisfaction of others. This frequently resulted in heated and aggressive debate, which in itself allowed boys to test out and practice ways of reaching reasoned decisions short of physical aggression, bogarding, monopolizing, conning, or other customary means of domination. Thus, the meetings were a place where boys could collectively examine and contemplate their life situations and potentials. However, it was in the day-to-day activities outside the meetings that this mutual introspection and exchange could be put to the test. It is to these activities that we turn in the following chapter.

NOTES

1. Matza indicates this function of group meetings in his discussion of the public revelation of shared misunderstandings that may take place in them. He contends that delinquents may be personally uncommitted to delinquency, but in "the situation of company," among delinquent peers, receive and transmit "miscues suggesting commitment." This pluralistic ignorance supports and maintains a mutually shared illusion of adherence to a delinquent subculture. Unless penetrated by deeper, informal peer interaction, affiliation with adult roles, or the more formal mechanism of group therapy such as guided group interaction, delinquents may drift into greater involvement in the subculture of delinquency and, eventually, adult criminality. See David Matza, *Delinquency and Drift* (New York: John Wiley and Sons, Inc., 1964), pp. 50-59.

2. To the extent that this sequence has a discernible patterning common to all groups, Mr. Albert Elias, formerly of the Highfields staff and Superintendent of the New Jersey State Youth Reception and Correction Center, has described the pattern in terms of four stages. The discussion that follows draws from his observations presented privately to the authors. For further comment, see John M. Wall, Albert Elias, and Albert Axelrod, "The Residential Group Center as a Treatment Method for Selected Youthful Offenders Age 16 and 17," a four year report on the Southfields Residential Group Center (March 1966, mimeographed): 6-10.

5

Work and Leisure

The work program, the leisure time between work and meetings, and the nights and weekends at home were integrated parts of the total program at Essexfields. Each of these areas of activity played a role in the process of "helping boys" and, together, they constituted a major source of group discussion at the evening meetings.

THE WORK PROGRAM

The work program at Essexfields performed two major functions. One was to develop attitudes and habits that would orient a boy towards job responsibilities. The other was to provide a relatively realistic setting for interpersonal relationships and to give the boys a common experience in which they could get to know one another and develop some sense of mutuality and common identity.

Work Attitudes

Contrary to some traditional conceptions of the role of work in corrections, Essexfields placed little emphasis on learning a trade or developing specific occupational skills. Although the period of time spent in the program was short, a very concentrated job training program might have been successful in developing certain skills in demand in the job market. It is unlikely, however, that such effort would contribute much to "changing boys" or even develop the initial orientation to work necessary to apply learned skills to the job.

The school, work, and delinquency history of these boys gave little support to traditional work roles. Repeated failure in school, a spotty record of part-

or full-time employment, irregular hours of aimless leisure, and a delinquency code that tended to relegate work to "suckers" and "squares" had not prepared these youths for regular employment even in unskilled or semi-skilled jobs. Therefore, priority was given to the development of motivation and orientation rather than specific skills, and the emphasis was upon learning such patterns as consistency, regularity, planning, and responsibility on the job.

The boys reported to Essexfields at 7:30 each morning. This was a new experience for most of them, since they were more accustomed to late night prowling and getting up late in the morning with little planned or scheduled activity in mind. Reporting on time to a particular place and following through a supervised work schedule provided a structure within which new attitudes and habits might be fostered. This structure did not make them enjoy work, but it provided the opportunity and motivation to become involved in its regular processes and to experience success where previously they had only failed.

In the final analysis, they had no alternative but to join the work program, since they could be returned to court if they failed to do so. However, it is unlikely that this was the primary motivation or even a very significant one for most boys, especially after they had been at Essexfields for a while. What seemed to be far more important was the pressure brought to bear by the group upon a boy who failed to "shape up" at work.

A boy who failed to work satisfactorily was known as a "slicker," and loafing on the job or doing poor work was called "slicking." Although the work supervisor, a member of the adult staff, set the task for the day, seeing that a job got done was largely the responsibility of the boys assigned to it. Individual expectations of job performance were based partly on physical capacity and partly on readiness to perform as evidenced by length of time in the program and progress towards being helped. Two semi-formal sanctions could be applied to boys who were slicking. Upon his own initiative or the recommendation of one or more of the boys, the work supervisor could place a boy "on report." This meant he lost his work pay for a specified period of time, usually a day. As an alternative, a boy might be given "extra duty," which could deprive him of smoking privileges, having desserts at meals, engaging in recreational activities, or require extra hours of work.

The symbolic significance of being on report or getting extra duty was probably more important than the actual penalties involved, since it meant that a boy was not making progress or helping himself. The major emphasis of such sanctions was to make them a learning experience, and they were defined by the boys as help rather than punishment. A boy who failed to conform to work expectations was expected to account for his behavior, to understand why he had violated a group norm, to think of alternative ways of handling the situation, and to relate his deviance to his broader problems. Since what happened at work was always subject to possible discussion at the evening meetings, penalties attached to slicking involved considerably more than simply ritualistically "paying the price" of deviance by losing pay or doing extra work.

The emphasis upon transforming negative punishment to more positive help demanded a flexible and adaptable approach to the boy who violated group norms. Negative response to deviance presents three major hazards. First, a purely punitive response might give rise to a counter-response of hostility and further deviance. Second, a predictable, institutionalized response might provide a structure to which a boy could respond in a calculating, "learn the ropes and beat the system" manner which reinforces his deviant orientation. Third, a "constructive" sanction, such as doing a useful piece of work, could be self-defeating, since a boy might concentrate on the mechanics of getting the job done rather than "thinking about" and "working on" his problems. Furthermore, there is the more general danger that the response might confer status on the deviant.[1] These consequences were minimized by encouraging the boys to be innovative in controlling the work situation. On one occasion, a boy might be required to stand idle until he convinced the group he intended to work properly; at another time, he might be required to dig a large pit and fill it up again. For the same offense, he might simply be given extra duty or be placed on report, and on occasion he might receive no penalty at all. The intent was to keep the potential deviate off balance, so that he could not calculate probabilities, and to keep him thinking about his problems, rather than concentrating on the penalty of a particular work task.

The dollar a day that boys were paid for their work was a small sum, but it was conceived to be an important component of the work program.[2] Loss of pay while on report had some meaning to the boys, since work was their only source of spending money. Hence, it offered some measure of control in the work situation. Boys also might be fined a small sum for program infractions. It probably was more important that token payment gave some tangible and meaningful reward for work well done, symbolizing respect for the job and a non-exploitative attitude towards the boys. This function of money was reflected in the general rule that boys be paid small sums if they were to be employed in any situation where their time or effort was requested. For example, persons who had a legitimate interest in interviewing the boys were asked to pay them a small fee, and boys were paid fifty cents for the Saturday morning clean-up of the Essexfields building. The use of money also required some anticipation, planning, and orientation to the future, if only on a modest scale. The weekly payday became something of an event in the boys' lives, and management of money during the week was sometimes a source of lively discussion.

More positive work motivation was provided by the boys' mutual dependence while working, so that the slicker was letting down the other boys. This group pressure was accompanied by self motivation, since a boy's progress in the program was partially linked to work performance, and early release could be jeopardized by poor work habits. However, work was geared to general development in the total program so that a boy would not easily get by through mechanically fulfilling work requirements but not changing in other respects. Thus, an attempt was made not only to develop a more positive orientation to work, but to integrate work into the day-to-day activities that together were calculated to move boys towards the major goals of the total program.

Providing a Mutual Experience

After the boys arrived at Essexfields in the morning, they were bussed to the county hospital grounds where they started their day's work. Thus began the first of a series of interpersonal relationships that the boys shared and that constituted their day as a group. Because the work was not specialized and was easily rotated among the boys and the number engaged in the joint activity was small, boys could get to know one another quickly in a relatively realistic setting of shared experience. At the meetings, a clever boy might be able to favorably impress the others by his verbal dexterity; in the informal relations that took place while waiting for the meeting or during recreation, he might present himself in a personable manner. However, the work situation was more demanding because stresses and strains were likely to arise naturally during the course of the work day. Thus, the work situation provided an opportunity for a boy to "show his true self" and for other boys to "find out about him."

The problems that arose during work were subject to discussion in the evening meetings. A boy who had been doing poor work would be certain to have his performance discussed by the other boys. Therefore, work offered a daily source of interaction for reality testing of what boys professed at the meetings. A boy who claimed he was making progress towards helping his problems would be challenged by the group if he had been slicking on the job. This confrontation could be devastating to the boy who had been able to convince the others of his good intentions, since even the least verbal boy in the group could readily indicate where he had specifically failed. At the same time, a boy who was doing well on the job presented visible evidence of the progress he was making because what he said took tangible form in what he did.

The common network of interactions involved in carrying out the specific tasks of the work program was supplemented by informal discussion while working. Boys were expected to talk over their problems and to get acquainted with new boys during the day. On particularly cold or rainy days, when work outside was not possible, all the boys might gather in one of the buildings for general discussion. However, most of the time they were placed in small groups on the hospital grounds where they raked leaves, cut grass, transplanted trees, and performed other tasks relative to the maintenance of the property. During the winter months, snow removal was the major work, followed in priority by chopping wood that had accumulated from tree trimming on the grounds. Small groups of boys also might be placed in the carpenter shop where they sanded furniture for painting; sometimes they cleaned motors in the work shop or painted in various parts of the buildings. In making his rounds, the work supervisor not only checked on the work done, but encouraged discussion by asking boys questions about their problems and their knowledge of other boys and where they stood in the program.

Occasionally, a boy would use the work situation instrumentally. He would become involved in the work in order to avoid interpersonal relations. He would be recognized as a good worker but one who failed to talk with the other boys. This, too, was criticized at the meetings, because the boy who concentrated only on the job was failing to meet his other responsibilities to the group. He also might be suspected of role playing or simply trying to "do his time" in order to get out as soon as possible.

Group Leaders

In conformity with the rest of the program, there were few formal rules and regulations governing work. Because work took place on hospital grounds and the boys had their lunch and dinner at the hospital cafeteria, swearing was taboo when patients or staff were around. Boys were also responsible for the care of the tools they used and the safety of other boys with whom they worked. Since the hospital cared for mental patients, the boys were prohibited from conversing with them. Swearing in the presence of patients or staff, talking with patients, careless use of tools, or endangering other boys on the job were occasions for extra duty or going on report.

The work supervisor assigned work and evaluated results. He was helped in his task by appointed "group leaders," selected from the old boys in the program. This practice developed when it became necessary to disperse the boys into small groups to perform a variety of tasks at different places throughout the hospital buildings and grounds. The boys recommended group leaders to the work supervisor, who had the option of final selection. Occasionally, a newer boy would be placed as group leader to test his progress in the program or help him develop confidence and responsibility. To be a group leader conferred some status, since it implied limited authority over other boys and represented recognition of being helped towards release from Essexfields.

The group leaders assigned boys to care for water, tools, and a first aid kit, and were responsible for seeing that assigned tasks were done. They reported to the work supervisor on the progress of the group with which they were charged. As the work program developed over time, an informal practice known as "recommendations" was instituted. After work, on the bus ride back to Essexfields, the group leaders recommended extra duty for boys who had been slicking during the day. Considerable discussion might take place concerning the charge and it could be taken up at an evening meeting. Usually the work supervisor, after hearing both sides, decided whether a boy should be given extra duty. This public revelation inhibited abuse of authority by group leaders, since they had to be prepared to defend the charge. Also, the work supervisor exercised authority over the group leaders and could assign them extra duty if they failed to perform their tasks or abused their authority. In addition, a group leader who abused his position was particularly vulnerable to criticism at the evening meetings, since he was usually an "old boy" in the terminal stages of release from the program. Failure on his part indicated that he had not been helped and had not made the expected progress towards release. A group leader who misused his position could be removed from it by the work supervisor or by the boys themselves. This was a severe penalty, because considerable prestige was attached to the position and most boys looked forward to the time they would be group leaders.

The stratification of authority implicit in the use of group leaders represented a departure from the usual structure of relations among the boys. Although the "old boy" and more particularly the helped boy statuses conferred some prestige, no special authority accompanied them. Both the Director and his Assistant expressed some ambivalence towards the status of the group leader because of a desire to avoid institutionalizing relationships and to spread responsibility to all boys and to the group as a whole. However, the practice was not abandoned for several reasons. It worked out reasonably well, did not give rise to serious problems, and the practical needs of the work supervisor seemed to require it. Furthermore, for the Director to demand a nonessential structural change that was not initiated or strongly supported by the boys would violate the general principle of encouraging initiative, constructive innovation, and flexibility in the program. It perhaps is worth noting that the work situation was the only occasion for stratifying authority in the group, if only in a limited way, and came closest to formalizing relationships among the boys. It may well be that even the limited division of labor in joint work tasks required it.

Work Alternatives

It has been indicated earlier that work expectations varied with the capacity of a boy to assume a particular job. This general principle was extended to what the boys called an "easy day," which was one that required no work. This was granted to a boy who had a particular problem that was bothering him or to one who had been ignored by the other boys. If a boy was being ignored, the work supervisor could assign him to another boy so he could discuss matters without any assigned job. The group also might permit a member to circulate freely among boys who were working to get their opinions and impressions on a problem that was giving him difficulty. Boys might be excused from work to see a doctor or lawyer, but without pay. On occasion, a boy might be needed at Essexfields for the day and received payment for work there. Working alone at Essexfields for the day without pay could be required of a boy who needed isolation from the group to think about his problems or some violation he had committed. Further flexibility in the work program was provided by the previously discussed opportunity to seek employment and work or to attend school outside the program.[3] This provided a bridge between Essexfields and the community for the boy and the other members of the group. It also afforded a stabilizing force when the boy was released from the program.

Meals

At work, boys were provided with lunch and dinner in the hospital cafeteria. This was a new experience for many of them. Few were accustomed to being served complete, well-prepared meals regularly. There was the additional novelty of eating meals in public. The prohibition of swearing was the only formalized rule at meals. However, the boys themselves placed considerable emphasis on manners and decorum while eating. Although most boys had little schooling in table etiquette, and meals provided an opportunity for relaxation and accustomed eating styles, meals became formalized in terms of table manners and politeness. This was different from their interpersonal relations at other times and situations. They seemed to insist on conformity to conventional "company manners" at meals and were strict in their enforcement of them. This may have resulted from what essentially was a new eating experience for many of the boys. It might have been a consequence of the presence of the hospital staff or others who were in the cafeteria. However, this apparent desire to make a good impression is paradoxical, since "impressing" violated the general norm that they should not simulate behavior to seek the favorable response of others. It seems likely that there was some genuine desire to learn and practice conventional eating habits, perhaps in response to the general structuring of the program towards a more conventional orientation. Furthermore, holding down loud talk and noise and controlling behavior associated with the use of food served an instrumental purpose, since the boys realized the program depended upon the hospital cafeteria for meals.

Boys were expected not to leave large portions of food uneaten. One way they controlled this was through three boys appointed by the group leaders to supervise each of the tables where the boys ate. As one of their functions, these boys passed through the cafeteria line early, tasted the food at their table, and then passed the word along to the others who were in line as to the quality and tastefulness of the meal. Also, since they were permitted second helpings, they discouraged large servings on the first time through the cafeteria line. Because desserts were less plentiful and more desirable, the informal rule was that boys must wait until everyone had finished his first helping before trying for seconds.

The various norms governing behavior in the cafeteria were largely worked out by the boys themselves. However, the work supervisor ate with them and helped mediate conflicts that arose, and supervised penalties, which involved withholding dessert privileges. The way that boys controlled eating behavior varied over time, so that there was no rigidly set pattern. The examples given here indicate the innovative nature of group controls. The general flexibility of the program permitted change in group norms and means of enforcing them that were appropriate to particular groups of boys at Essexfields at any given time. For this reason, practices that the boys considered very important at one time might be discarded at another.

RECREATION AND LEISURE

After lunch and during favorable weather, a short period of recreation was available before returning to work. Here the boys freely indulged in rough verbal and physical give-and-take. Football and softball were played in season.

Another occasion for recreational activity was offered before meetings and after return from work. This period usually was less game oriented. A ping-pong table was provided inside, and the back yard at Essexfields afforded some opportunity for play. However, some of the time available for recreation might be given over to "having store." This consisted of electing one or two boys to buy soda and candy at the neighborhood store for those who wished it. Also, some boys were tired after work and wished to rest. Others engaged in informal discussions or began to decide who would have the first meeting that evening. A few might be working off extra duty hours.

The bus ride to and from work was another occasion for informal interaction. This time, however, was devoted primarily to discussing problems and getting acquainted with new boys. This purpose was not rigidly observed and some of the time might be spent in aside remarks on people and events observed from the bus. Boys did not permit sleeping on the bus in the morning unless a boy had a good reason for it. Sleeping would not allow discussion, and would be inferential evidence that the boy had been "clicking with himself"; that is, he did not go straight home after the meeting, and, therefore, did not get enough sleep to report for work the next day.

Before the meetings boys usually were scattered about the building engaged in intense discussion and debate about the day's events and the problems that developed or remained to be resolved. One of the building's several rooms, known as the "back room," had been set aside for general leisure use. Several old but comfortable chairs were scattered about and a bulletin board hung on the wall. Names of recent Essexfields graduates were printed in boxes there, and a running account of their progress after release was kept. The word "busted" was written across the name of boys who had failed to "make it on the outside," sometimes accompanied by derogatory remarks. Great interest was sustained in Essexfields graduates, and boys who did well served as models. Successful graduates often returned to Essexfields and could be seen mingling with the boys during the leisure hours of the evening. They might also be asked to sit in on the meetings, particularly when the meetings were not going well or some problem had developed.

The back room also provided a place to post signs and drawings. These were usually devoted to comments about the state reformatory for youthful offenders, which was the next probable step for boys who failed at Essexfields. Although none of the boys had been institutionalized previously, they knew reformatory boys, and a court disposition to a reformatory carried a certain amount of prestige that one to probation did not. At the same time, they recognized that Essexfields was a "better break" than the reformatory. The boys used this ambivalence to capitalize on the fear and deflate the prestige. Posted around the walls were such signs as "The Reformatory Is Real," or drawings of a boy behind bars with the caption, "Your Next Stop May Be The Reformatory." This received verbal support in the notion that the reformatory was for "punks" and that Essexfields was an elite program, and by frequent reference to the reformatory in the meetings, when boys failed to "shape up" in the program.

Although there was no formal structure to these leisure and recreation periods, they nevertheless played an important role in the program. Precisely because of their loose and uninhibited nature, they gave boys an opportunity to show their true selves and to get acquainted with one another in an atmosphere more nearly approximate to that of the outside.

Sports were important to most of the boys and provided a source of prestige for those who excelled in them. It was important that the boys achieve success and recognition in some aspect of the program reasonably early in their stay at Essexfields, and sports provided one source of group approval, especially for those who were less adept at work or in the evening meetings. However, good sportsmanship was demanded by the boys in an apparent elaboration of street codes. The boy who cheated or "played dirty" was derided, and boys responded favorably to those who "played fair." The character and intensity of play also suggests that it served as a safety valve for the intense and serious interactions that took place in most of the other aspects of the program.

Leisure activities offered opportunities for developing social ties among the boys, and the relationships established in meetings and at work often carried over into leisure. Social relationships had a potential for both positive and negative consequences for the program. They might be instrumental in giving boys mutual support during the many personal crises and difficult interpersonal encounters they were likely to experience during their stay at Essexfields. Such relations also might help a boy through a particularly trying crisis in a milieu that could initially be confusing, bewildering, and threatening. This was particularly true for new boys or weak boys. However, the program emphasized self-confidence and self-reliance, and dependent bonds could interfere with these goals. Furthermore, strong cliques might destroy the effectiveness of the group as a whole. Some boys might be excluded or ignored. Others might form tight cliques that protected members from the impact of the larger group or maintained and gave mutual support to deviant orientations and behavior.

For these reasons, cliques were regarded with some ambivalence by the staff and the boys. When boys established instrumental relationships in opposition to program goals, they were said to be "cliquing together." In its most gross form, boys who were cliquing together might be engaging in delinquency in the community, slicking at work, or violating other program norms and concealing one another's deviance. In milder forms, they might simply "stick up" for each other in the meetings or form a "revenge squad" that tried to dominate other boys and make trouble for them. When boys were found to be cliquing together, it was taken up at a meeting. They would be told that they were only destroying their chances for helping themselves or for the group to help them, that this kind of cliquing was what got them into trouble on the outside, and that they were failing in their responsibility to help other boys who needed it. If they were old boys, they received scathing criticism from new boys for not setting a good example; if new boys, for failing to understand what the program was all about. They might be given extra duty to think about their cliquing together problem or placed in different work groups on the job. New boys were expected to do some cliquing together, and because of its positive potential for them, it was tolerated by the staff and the boys. Old boys, however, were expected to have developed enough self-confidence that they no longer needed to clique together.

NIGHTS AND WEEKENDS AT HOME

The fact that boys spent nights and weekends at home presented a serious, potential hazard to the program. Boys returned to their homes unescorted after meetings and the Saturday morning clean-ups. Some walked to homes nearby; others took the local buses, alone or in the company of other boys. They were expected to go straight home and get sufficient sleep for the day's work to follow and to stay out of trouble over the weekend. This sort of regularity was a new experience for most of the boys and alien to their delinquency history and general life style.

In character with the general program, control of the outside activities was largely carried out by the boys. Probably one very general factor that inhibited delinquency was the culture that developed among the boys. This culture, as noted, depreciated delinquency, downgraded prior delinquent associates as "undesirables," rewarded honest conformity to group norms, defined delinquents as boys with problems that could be solved, stipulated alternatives to delinquency, posed dire consequences for continued delinquent behavior, and presented models of success in boys who had avoided trouble after release.

Behavioral Visibility

For new boys not inducted into this culture and those in the process of assimilating it, a number of controls were informally developed and changed as the situation seemed to demand it. Because boys lived in surrounding communities, some knew each other before Essexfields or had mutual friends and acquaintances. Most had been involved in delinquency for some time and were wise to street ways and the subterfuge, rationalization, and deviousness that often accompany delinquency. Under these conditions, it was difficult at best for a boy to engage in delinquency without the knowledge of some of the other boys. Not to reveal such knowledge to the group would be failing to help a boy who needed it badly. Therefore, boys who engaged in behavior on the outside that might lead to trouble were very likely to come to public attention at Essexfields. Putting this public revelation in terms of "help" seemed to legitimate it with the boys and denied the usual connotation of "ratting" or "squealing" which is one of the strongest taboos of the street code. Moreover, boys who got into trouble were viewed as "defying the group" and might give Essexfields a "bad name," so that deviance became both an individual and a group concern.

The full work schedule each day and the early hours for reporting in each morning offered little inducement for late night hours, but weekends presented a more serious problem. Saturday night was a traditional occasion for celebration, with opportunity for late night prowling and visits to New York City. Frequently, the boys' parents or guardians were out late themselves or engaged in Saturday night parties at home. In this setting, boys might not only be strongly tempted by activities that could get them into trouble, but had an opportunity to seek reinforcement of prior orientations and attitudes. At home and in the streets, they could "lick their wounds," and might seek out "undesirables" to get support for behavior and values that were downgraded or prohibited in the program. It was urgent, therefore, that the time away from work and meetings be viewed as an integral part of the process of getting helped and working on problems.

Saturday Morning Clean-Up

Partial contact with the boys during weekends was maintained by the Saturday morning clean-up. This time was devoted to cleaning, painting, and repairing the building and tending to the small grounds surrounding it. A new boy usually was paired with an old boy in the various assigned tasks in order to facilitate assimilation into the group. On Saturday, boys also received their weekly wage for work done during the week and for the Saturday morning clean-up. They were paid in order of length of time in the program. The oldest boy in the house would then collect fines from boys who had gone on report. This money was put aside as a general fund to buy recreational equipment, to lend to boys who needed it, or to purchase special equipment for use in the building.

At various times, boys who had been released from Essexfields returned to visit Saturday mornings. These visitations resulted in "help meetings" which might be devoted to a boy currently in the program or one who had been released. Sometimes a released boy would come in on Saturday mornings to discuss a problem with the other boys. Frequently, helped boys were asked to hold a meeting for some boy in the program who the Director or the boys felt would benefit from it. Released helped boys carried considerable prestige as successful graduates. Because of his prestige and the fact that he was not involved with the boys currently in the program or subject to criticism (since he had made it and they had not), these meetings could be very effective. Several helped boys in a meeting, with their skill in Essexfields techniques, could be particularly perceptive in discussion with the boy who had the meeting.

Although boys in the program were much less sure of themselves and their chances for success on the outside, they were quick to spot a helped boy who abused his prestige. They were particularly sensitive to helped boys, since they were regarded as models to emulate. There was great dissatisfaction with a helped boy who seemed headed for failure and an almost morbid fear that a helped boy might fail. Therefore, they demanded a clean image of a helped boy, which served to help him in his progress on the outside, as well as to reinforce the program standards among boys currently in the program.[4]

Checking Up

After the Saturday morning activity, boys were "on their own" until Monday morning. Two major ways of helping boys stay out of trouble during this period were developed. If a boy had some problem and the group felt he needed help, another boy could be assigned to him over the weekend; sometimes a boy would ask that another boy spend the weekend with him. "Old boys" usually volunteered for this duty. They accompanied a boy to his home at noon Saturday, stayed with him overnight, and reported in with him Monday morning. During this time, the old boy would discuss the program, try to help the boy with his problems, and see that he avoided trouble. He also might discuss the program with the boy's parents and, in a general way, try to convince the boy of the value of the program and encourage him in handling his problems. These home visitations frequently took place when the group felt a boy was facing a personal crisis or the boy himself knew he was likely to have a problem over the weekend.

If the group felt that a boy was not leveling with them about his weekend activities and there had been reports of drinking, stealing, fighting, or other evidence of failure to be helped, an alternative measure might be employed. This was called "checking up." A boy's home might be called to check what he had told the group or to find out if he was at home as he had reported that he would be. Information might be solicited from friends or relatives concerning his activities or his whereabouts. Rumors about his behavior might be verified or denied by checking up, and then discussed with the boy. Although such activity ordinarily would be viewed with scorn by the boys, they accepted it in the name of helping a boy with his problems. They would tell him that he could not be helped unless he showed his true self, and that lying to the group was "only hurting yourself" and endangering progress in the program. Whatever checking up revealed would become subject for a meeting, where a boy would have full opportunity to explain his activities and other boys could freely express their opinions and impressions of him, their concern about his progress, and ways he could help himself with his problems.

Because boys were aware that weekends were a sensitive period for all of them, and particularly for new boys, what happened at this time became an integrated part of the total program. The staff and the boys expected some deviance, and the weekend was viewed as an opportunity to learn from such experiences. Mondays frequently became an occasion for "confessing on yourself" and boys would discuss difficulties, trouble, or problems they had encountered. Since deviance was expected—especially of new boys—such confessing was taken as a matter of course; the boys who had nothing to say about their weekends were suspected of not leveling. On occasion, this resulted in a flurry of Monday self-reports that the staff or the boys quickly spotted as "impressing." Trying to impress the staff or the other boys in order to "look good" was regarded as a serious violation of group norms and would lead to a discussion of the "impressing problem."

The integration of outside activities into the total program at Essexfields performed two vital functions. First, it maintained community contacts and provided an opportunity to test and practice new modes of behavior in a realistic milieu. At the same time, failure or success encountered at home could be analyzed and discussed in the meetings so that experience on the outside assumed meaning and purpose for both the individual and the group. Second, the very practical need for controlling delinquency could be accomplished in a non-residential program that understandably was viewed with some anxiety and skepticism by authorities and residents in the community. That this control was largely successful is confirmed by the fact that the percentage of boys returned to the courts as in-program failures while at Essexfields was slightly lower than probationers (see chapter 7). Although Essexfields boys were under closer supervision during the day than probationers, offenses were more likely to be detected by the group or the staff, since they were in daily interaction. Essexfields boys also had more extensive delinquency histories and were under greater tension and pressure that might be expressed by trouble in the community. This control is the more remarkable for the fact that nearly a third of the Essexfields in-program failures were sent to the court as unsuitables, involving no delinquency, and none of the delinquencies involved offenses against persons.

COMMENT

In the first chapter, the role played by social structure in the etiology and maintenance of delinquency was stipulated as the basis for a correctional program that would intervene in and reverse the processes that give rise to delinquent conduct. According to this analysis, if change is desired, it can most effectively be accomplished by means of the associations and processes that developed and supported the behavior to be changed.

At Essexfields, boys continued to associate with others significant to them and were subject to group processes similar to those previously experienced. However, the content of these associations and processes was radically different. In the meetings, verbal support for delinquency was withdrawn in favor of critical evaluation of its consequences for others and oneself, probing search for underlying problems submerged by familiar rationalizations, and examination of viable solutions. Outside the meetings, the group pressures and processes that previously gave status and support to delinquent attitudes and values were brought to bear on revealing, assessing, and developing ways of handling everyday problems that arose at work, leisure, and in the community.

Each of the activities described in this chapter was regarded as an integral part of the total Essexfields program. Each was controlled, carried out, and integrated into the program by means of an innovative, flexible, and calculatedly permissive group culture particular to each activity, but also common to the program as a whole. Together, they provided a relatively realistic setting for interpersonal relations for both deviance and conformity, and for testing and practicing what was learned in the meetings. In turn, these activities assumed relevance and meaning as they were discussed, questioned, and probed in the evening sessions. They also validated or denied what was declared in these meetings and provided continuing and visible bench marks of progress (or lack of it) for each boy and for the group as a whole.

NOTES

1. The negative consequences of public or official response to deviance have received considerable attention recently in the literature. One of the best, most concise, and thoughtful discussions of the subject is Edwin M. Lemert's "The Concept of Secondary Deviation" in his *Human Deviance, Social Problems and Social Control* (Englewood Cliffs, N. J.: Prentice-Hall, Inc., 1967), Chapter 3.

2. The use of money in institutional settings presents potential problems, but also helps to provide a dimension of reality and may be used as a technique for behavior modification. Token economies have been used for this purpose in treating retardation and mental illness. An example of this more elaborate use of economic incentive and management in correctional work is found in the Federal Youth Center at Morgantown, West Virginia; see Roy Gerard, "Institutional Innovations in Juvenile Corrections," *Federal Probation* (December 1970): 37-44.

3. This practice is increasingly being instituted in adult correctional programs in the form of work release or work furloughs. One advantage that Essexfields brought to this innovation was that non-participants could profit from it through participation in the selection of candidates and by discussion and evaluation of their work experience. For discussion of work release programs see Sapario R. Zalba, "Work Release—A Two-Pronged Effort," *Crime and Delinquency* 13:4 (October 1967): 506-512 and Alvin Rudoff, T. C. Esselstyn, and George L. Kerkham, "Evaluating Work Furlough," *Federal Probation* (March 1971): 34-38.

4. The use of offenders and ex-offenders in corrections has been practiced in a wide variety of ways in recent years. For a review of current programs, see Albert Morris, "The Involvement of Offenders in the Prevention and Correction of Criminal Behavior," Massachusetts Correctional Association, *Correctional Research*, Bulletin No. 20 (October 1970).

6

Evaluation Research:
Design and Population

Thus far, we have attempted to show the group basis of crime and correction and, in the last four chapters, how one correctional program based upon group principles of behavioral change actually operates. There is often a profound difference, however, between the feasibility and the effectiveness of a therapeutic program. In this chapter and the next, therefore, we shall attempt to evaluate how effective the Essexfields program actually was in achieving its correctional objectives.[1]

It is a well-known and frequently deplored fact that until recent years there has been little evaluative research on the relative effectiveness of treatment or prevention programs in the field of social welfare and rehabilitation. Nowhere is this more apparent than among correctional programs for juvenile and adult offenders. The scattered and intermittent research on traditional adult incarceration programs has been concerned largely with the recidivism of releasees from a single institution without benefit of control groups or comparison with similar facilities or alternative correctional measures. In the absence of such comparison, there is little basis for judging the effectiveness of a program, and one is left to deplore or applaud the findings according to his predispositions.[2] Evaluation of treatment or prevention-oriented programs for juvenile delinquents has fared somewhat better. Probably because there has been greater opportunity for experimentation and a growing insistence that tested methods of treatment and control be instituted, research has gradually increased.

Essexfields provided an opportunity to continue in this tradition and to extend the earlier evaluative studies of Highfields,[3] the first of the Group

Centers in New Jersey. Although the program of treatment at Essexfields was similar to Highfields, Essexfields was non-residential and boys were free in the community at nights and on weekends. It seemed desirable, therefore, to extend the comparison of treatment facilities to probation, to Annandale, the state reformatory, and to the state's three residential Group Centers. This, then, permitted an evaluation of the full range of the major alternatives available to the juvenile court of Essex County. The earlier Highfields research had compared recidivism at Highfields with but one alternative—Annandale.

In New Jersey, probation is supervised by the county. Treatment consists primarily of weekly or bi-weekly meetings with a probation officer, who acts as a counselor and advisor, helping the boy with his problems, lending support and encouragement, and attempting to keep the boy out of further difficulty. Treatment lasts an average of about nine months. Group Centers (Highfields, Ocean, and Warren) are state facilities. The size and nature of these programs are similar to Essexfields. Group Centers are residential, however, and located in rural or semi-rural settings. Treatment lasts an average of four to five months. Annandale is the State reformatory for youthful offenders. Due to a lack of facilities, funds, and staff, the treatment program is restricted and irregular. As conditions allow, a three-stage program is attempted. It consists of a period of approximately two months of half-time social reeducation classes and half-time vocational training or work detail, followed by classification and assignment to cottages and work details, and terminated by a two-month period of community reorientation consisting of parole planning and pre-release classes. The treatment period averages about nine months.

PERIOD OF EVALUATION

Although boys were first admitted to Essexfields in April 1961, this study did not begin intake of cases until January 1962. Since the first boys in the program were transfers from Highfields, they could not represent boys who had only the Essexfields experience. Furthermore, it seemed desirable to allow a period of time for the program at Essexfields to cope with initial operational problems that are likely to confront any new facility.

Because of the nature of the program at Essexfields, only delinquents who met the following criteria were eligible for admission: male, Essex County residents, 16 or 17 years of age, no psychosis, severe neurosis or serious mental retardation, and no prior commitment to a correctional institution. With the exception of Essex County residence, the same criteria for admission apply to the Group Centers. Since the Group Centers and Annandale are state facilities, they receive boys from all counties. Because it was desirable to have a reasonably homogeneous universe of boys, only those who were assigned to these institutions by the Essex County Juvenile Court were included in this study. In addition, only boys who met the criteria of admission to Essexfields were selected to represent the Probation and Annandale treatment programs. Thus, all boys in the study are similar with respect to admission criteria to Essexfields.

It was planned to take cases into the study until a base figure of 100 was reached for Essexfields and Annandale. This, of course, would result in many more boys in the Probation group and some fewer in the Group Centers group. This is because many more boys of the type included in this study are placed on probation than in the other facilities; and fewer boys are placed in the Group Centers, since they are small and receive from all counties, and some Essex County boys eligible for Group Centers were placed in Essexfields, which is not available to other counties. The base figure was reached by January 1965, at which time there was the following distribution of boys in the study: Probation, 943; Essexfields, 100; Group Centers, 67; and Annandale, 100.

All boys were followed up for recidivism until June 1966. This was necessary to assure that the last cases taken into the study by January 1965, would have sufficient time to complete their treatment and return to the community for a period of at least six months. It would then be possible to compare treatment groups for recidivism for six-month periods ranging from six months to approximately two and one-half years.

BACKGROUND DATA

Assurance of reasonable comparability among cases, with respect to such differentiating factors as social background, psychological profile, and delinquency history, presents a major problem in any comparative study. Ideally, it would be desirable to have the court assign boys to the four facilities to assure such comparability or, at least, on a random basis.[4] This was not possible. However, it was felt that it would be possible to match boys across facilities on pertinent variables so as to control to some extent differences that might be found among the four groups of boys.

In order to obtain data upon which to match boys by treatment programs and to see how such data are related to progress in a facility and recidivism after release, information was sought on the boys' social background. This consisted of a series of data that fall into the following general categories: race, education, work experience, mental history, family situation, and socio-economic status. This information was obtained from the pre-sentence investigation report of the Probation Department by a research assistant at the time a boy was assigned by the court to a treatment facility.

Second, a delinquency history for each boy was obtained from court records. This consisted of all previous court appearances and dispositions, number of times a petition was sustained, number of times on probation, age of first court appearance, and any institutionalization in a private training school. In addition, a boy's status at the time he entered the study was obtained. This consisted of the type of offense that brought him into the study, the number of associates involved in the offense, the agency of referral, and age at present offense.

Third, some indication of a boy's psychological make-up seemed desirable. Of the several psychological instruments available, the Minnesota Multiphasic Personality Inventory (MMPI) appeared to be most feasible for this purpose. Resources would not permit an exploration in depth, nor was it possible to design, test, validate, and complete an instrument more suitable for this particular study. On the other hand, the MMPI has been widely used, is readily administered, and gives a reasonably broad psychological profile. Moreover, a number of studies have used the MMPI on both delinquent and non-delinquent populations.[5] Therefore, this inventory was given whenever possible to each boy after his court appearance and before entrance into one of the treatment programs. Because of the large number of probationers relative to the other treatment groups, the MMPI was not administered to members of this group after January 1964. The inventory was administered by the same research assistant attached to the court who collected the data discussed above. In order to test for changes in the MMPI during treatment, boys were again given the inventory at the time of release from their treatment program. This was given by the Superintendents at Essexfields and the Group Centers and the parole officer attached to Annandale. Upon release from probationary supervision, probationers were given the post-treatment MMPI by the research assistant.

Since some of the boys were non-readers or failed to cooperate, it was impossible to test all in both pre- and post-treatment situations. Further attrition of cases was occasioned by changes in institutional personnel administering the tests, in-program failures, and a variety of administrative circumstances.

TABLE 1

Distribution of Available MMPI's by Treatment Facility

	Probation		Essexfields		Group Centers		Annandale		Total	
	N	%	N	%	N	%	N	%	N	%
Received both pre- and post- MMPI	310	32.9	71	71.0	40	59.7	24	24.0	445	36.8
Received pre- MMPI only	162	17.2	19	19.0	22	32.8	41	41.0	244	20.2
Received post- MMPI only	24	2.5	6	6.0	1	1.5	7	7.0	38	3.1
Received neither pre- nor post- MMPI	447	47.4	4	4.0	4	6.0	28	28.0	483	39.9
Total cases	943	100.0	100	100.0	67	100.0	100	100.0	1210	100.0

Table 1 presents a tabulation of both pre- and post-tests available on boys from each facility and the total number of cases in this study.

The MMPI answer sheets were scored on the fourteen regular clinical and validity scales, and these scores were used in the psychological analysis of the study population. Fifteen additional measures, selected from Dahlstrom and Welsch's summary of scales and scoring procedures, were also used.[6] They were selected as having potential relevance to the problem of juvenile delinquency, even though the validity evidence available on some of them was minimal. (Consult Appendix B for a description of all MMPI scales used in this study.)

After the inventories had been scored, they were examined for validity on the *?, L, F,* and *K* scales designed for this purpose. They were not analyzed further if any one of the validity scales fell above the following cut-off points:

?: 37 and above (i.e., 37 or more questions where neither or both alternatives were indicated);

L: 10 or more (indicating an excessive amount of naive lying in a socially desirable direction);

F: 22 or above (indicating enough deviant responses to suggest either deliberate distortion, inadequate reading ability, or some other invalidating condition);

K: 23 and above (suggesting the presence of a set toward subtle distortion in a socially desirable direction: i.e., "defensiveness").

TABLE 2

Distribution of Valid MMPI's by Treatment Facility

	Probation	Essexfields	Group Centers	Annandale	Total
Pre-MMPI	340	66	49	36	491
Post-MMPI	221	44	34	26	325
Both pre- and post-MMPI	160	34	30	15	239

Table 2 gives the distribution of inventories available for analysis after elimination of those determined to be invalid. Means and standard deviations were calculated for all MMPI scales on the pre-test and post-test, and tests of significance were made on the pre-treatment differences between each facility (Probation, Essexfields, Group-Centers, and Annandale). This procedure was carried out on three different groupings of data as follows:

> (1) All subjects who had validly taken either or both pre- and post-tests, using the four validity scales (*?, L, F,* and *K*).
> (2) All subjects who had validly taken either or both pre- and post-tests, using only the *?* scale as a criterion of validity.
> (3) Only subjects who had validly taken *both* pre- and post-tests, using the four validity scales (*?, L, F,* and *K*).

The major analyses were done on grouping 1. However, groupings 2 and 3 were examined to ensure that the criteria employed in arriving at grouping 1 did not lead to significant distortions in the data. It should be noted that grouping 2 included more cases because of the less rigorous use of validity tests, while grouping 3 excluded many cases, since it was composed only of boys who validly completed both the pre- and post-tests.

With these social and psychological data in hand, it would be possible to assess the character of the universe of boys studied, to see to what extent facilities differed with respect to them, and to indicate their relationship to in-treatment progress and post-treatment recidivism.

IN-PROGRAM PROGRESS

It was recognized that some boys would commit offenses while in treatment and be returned to court for further disposition. Others might be recalled to court, escape from an institution, or in other ways drop out of a program. Therefore, information was collected on in-treatment progress. A running account was maintained of all boys who failed to complete the program to which they were assigned. Most of them were boys who were returned to the court because of a new offense, except at Annandale where the boys were in full confinement. However, Annandale boys might be transferred to the reformatory at Bordentown if they proved to be unsuitable; recall to court, escape, death, or extended medical treatment might add to this attrition.

Boys returned to court while in treatment and reassigned to another program constituted in-program failures. They were not picked up as new cases in the facility to which they were reassigned, since they had already been exposed to one treatment program and would represent cases unlike those being studied in the respective facility. The number of weeks between commitment to treatment and court appearance leading to reassignment while in treatment was recorded for in-program failures. For boys who successfully completed a program, the number of weeks in the program was recorded. A record was also kept of the probation or parole officer's notation of "discharged with improvement" or "discharged without improvement" on all boys who terminated probation or parole. It should be noted that Essexfields and Group Center boys returned to probationary supervision after completing their treatment in these programs, and Annandale boys were placed on parole after their release.

RECIDIVISM

Just what constitutes recidivism is not easily determined, and any discussion of the matter is largely determined by definition. The definition, in turn, depends upon the nature of the program studied, the data available for analysis, and the predispositions of the analysts. The problem is compounded when different programs are compared. In this study, several barriers to a simple, one-dimensional analysis of recidivism are apparent.

The first of these problems concerns what constitutes a period of treatment. No difficulty arises from Probation, since release terminates the period of treatment. However, boys are assigned to Essexfields and Group Centers as a condition of probation. When they are released from these programs, they return to probationary status and are under this supervision until probation is terminated. Furthermore, boys released from Annandale ordinarily are placed on parole and are under supervision until it is terminated. This means that boys on Probation have a treatment program of approximately 9 months;

Essexfields and Group Centers boys, a program of 4 to 5 months plus probationary supervision for 4 or 5 months; and Annandale boys, a program of
approximately 9 months plus parole time. It was decided, therefore, to collect
data so as to permit comparison of facilities by both treatment time in a facility and treatment plus post-treatment supervision under probation or parole.

A second problem was the selection of an indicator of recidivism. In this
study, a court appearance indicated that a boy may have committed a new
offense after treatment. However, a court appearance alone does not necessarily indicate an offense has been committed. A judge may dismiss the case
or the petition to the court may be withdrawn. If the judge feels that some
kind of court action should be taken, indicating a judgment that some sort of
offense has taken place, several alternatives are available. The court may
counsel the boy and close the case, restitution may be ordered, or the boy
may be placed with a private agency. If the boy is still on probationary status,
the judge may simply continue or extend probation or recommend that the
boy's adjustment be reviewed. None of these court responses seemed sufficient
to define a case as a recidivism. However, such court appearances were recorded in order to have as complete a post-treatment history as possible.

In some instances, final disposition of a case could not be determined because court action had not taken place by the terminal date of the post-treatment follow-up. Such is the case where a bench warrant has been ordered, a
case has been referred to the Prosecutor or to other counties or states, or is
simply pending court action. Although serious offenses may have been committed in such cases, guilt has not yet been determined. Such cases cannot
objectively be called recidivism, although they were recorded for purposes
of completing the record. The same is true of those few cases that the court
may commit to mental institutions.

Court dispositions of a fine, probation, placement at Essexfields or Group
Centers, sentence to Annandale or Bordentown reformatories, commitment to
a county jail or penitentiary or to a State Prison or a federal institution are
less ambiguous. All such cases were, of course, recorded and defined as recidivism.

A third problem was determining the period of post-treatment follow-up.
Since boys came into the study at different times over a period of several
years and were released after varying periods of confinement or supervision,
it was necessary to record both the date of entrance into a treatment program
and the date of release from it. For Essexfields and Group Center boys, the
date of release from probation was also recorded; and for Annandale boys, the

date of release from parole. The drop-out date for all boys who failed to complete a program was also recorded. This information made it possible to identify boys by amount of time in post-treatment follow-up, permitting comparative analysis of recidivism by equal time periods for each treatment program. It would be possible to assess recidivism both after release from a program of treatment and after release from probationary supervision for Essexfields and Group Center boys and from parole for Annandale boys.

THE STUDY POPULATION

From January 1962 to January 1965, nearly 15,000 children appeared before the Essex County Juvenile Court. Some 4,761 of these youths were boys sixteen or seventeen years of age. Confronted with over 1,500 young men in trouble each year, what alternatives are available to the court?

Considering, first, boys who are not in some correctional program at the time of court appearance, the case may be dismissed or the petition withdrawn and no further action taken. On the other hand, a boy may simply be counselled and the case closed. He may be fined, restitution may be ordered, or private placement may be arranged with the aid of a private agency or the family. Some boys may be committed to a mental institution; others may be referred to the State Diagnostic Center or to private psychiatric services and later returned to the court for final disposition. Finally, a youth may be placed on probation or assigned to Essexfields, one of the Group Centers, or a State reformatory.

If a boy is brought before the court on a new offense while on probation or at Essexfields or Group Centers, these same alternatives are available. In addition, if a boy is already on probation, it may be continued or extended or the case may be referred to the Probation Department for action or for review of the boy's adjustment. A probationer may also be removed from probation and assigned to Essexfields, Group Centers, or Annandale. In some cases, probation may be "vacated," which usually permits a boy to join the Armed Services, live with relatives in another state, or in some other way terminate probation without serving out the usual probationary period. A boy brought to the court from Essexfields, Group Centers, or Annandale may be reassigned to another facility or returned to the referring facility. It should be noted that Essexfields and Group Centers boys may be returned to the court as "unsuitable," without committing a new offense. Occasionally, such a boy is returned to the program, but usually he is sent to Annandale. The parallel but less frequent case at Annandale is the escapee, attempted escapee, or incorrigible, who may be transferred to Bordentown, the State Reformatory for older offenders. If a boy is brought before the court while on parole, most of the options already discussed may be used, except assignment to probation, Essexfields, or Group Centers.

The boys taken into this study are a special sample of sixteen- and seventeen-year-olds appearing before the Juvenile Court of Essex County. Although many have had a history of court appearances and some have been on probation, none have been previously institutionalized, and none were in a correctional program when brought to court. They are further distinguished from other court cases in this age category in that they constitute only those who met the criteria of admissions to Essexfields and were placed on probation or assigned to Essexfields, Group Centers, or Annandale. From January 1962 to January 1965, there were 1,210 such boys.

SOCIAL BACKGROUND

Although race is a biological fact, its social implications are such that it cannot be ignored in considering the boys' social background. Fifty-two percent of them were Negro; 48 percent, white. This distribution reflects the relatively high percentage of Negroes in the metropolitan area of this county and the fact that 70 percent of the boys in this study were from the city of Newark.

These boys came from families that may generally be described as in the lower reaches of a socio-economic continuum. Total family income ranged from welfare subsistence to $10,000 or more. However, 16 percent of the families were on welfare and an additional 3 percent had an income of $2,000 or less. Twenty-one percent had an annual income between $2-4,000, and 28 percent between $4-6,000. Only 7 percent had incomes of $10,000 or more. At the same time, family size was relatively large, ranging from two to seventeen. The mean number of family members was slightly over four. Fifty-three percent of the boys came from families having five or more members, and of these, 5 percent had ten or more.

The occupation of the family breadwinner reflected the family income. Eighty percent were blue collar workers, 75 percent of whom were either unskilled or semi-skilled laborers. Only 9 percent could be classified as owners, managers, or professionals, and 11 percent as lower white collar employees.

The education of the family breadwinner ranged from none (8 cases) to as many as nineteen years (1 case), with a median of nine. Fifteen percent had six years of education or less. Nineteen percent had completed twelve years of education, which ordinarily would indicate high school graduation. Six percent had more than twelve years of education, but of these, less than 3 percent indicated sufficient education to be considered college graduates (16 years or more).

Although detailed information on the homes of these boys was not available, some indication of the status of their family life may be inferred from the following. The marital status of 1 percent of the boys' parents was unknown, and 2 percent had parents who were never married. Thirty percent came from families broken by separation or divorce, 19 percent by death of one or both parents. At the time of their court appearance, 48 percent of the boys were living with both parents and 11 percent with one parent and a step-parent. Thirty percent lived with their mothers only. The rest were living with their fathers, other relatives, or were in foster homes or institutions. Ten percent of the families had a known history of correctional institutionalization of family members, 7 percent of which involved siblings. Family members of 2 percent of the boys had a known history of mental hospitalization. The families appear to have been relatively mobile. Only 18 percent had no history of changing residence prior to the sons' entering this study. Forty-nine percent had made one or two moves; 37 percent, three or four. Six percent had moved five times or more.

The education of these boys leaves much to be desired when compared with ideal standards or other boys in this age group. At the time of their court appearance, half of these boys had dropped out of school or been expelled or excluded. Seventy percent of the out-of-school group were unemployed. Fifty-six percent of all boys were or had been retarded one or more years in school, nearly half of these for two or more years. Nearly 10 percent were or had been in ungraded classes. Of the 114 boys who had been in ungraded classes, 27 were still in school, 52 had quit, 5 had been expelled, 24 were excluded, and 6 had graduated.

DELINQUENCY HISTORY

Although none of these boys had been in a correctional institution prior to the court appearance bringing them into this study, most of them had been known to the juvenile court and many of them to the Probation Department. Over 60 percent had at least one previous court appearance. Three boys had as many as eight appearances. Collectively, these boys had appeared before the court on a total of 1,548 offenses. Although many of these were relatively minor offenses that were ultimately dismissed by the court, over half of the petitions were sustained and many of the offenses were relatively serious. A third of the boys in this study had previously been on probation at least once; a few, two or three times. Sixteen percent had appeared in court before they were fourteen years old; 45 percent, before they were sixteen. Twelve boys had been known to the court since the age of nine.

PSYCHOLOGICAL CHARACTERISTICS

The Minnesota Multiphasic Personality Inventory (MMPI) was used to assess the psychological characteristics of the study population. Of the total sample of 1,210 boys, 769 were administered this inventory. It should be recalled that not all the probationers were given the inventory, since their number was greatly in excess of boys in the other programs. Furthermore, cases were lost because some boys were non-readers or because of administrative difficulties. As anticipated, further attrition of cases resulted when the inventories were examined for validity. Of the 769 boys who took the inventory prior to treatment, 491 had valid MMPI's.

Two conditions should be noted before assessing the general group profile that emerges from these inventories. First, one of the criteria of admission to Essexfields, and hence to this study, excluded psychotics and boys with the more obvious symptoms of neurosis. Second, it seems likely that boys who did not have valid MMPI's may represent the more deviant cases, since invalidity was based on indications of non-cooperation, lying, deliberate distortion, or defensiveness. Hence, these boys might not be expected to vary greatly from central tendencies established by prior use of the MMPI with non-deviant groups. Indeed, such was the case.

A summary of the profile of these 491 cases based on the mean scores of the ten clinical scales reveals that, although all scale scores fall above the mean of 50 established on the Minnesota normal reference group,[7] only the psychopathic deviance (*Pd*) scale reaches a point slightly above the seventy point limit set for normality. The profile summary is presented in Figure 1.

However, these boys conform to the pattern generally found among delinquents.[8] The *Pd* scale, measuring antisocial hostility and rebelliousness, especially the kind common in adolescence, is the significant high point among the ten clinical scales. The second significant characteristic of these boys is an elevated schizophrenia (*Sc*) scale, suggesting a less than optimal grasp of reality, inefficient and perhaps distorted thinking, a tendency toward

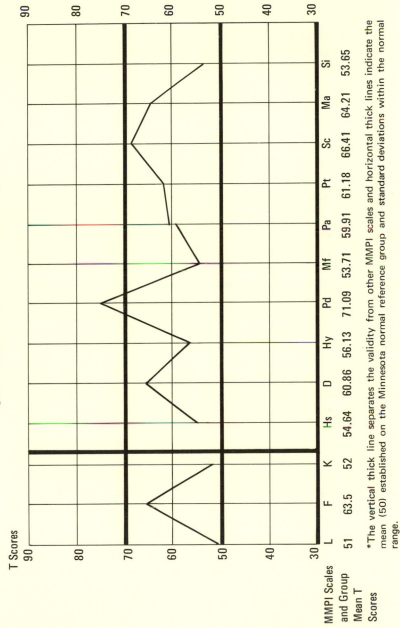

Figure 1. MMPI Profile of 491 Male Delinquents*

MMPI Scales and Group Mean T Scores	L	F	K	Hs	D	Hy	Pd	Mf	Pa	Pt	Sc	Ma	Si
	51	63.5	52	54.64	60.86	56.13	71.09	53.71	59.91	61.18	66.41	64.21	53.65

*The vertical thick line separates the validity from other MMPI scales and horizontal thick lines indicate the mean (50) established on the Minnesota normal reference group and standard deviations within the normal range.

unusual thought processes, and general difficulty in getting close to others. Another significant feature, the elevated hypomania (*Ma*) scale, suggests a relatively high energy level with some lack of the usual controls over expression of immediate impulse. The elevated *F* (deviant response) score is typical of people who show lack of conformity in one respect or another. Taken together, these four highest scores reflect hostility towards society, with some feelings of isolation and alienation, rebelliousness, and relatively high energy level with lack of impulse control, suggesting that immediate pleasure will take precedence over careful planning.

COURT DISPOSITIONS

There has been a good deal of speculation about the process of judicial decision in the juvenile courts.[9] What considerations lead to a dismissal, to counselling, a fine, or other action that does not involve probation or some form of confinement? Why is one boy placed on probation and another in a more supervised program? And among facilities that involve varying degrees of close supervision or confinement, what determines which boy is placed where?

Although the information available in this research cannot answer all such questions, it is possible to use these data to indicate to what extent, if at all, certain known differences among the boys are associated with court dispositions. Such patterns of association may indicate to some extent what factors accompany varying court decisions. At the very least, such exploration would suggest that decisions are either a matter of caprice or chance or that boys are distinguished by certain conditions that differentiate their assignment to a facility. Such information is essential for a comparative study of recidivism, irrespective of its implications for judicial decision.

The four facilities to which boys were assigned in this study represented a rough continuum of supervision and confinement. They ranged from the minimal supervision of probation; to the non-residential but supervised day program at Essexfields; to the 24 hour, minimum security supervision of the residential Group Centers; on to the full confinement of Annandale. The judges who assigned boys to these programs had essentially the same information before them for each case—social background and delinquency history presented in the foregoing discussion. When warranted, information of a more qualitative sort was available from the Probation Department, New Jersey Diagnostic Center, or other services. They did not have, of course, the psychological data derived from the MMPI's. The 1,210 boys in this study were assigned by the court as follows: 943 to Probation, 100 to Essexfields, 67 to Group Centers, and 100 to Annandale.

The general pattern of the distribution of social background variables, delinquency history, and psychological profiles indicated that boys who are more disadvantaged, more delinquent, and more psychologically atypical increase in relative number from Probation to Annandale. Differences among facilities are not great in some instances, the pattern of progression is not always consistent from one facility to another, and sometimes there is considerable variation in distribution within a facility. Nonetheless, the broad, general pattern is one in which Probationers fall at one end, Essexfields and Group Centers boys in the middle, and Annandale boys at the other end of a continuum with respect to these considerations.

SOCIAL BACKGROUND AND TREATMENT PROGRAM

Table 3 indicates that over 70 percent of the Annandale boys are Negro. Group Centers have the smallest percentage of Negroes, followed by Probation and Essexfields.

The distribution of total family income and the occupation and education of the family breadwinner is presented by facility in Table 4. The Annandale boys seem less advantaged in economic placement. A considerably higher proportion of their families receive welfare aid. Over half have incomes of $4,000 or less or are welfare cases, compared with somewhat more than a third of the families of Probationers and with the 40 and 43 percent of the families of boys at Group Centers and Essexfields. Although the pattern of incomplete data on

TABLE 3
Percentage Distribution of Race by Facility

	Probation (N = 943)	Essexfields (N = 100)	Group Centers (N = 67)	Annandale (N = 100)	Total (N = 1210)
White	50	41	55	29	48
Negro	50	59	45	71	52

occupation of family breadwinner is not entirely clear, Group Center boys seem to be the most favorably placed. They have a lower percentage of unskilled and semi-skilled breadwinners, and a higher percentage of owners,

TABLE 4

Percentage Distribution of Family Income and Occupation and Education of Family Breadwinner by Treatment Program*

	Probation (N = 938)	Essexfields (N = 100)	Group Centers (N = 67)	Annandale (N = 95)	Total (N = 1200)
Family Income:					
Welfare	15	18	12	26	16
Less than $2000	2	6	3	1	3
$2000-$4000	20	19	25	25	21
$4001-$6000	28	33	28	24	28
$6001-$8000	19	15	21	12	18
$8001-$10,000	9	4	8	8	8
$10,000 or more	8	5	3	3	7
Occup. of Breadwinner	(N = 737)	(N = 76)	(N = 52)	(N = 67)	(N = 932)
Unskilled	21	35	25	33	24
Semi-skilled	44	41	27	39	43
Skilled	14	12	19	8	13
Clerical	12	7	14	8	11
Owner-Manager	5	3	8	13	5
Professional and Semi-professional	4	3	8	–	4
Educ. of Breadwinner	(N = 891)	(N = 99)	(N = 61)	(N = 56)	(N = 1107)
Grammar school grad. or less	16	15	5	27	16
Some high school	59	65	66	54	59
High school grad.	19	17	21	11	19
Some college or post-high school	3	3	5	7	4
College grad. or four yrs. or more of post-high school	3	–	3	2	3

*Percentages are based on the N's indicated. Unknown cases represent difference between these N's and 943 cases for Probation, 100 cases for Essexfields, 67 cases for Group Centers, 100 cases for Annandale, and 1,210 cases for the total.

managers and professionals. Annandale and Essexfields boys appear to be less well placed with respect to unskilled and semi-skilled occupations. The 13 percent of the Annandale boys whose family breadwinners are classified as owners or managers is puzzling in the total pattern, although the number is small and this category is extremely broad, embracing anything from the owner of a marginal, one person business to the manager of a large corporation. Also, no family breadwinner of an Annandale boy falls in the "Professional and Semi-Professional" category. Perhaps it is worth mentioning that the Annandale group also has the highest number of cases in the "Unknown" category, since it is likely to indicate an absence of the family breadwinner, a history of transitory employment, or a lower occupation.

Of the four groups, the education of the family breadwinners of the Annandale boys appears the least satisfactory. Twenty-seven percent of the Annandale boys have breadwinners who did not progress beyond grammar school, while Group Centers boys have only 5 percent and Probation and Essexfields boys about 15 percent in this category. Annandale boys generally show less favorably at each successive educational level through high school graduation. Although post-high school education improves, the number is probably too small to be significant. What is likely to be more significant is the large percentage of Annandale boys whose family breadwinners' education is "Unknown." The Group Centers boys seem to have the best educational background in their families, since only 5 percent of the breadwinners had less than a grammar school education and 21 percent graduated from high school.

Although differences are not great, the family organization of the Annandale boys is somewhat less desirable than that of the boys in the other programs. They have a slightly higher proportion of families broken by separation, divorce, or death; fewer live with both parents; and a considerably larger proportion are from foster homes or institutions, or live with relatives. There is little difference among boys in the other three facilities, but probationers seem to be in a slightly better position.

In assessing the boys' educational experience, their age at the time of the most recent court appearance is a conditioning factor. Annandale has slightly more boys who are seventeen years of age than do the other programs. The central pattern, however, is that Essexfields and Group Centers have more younger boys than either Probation or Annandale.

Over 70 percent of the Annandale boys have quit school or have been expelled or excluded, compared with approximately 50 percent of the Probation and Group Centers boys and a low of 31 percent of the Essexfields boys. Although Annandale boys are somewhat older than those at Essexfields or Group Centers, fewer have completed the tenth or eleventh grades and considerably more have been in ungraded classes. They compare even less favorably with probation boys, 37 percent of whom have completed the tenth grade or more. However, it should be noted that at some levels the boys are not sharply differentiated by treatment program, nor are the differences found consistently at each level.

Although 52 percent of these boys were not in school at the time of the court appearance that brought them into this study, only 13 percent had full-

TABLE 5

Percentage Distribution of Delinquency History Data by Treatment Program

	Probation (N = 943)	Essexfields (N = 100)	Group Centers (N = 67)	Annandale (N = 100)	Total (N = 1210)
Past Court Appearances:					
None	47	6	7	7	38
One	32	24	15	12	29
Two	12	33	38	19	15
Three	6	21	18	29	10
Four	1	10	7	13	4
Five	1	2	9	11	2
Six	1	3	4	6	1
Seven	*	1	2	1	1
Eight	*	–	–	2	*
Petitions sustained:					
None	60	6	9	7	48
One	27	35	30	27	28
Two	8	32	36	25	13
Three	3	17	16	22	7
Four	1	6	2	8	2
Five	*	2	6	9	2
Six	*	2	2	–	1
Seven	*.	–	–	1	*
Eight	–	–	–	1	*
Times on Probation:					
None	80	15	13	19	66
One	19	67	70	62	29
Two	1	16	16	18	5
Three	–	2	–	1	*
Age first known to court:					
Nine	1	2	–	2	1
Ten	1	1	2	1	1
Eleven	2	8	6	2	2
Twelve	3	2	6	10	4
Thirteen	5	10	12	21	7
Fourteen	11	16	16	15	12
Fifteen	15	33	37	19	18
Sixteen	35	22	19	22	32
Seventeen	28	6	2	8	23

*Less than 0.5 percent

time employment. Annandale boys have the largest proportion of unemployment and the smallest proportion of boys in school. Few boys in any group have an extended work history, and the general pattern suggests short-term intermittent employment. The largest percentage of boys in each facility having one through six months of full-time employment had only one month or less. Although these boys are only sixteen and seventeen years of age, it should be noted that a significant number probably have been out of school long enough for a better employment history than is indicated by these data.

DELINQUENCY HISTORY AND TREATMENT PROGRAM

A fairly clear pattern of progression with respect to the association between delinquency history and treatment program emerges upon examination of the data presented in Table 5. This pattern indicates that the extent of delinquency tends to increase from Probation through Essexfields and Group Centers to Annandale. This progression is most clearly indicated by the number of past court appearances. Nearly half of the probationers have had no prior court appearance, while only 6 or 7 percent of the other boys fall into this category. Twenty percent of the boys at Annandale, 15 percent at Group Centers, 6 percent at Essexfields, and 3 percent on probation have had five or more appearances. Only 40 percent of the probationers, but over 90 percent of the boys in the other groups had one or more prior petitions sustained by the court. Forty-one percent of the Annandale boys, compared to 5 percent of the probationers, had three or more petitions sustained. Eighty percent of the probationers, but only 19 percent of the Annandale boys, had never been on probation before. As a group, probationers were older and Annandale boys younger at the time of their first court appearance. Twelve percent of the probationers, 23 and 26 percent of the Essexfields and Group Centers boys, and 36 percent of the Annandale boys were thirteen or younger at the time of their first court appearance. Almost two thirds of the Probationers were sixteen or seventeen years of age; less than a third of the boys in any other group were that old. Insofar as previous court history and age of first court appearance are associated with continued delinquency, the probationers appear to be the best risk and Annandale boys the worst.

The type of past delinquency does not seem to be closely related to the present court disposition. As Table 6 indicates, boys in all facilities have appeared in court on a wide range of delinquencies, and the offenses of the Annandale boys do not appear to be any more or less serious than those of the other boys. Nor is any particular type of delinquency grossly associated with one or another of the programs of treatment.

If offenses are collapsed into more general types, again no clear pattern emerges. For example, sometimes offenses are typed as crimes against the

TABLE 6

Percentage Distribution of Type of Past Offenses by Treatment Program*

	Probation (N = 846)	Essexfields (N = 228)	Group Centers (N = 171)	Annandale (N = 303)	Total (N = 1548)
Type of offense:					
Manslaughter	**	–	1	–	**
Forcible rape	–	1	–	1	**
Robbery	2	2	5	3	2
Aggravated assault	10	7	7	9	9
Other assault	2	2	3	3	2
Auto stealing	12	10	16	11	12
Burglary/unlawful entry	16	17	10	14	15
Other stealing	15	13	11	12	14
Immorality	1	3	2	2	2
Sex offense	1	1	2	1	1
Drug offense***	2	2	1	2	2
Liquor offense	5	5	2	5	5
Motor vehicle violation	2	2	5	3	2
Truancy	3	8	5	3	4
Running away	3	4	6	5	4
Incorrigible	6	7	10	12	8
Carelessness/mischief	21	17	15	15	18

*If a boy is charged with more than one offense at the time of a court appearance, only the most serious offense has been recorded.
**Less than 0.5 percent
***Includes use of barbiturates

person, property or public policy. Using this typology and given the offenses in Table 6, manslaughter, forcible rape, robbery, aggravated assault, and other assaults are "crimes against the person"; auto theft, burglary and unlawful entry, and other stealing are "crimes against property"; and all other offenses are "crimes against public policy."

With this typology, few differences are again revealed among the four treatment programs. If present offense (the one bringing the boy into this study) is taken as the point of departure, there is some slight indication that the nature of the offense is associated with court disposition.

Annandale boys register highest in crimes against the person and lowest in crimes against public policy. However, Essexfields boys, rather than probationers, appear to reverse this pattern most markedly. This pattern suggests that both a boy's history of past court appearances as well as his present offense may be associated with the court disposition.

PSYCHOLOGICAL CHARACTERISTICS AND TREATMENT PROGRAM

When the psychological characteristics of the four groups are examined, rather distinct differences can be seen. As with many of the social background and delinquency history characteristics, the probation and Annandale groups are the most different, with the Essexfields and Group Centers groups falling between these two extremes.[10]

The probation boys, although exhibiting a distinctly delinquent personality pattern, are significantly less deviant than each of the other three groups on the majority of the characteristics. Thus, they are significantly lower than all other groups on most of the usual clinical scales: hypochondriasis (Hs), depression (D), psychopathic deviancy (Pd), psychasthenia (Pt), schizophrenia (Sc) and hypomania (Ma). They are also lower on the F or deviant response scale. These results suggest that the probation boys as a group are somewhat less antisocial, less delinquent, and better emotionally adjusted than the boys in the other groups. The additional MMPI scales suggest further differences of a similar nature. Probation boys are less anxious than boys in all other groups (lower A scores), less hostile (lower Ho and Ha scores), and exhibit a slightly better attitude toward themselves (generally lower As scores). They are also lower than all other groups on the Dq (delinquency), Ec (escapism), and Rc (recidivism) scales. They score better than the other groups in work attitude (lower Wa scores) and higher in social responsibility (higher Re-r scores). They score lower on the Ps (psychotic signs) index and on the As (attitude toward self) scale than the Essexfields, Group Centers, and Annandale boys. In addition, they are higher in dominance (Do scale) than Group Centers and Annandale boys.

In summary, despite the relatively small absolute differences between the probation boys and the boys in the other groups, the consistency with which a wide variety of differences occurs does suggest that the Probation group is in fact reliably different. While unquestionably identifiable as delinquent (as stated above, the mean high points of F, Pd, Sc, and Ma are usual among delinquent groups), the probation group is less delinquent than the others. These boys show a lesser capacity for antisocial behavior, slightly better control over impulses, fewer signs of maladjustment and, specifically, a lower likelihood of psychiatric disturbance. They are less anxious or hostile, have a better work attitude, and are somewhat more dominant and better socialized.

The Essexfields boys, and to some extent the Group Centers boys, fall somewhere between the probation group and the Annandale group on most characteristics. However, they appear to be somewhat more like the Annandale group than the probation group. They tend to be slightly less deviant than the Group Centers boys from a delinquency standpoint (lower *Pd* score) and to show less anxiety and fewer neurotic signs as well.

The Group Centers boys score higher than all other groups on the *D* (depression) scale, and tend to have somewhat higher scores on the *Hs* and *Hy* (hysteria) scales. They score higher than probation and Essexfields boys on the *Pt* scale. These findings suggest that Group Centers boys are slightly more neurotic than the other groups and have slightly more motivation for change; although taken alone, their motivation for change is still quite minimal.

Boys at Annandale scored higher than all other groups on the *Pa* (paranoia) and *Ma* scales, and tended to score higher than all others on the *Pd, Pt,* and *Sc.* These findings suggest that the Annandale boys have somewhat greater tendencies toward delinquency than the other boys. In addition, they show a greater tendency toward psychiatric difficulty. The Annandale boys also score higher than all other groups on hostility, an overall degree of psychiatric maladjustment (*OE* index), and on the psychotic sign index (*Ps*) while tending to be lower in dominance (*Do* scale).

In summary, Annandale boys are psychiatrically more disturbed than the other groups, but there is conflicting evidence as to whether they should be called more "delinquent." They are most hostile and impulsive, but somewhat less dominant. This description suggests that they are a little less aware of social realities, and might be less likely to initiate a delinquent act; but once involved, they might have stronger impulses and somewhat less control.

SUMMARY

From January 1962 to January 1965, 1,210 boys who were sixteen or seventeen years of age and had no prior correctional institutionalization or serious mental disorder or retardation were assigned by the Essex County Juvenile Court to one of four treatment programs. These boys tended to have a low socio-economic background, a relatively unfavorable family situation, and a poor educational experience. Sixty percent had appeared in court one or more times, and one third had been on probation at least once. Age of first court appearance ranged from nine to seventeen, with 45 percent appearing before the age of sixteen. Collectively, these boys accounted for over 1,500 offenses prior to the court appearance that brought them into this study. Psychologically, they conformed to the personality pattern generally found among delinquents in previous studies using the Minnesota Multiphasic

Personality Inventory. Collectively, their scores revealed hostility and rebelliousness, feelings of isolation and alienation, and relatively high energy levels with lack of impulse control.

Nine hundred and forty-three of these boys were assigned to probation, 100 to Essexfields, 67 to Group Centers, and 100 to Annandale. Their social background, delinquency history, and personality characteristics were roughly associated with assignment to these facilities. Although the association was not always marked nor consistent, Annandale tended to have a greater proportion of boys who were Negro, in the lower socio-economic range, and more likely to terminate their education before high school graduation. Essexfields and Group Centers boys were somewhat younger than either probationers or Annandale boys. Nearly half of the probationers had no prior court appearance, compared to only 6 to 7 percent of the other boys. Similarly, 80 percent of the probationers had never been on probation before, compared with 13 to 19 percent of the boys in the other facilities. Probationers were also generally older than the other boys at the time of their first court appearance. There appeared to be little association between the type of past offenses and court disposition to a particular treatment program, however.

The results of the MMPI suggested that probation boys as a group were somewhat less antisocial, less delinquent, and better emotionally adjusted than the boys in the other programs. The Essexfields boys, and to some extent the Group Centers boys, fell somewhere between the Probation and Annandale boys. The Annandale boys appeared to be more disturbed than the others, and tended to score higher on the scales associated with delinquency.

NOTES

1. This chapter and the next are adapted from the authors' final report to the Ford Foundation, *The Rehabilitation of Delinquent Boys*, mimeographed, (1967): 14-113.

2. Daniel Glaser's *The Effectiveness of a Prison and Parole System* (New York: The Bobbs-Merrill Co., Inc., 1964) presents a review and critique of earlier evaluative research and an extensive study of the Federal Prison Service. Correctional research in California has been notable for evaluative studies. See, for example, Stuart Adams, "Some Findings from Correctional Caseload Research," *Federal Probation*, 31 (December 1967): 48-57 and Marguerite Q. Warren, "The Community Treatment Project: History and Prospects," *Law Enforcement Science and Technology*, 1 (1967): 191-200. Evaluation of preventive programs may be found in Edwin Powers and Helen Witmer, *An Experiment in the Prevention of Delinquency* (New York: Columbia University Press, 1951) and Walter B. Miller, "The Impact of a 'Total-Community' Delinquency Control Project," *Social Problems*, 10 (Fall 1962): 168-191. In abstract or original form, all of these studies are pre-

sented in Norman Johnston, Leonard Savitz, and Marvin E. Wolfgang, eds., *The Sociology of Punishment and Correction,* 2nd ed. (New York: John Wiley and Sons, Inc., 1970).

3. Lloyd W. McCorkle, Albert Elias and F. Lovell Bixby, *The Highfields Story* (New York: Holt and Co., 1957); H. Ashley Weeks, *Youthful Offenders at Highfields* (Ann Arbor: University of Michigan Press, 1958).

4. Random distribution is probably the more feasible of the two. However, personnel and policies beyond the control of the researchers are likely to change over the course of an extended study, and agreements made at one phase of research may not be carried out in another. Furthermore, even where some system of random assignment is worked out, problems may arise that inhibit adequate instrumentation. (See, for example, the Annual Progress Report to the Ford Foundation for 1964 on the Provo Experiment in Delinquency Rehabilitation; and Second Progress Report, Evaluation of Southfield's Treatment Center, to the Ford Foundation, August 10, 1965).

5. See S. R. Hathaway and E. D. Monachesi, *Analyzing and Predicting Juvenile Delinquency with the MMPI* (Minneapolis: University of Minnesota Press, 1952) and *Adolescent Personality and Behavior* (same press, 1963); W. G. Dahlstrom and G. S. Welsh, *An MMPI Handbook* (same press, 1960); G. S. Welsh, *Basic Readings on the MMPI in Psychology and Education* (same press, 1956).

6. W. G. Dahlstrom and G. S. Welsh, *An MMPI Handbook* (Minneapolis: University of Minnesota Press, 1960).

7. Dahlstrom and Welsh, *An MMPI Handbook,* Chapters 1 and 4.

8. The authors are indebted to Professor Richard I. Lanyon, Department of Psychology, University of Pittsburgh, who assisted in the interpretation of MMPI data.

9. See, for example, Frank R. Scarpitti and Richard M. Stephenson, "Juvenile Court Dispositions: Factors in the Decision-making Process," *Crime and Delinquency* 17 (April 1971): 142-151.

10. Since the MMPI was given after court disposition, the differences may be a consequence of the response by the subjects to the relatively favorable or unfavorable disposition they received. However, the variety of scales used, the fact that most items in the scales are not time- and situation-bound, and the presence of scales ($?$, L, F, and K) to test validity may mitigate this possibility somewhat. Furthermore, the differences in the delinquency history of the subjects raise the question of the *relative* impact of the current court appearances and disposition. Nearly half of the probationers had never appeared in court before, and 80 percent had never been on probation. Even though they were placed on probation, the experience of a court appearance and the implications of a delinquency status may be quite as devastating to them as the harsher disposition of boys who have longer delinquency histories, have had one or more court appearances, and have been on probation before. For the latter boys, both their past experience and the present expectations concerning probable court disposition based on their delinquency history may mitigate the impact of the more severe disposition for them. Finally, if test-taking were of major significance in test scores, post-release scores might also be expected to manifest this relationship. We could conclude that reformatory boys would show more favorable scores on the post-treatment tests than on the pre-treatment tests and would have scores equal to or more favorable than probationers', since their release would seem to be a much greater gain than simply being released from probation. This was not the case. Reformatory boys showed the least improvement and even evidenced some decline on some of the crucial scales. (See Chapter 7, Section II.)

7

Evaluation Research:
Assessment of Impact

In this chapter, three types of data are examined in order to evaluate the overall effectiveness of the various treatment programs. First, those boys who failed to complete their assigned programs are compared with those who did successfully complete them. Second, the psychological changes occurring during treatment are examined for the boys who completed their treatment programs. Third, the amount and nature of recidivism is determined for all program participants. Through an examination of these data, the impact of each program can be seen in terms of its ability to hold the assigned delinquents during treatment, to affect any personality change as measured by the MMPI, and to deter further law violation after release.

I. IN-PROGRAM FAILURES AND SUCCESSES

"In-Program failure" is used to refer to any boy who was sent back to the court during the course of the treatment program and who was not returned by the court to the same program. It refers to those boys returned to court for committing a new delinquent offense, being incorrigible and unmanageable while in the program, or, in the case of Essexfields and Group Centers, being unsuitable for the program. "Unsuitability" refers to boys who are returned to the court by the program director because they could not be integrated into the program of treatment. "Unsuitables" usually are boys who are too emotionally insecure or socially immature to interact meaningfully with the group and participate in the guided group interaction sessions. In-program failures do not include those cases recalled by the court for a reason other than those listed above. Nor does it necessarily mean that the court's new disposition was more severe than the original placement. In essence, the in-program failures were those boys upon whom the various rehabilitation programs had the least immediate effect, not even providing them with an opportunity to experience the entire treatment process.

As might be expected, Annandale, the only custodial institution of the four facilities studied, had the greatest success rate in this respect. Of the 100 boys committed to Annandale, 97 successfully completed the program, two were transferred to the more secure Bordentown Reformatory for incorrigibility and drug use while in the institution, and one was still incarcerated at the termination of this study. Since in-program success and failure for Annandale inmates is not the same phenomenon it is for the other groups studied, they will not be considered further.

Aside from Annandale, the in-program success and failure rates for the other facilities were strikingly similar. Although the failure rate for Essexfields, 23 percent of the committed boys, is lower than that for probation and Group Centers by 5 and 4 percent respectively, these differences are not significant. These rates indicate that the overwhelming majority of the boys in the non-custodial programs do complete their treatment experiences without becoming involved in further difficulty.

The in-program failures committed a wide variety of offenses leading to their return to court. Because of the small number of failures in the Essexfields and Group Centers programs, comparing their distribution by offense with that of the probation group is not particularly meaningful. However, it can be pointed out that of these boys who committed offenses while in treatment, over one-half of each group committed offenses against public policy rather than person or property. Whereas some 27 Probation failures committed a personal offense, none of the failures in the other two groups did so. In addition, seven Essexfields boys were returned to the court because of unsuitability for the program.

The court dispositions for those boys returned as program failures reveal that 52 percent of the probation failures were committed to Essexfields or Group Centers, an alternative disposition not available to Essexfields or Group Centers failures. Within these latter groups, most (83 and 78 percent, respectively) were committed to a state reformatory, as were nearly one-third of the Probation failures.

Essexfields program failures fail earlier than those in the other two groups. As Table 7 shows, nearly 74 percent of them are returned to court during the first twelve weeks of their program participation, with the great bulk (12 of 17) failing within the first four weeks. Slightly more than 61 percent of the Group Centers failures also fail within the first twelve weeks, but many fewer within the first four weeks (3 of 11). The difference in time of failure between these groups is not statistically significant. Probation failures are also slightly more prevalent within the first twelve weeks, but not to the extent of the other groups. Failure in this group is spread over a much longer period of time. To a certain extent, this is to be expected since probationers participate in their program for a much longer time than do participants in the other two programs. However, since the first twelve weeks constitute a time period shared by all, the difference in the failure rates between probation and the other two programs is striking.

TABLE 7

Percentage Distribution of In-Program Failures by Weeks Spent in Treatment Programs before Failing

Weeks	Probation (N = 255)	Essexfields (N = 23)	Group Centers (N = 18)
1-12	38	74	61
13-24	25	26	39
25 or more	37	–	–

The Essexfields failure rate during the early weeks of a boy's tenure is somewhat inflated as a result of seven boys' being returned to the court as unsuitable. This determination is made early in the program. When the unsuitables are taken into account, the Group Centers and Essexfields rates are more comparable. However, the probation rate is still considerably lower than that of the other groups. It is possible that one explanation for this difference may be that the Probationers are generally less delinquent and better able to withstand the pressures to deviate for a longer time. In addition, the pressures of the two group programs may be too great for some boys and, coupled with the looseness of the program structure and the availability of community contacts, delinquent behavior r' sumes. Furthermore, offenses committed by Essexfields and Group Cer .ers boys are probably more likely to come to the attention of the directors, who are in constant contact with boys in their facilities.

Social Background, Delinquency History and In-Program Failure

Of the many background variables available for analysis in this study, only three differentiated program failures from program successes, and these pri-

marily for one program, probation. Race, school status at time of admission
to the program, and educational status score were significantly different for
probation failures and successes. These factors were not significantly related
to program failure and success in Essexfields nor, with one exception, in
Group Centers.

Table 8 shows the racial distribution of the successes and failures in the
three groups. In probation, whites have a lower failure rate and a higher success
rate than Negroes. This difference is significant at the .02 level (x^2 = 6.46).[1]
Essexfields shows the same rates for success and failure by race. The Group
Centers data, on the other hand, show striking internal differences, with
Negroes having a much lower failure rate and a higher success rate. These
differences are statistically significant at the .01 level (x^2 = 7.51).

TABLE 8

Percentage Distribution of In-Program Failures and Successes by Race

	Probation		Essexfields		Group Centers	
	Negro *(N = 462)*	*White* *(N = 464)*	*Negro* *(N = 57)*	*White* *(N = 43)*	*Negro* *(N = 31)*	*White* *(N = 36)*
Failure	31	24	23	23	16	36
Success	69	76	77	77	84	64

In terms of school status at time of admission to the program, a more consistent picture emerges from the data. In all three groups, more program successes are either in school or graduated from school than are in-program
failures. Boys who were out of school at the time of their admission are more
likely to fail. Again, the significant difference occurs between the probation
groups (x^2 = 35.73; p = .005), but the same trend is found within the other
programs as well. In all but the Essexfields group, at least one-third of those
out of school do not succeed in their programs, whereas less than one-fifth
of those in school become program failures. The Essexfields data, on the other
hand, show much less difference between those in and out of school in terms
of failure and success, but the difference that does exist corresponds to that
found in the other groups.

Educational status score,[2] a composite index which includes present school
status, number of grades completed, and number of years retarded, presents
a very similar picture of the successes and failures within each treatment
group. With low scores representing positive educational status and high
scores the converse, program successes score more positively than failures in

every case. When the status scores are collapsed into two categories, positive (3-5) and negative (6-9), the differences between the failures and successes on this variable are statistically significant for the Probation group (x^2 = 16.02; p = .005), but not for the others.

Although nearly four-fifths of all boys with positive educational status scores succeed in their respective programs, a large percentage of negative scorers also succeed. Therefore, it would appear that a positive educational status enhances one's opportunity of program success, just as school status does, but is not solely responsible for it. Success or failure in the Essexfields program seems to be related less to educational status than it is in the other programs. Only in probation, for example, does a majority (56 percent) of the success group fall into the positive category. In both Essexfields and Group Centers, a majority of the program successes (53 and 54 percent, respectively) can be designated as having a negative educational status score.

Delinquency history data do not differentiate each program's failures from successes any more sharply than the social background data. The age at which the boy was first known to the court indicates that Probation and Essexfields failures were slightly younger when they first received official recognition for their delinquencies. However, the differences are only fractional and are reversed for the Group Centers.

The delinquency history score,[3] another composite index consisting of age first known to court, number of delinquent offenses, and types of delinquent offenses, was also used to differentiate between program successes and failures. Again, the results were not very informative. With scores ranging from 3.0 to 8.0 or more, a majority of the members of each group, failures and successes, are located in the less delinquent, low-score categories. When the scores are collapsed into a low (3.0-5.4)-high (5.5-8.0+) or positive-negative dichotomy, some 81 percent of the failures and 87 percent of the successes on probation fall into the positive category. Although the percentages are not high, a majority of the Essexfields failures (52 percent) and successes (65 percent), as well as the Group Centers failures (67 percent) and successes (57 percent), also place in the positive category. These findings verify what has been reported earlier, that the probation group is obviously less seriously delinquent than the other groups. Even probation failures generally have lower scores than successes in Essexfields and the Group Centers.

Nevertheless, in both probation and Essexfields the proportion of boys with low scores who succeed is greater than the proportion of success with high scores. Although the rates of program success and failure are not significantly

different for low and high scorers in Essexfields, they are statistically significant (x^2 = 4.43; p = .05) for the probation group. The distribution for Group
Centers, however, is not consistent with that of the other programs. High
scorers in the Group Centers have a better success rate (although not statistically significant) than do the low scorers.

Personality and Program Success and Failure

Pre-treatment MMPI scores were also used in attempting to differentiate
between program successes and failures. However, as with the factors examined thus far, this produced only modest results at best. The relatively small
number of failures in the Essexfields and Group Centers programs, coupled
with the fact that not all boys in any of the programs had valid MMPI tests,
produced the following number of cases in each group: Probation success—
239, failure—101; Essexfields success—51, failure—15; Group Centers success—
38, failure—11.

Again, the greatest differences are seen between the probation successes
and failures. Nineteen of the thirty-two MMPI scales used in this study differentiate these two groups at the .05 level of significance or better (derived from
the standard error of the difference between uncorrelated means). Among
those tests which distinguish between the groups are the *Pd, Ma, Sc* and *F,* as
well as the delinquency, escapism, and social responsibility scales. All of these
differences are significant at the .01 level or better, and, as with the other
tests which differentiate, the probation successes score more positively than
do the failures. The failures clearly have a more delinquent personality pattern,
conforming closely to the classic pattern for delinquents.

All of the scores for the probation successes indicate that they are not
very disturbed and are fairly well adjusted. Probation failures, as indicated,
are less so, but are similar to both the failures and the successes in Essexfields
and Group Centers. In these groups, there are practically no significant differences between program successes and failures as determined by the MMPI
tests. However, failures, in both programs generally score more negatively
than do successes on most tests. Although many of the success-failure differences in the Essexfields and Group Centers programs are in the same direction
as those found in probation, they are milder and less able to distinguish between the criterion groups.

These data seem to indicate that the Probation successes are less delinquent
and better adjusted than all other boys in this study, successes or failures. In
Essexfields and Group Centers, the successes and failures are more similar to
each other and to the probation failure group.

II. PERSONALITY CHANGES DURING TREATMENT[4]

The changes made by boys while on probation were relatively minimal. Although the large size of the sample resulted in a fairly substantial number of statistically significant differences, the greatest absolute changes were no more than two or three T-scores.[5] Of the basic MMPI scales, the only significant changes were an increase[6] on the D (depression) and K (defensiveness) scales, and a decrease on the Pa (paranoia) and Si (social introversion) scales. While this pattern of change is not readily meaningful, it becomes clearer upon examination of the remaining scales. Decreases occurred on the A (anxiety) and Ne (neuroticism) scales, although these changes tend to be inconsistent with the increase in D. Other changes were an improvement in Ao (attitude toward others), in As (attitude toward self), in Wa (work attitude), in Iq (intelligence), and in Do (dominance).

These scores suggest that a definite though slight change did take place in the boys during their probationary term. The changes were not in the scores characteristic of delinquency (Pd, Ma, and Sc), however, but in a variety of other areas.[7] Overall, the boys became a little less anxious, and more outgoing, secure, and intellectually efficient. Also, there was improvement in attitudes toward themselves, others, and work. The slight decrease in Pa seems to have little meaning, since larger decreases were shown by all other groups. Further, in light of the other scores, the increase on the D scale probably reflected no real change.

Changes shown by the Essexfields boys were somewhat more marked than those shown in the probation sample, but were by no means startling. The most noteworthy change was a decrease of almost six T-scores in the D scale, accompanied by comparable decreases in anxiety, social introversion, and neuroticism. There were also moderate decreases in several indicators of relatively severe disturbance (Pa, Pt, and Sc scales, overall profile elevations, and Peterson's psychotic signs), though these failed to reach significance because of the large variation. Other significant changes were a decrease in Ho (hostility), and in Ec, a scale predicting the likelihood of making an escape from a prison-like institution. Finally, there was a highly significant improvement in work attitude and a moderate improvement in attitude toward self.

Again, the scores suggest that definite changes occurred in the boys, though not necessarily the kind commonly associated with reduction in delinquent tendencies. There were noteworthy reductions in scores indicating general psychopathology, as well as improvements in attitudes.

The changes that took place in the Group Centers boys were again noticeable though not marked. The nature of these changes was a little different from those occurring in the probation and Essexfields boys. For the Group Centers boys, the only change for the regular MMPI scales was an increase on the *Mf* (masculinity-femininity) scale, indicating a change in the direction of more esthetic and cultural interests, passive pastimes, and verbal rather than physical expression. This change was supported by a sizeable decrease on the *Ho* (hostility) scale and on the *Dq* (delinquency) scale. Other changes were similar to those found in the two previous groups: an improvement in attitude toward self, attitude toward others, and work attitude, an increase in ego-strength, and a decrease in anxiety level.

Changes were generally smaller for the Annandale boys than for the other groups, although some caution should be observed in interpreting the results because the Annandale sample was the smallest. There were some moderate but not significant reductions on several of the regular MMPI major pathology scales, but no other notable changes. Scores on the *Ho* (hostility) scale *increased,* and there was a trend toward increase on the *Rc* scale (measuring tendency toward recidivism). The changes found in each of the other three groups—improved attitudes and ego-strength, and reduced anxiety—were absent.

Relationships Between Social Background and Changes During Treatment

Pre-treatment MMPI scores for the total sample were dichotomized on five variables: socio-economic status,[8] delinquency history, race, education, and parental status.[9] The effects of these dichotomies were studied within each treatment group, to see how they related to changes during treatment. The recidivism data are discussed later.

Socio-economic status (SES). Personality differences between high and low SES boys were minor, the only one of note being a higher score on the ego-strength scale for high SES boys. This suggests greater self-assurance and better prognosis in verbal therapy. The high SES boys also scored higher on the attitude toward others scale.

The changes made during treatment by high and low SES boys differed somewhat according to the treatment facility. For boys on probation, high SES was associated with greater change than low SES.[10] High SES boys showed a slight but definite improvement with respect to neurotic difficulties, anxiety, and general emotional adjustment and security, as evidenced by lower scores on the depression, social introversion, anxiety and neuroticism scales, and higher ego-strength scores. A decrease in K scores suggests a greater openness in their responses. Improvements also occurred in attitude towards self, attitude toward others, work attitude, and dominance. For low SES boys, the changes were much more modest, with some improvement in ego-strength, neuroticism, and attitude towards self and others.

At Essexfields, the changes were greater in magnitude, and more pronounced for the low SES boys. These boys showed improvement in general outlook on life, social facility, and anxiety, as indicated by changes on the D, Si, A, and Ne scales, and in overall profile elevation. Work attitude and attitude towards self also showed firm improvement. Another marked change was a reduction in the Pd scale, indicating less rebelliousness and increased acceptance of social standards. These changes took place in a less marked way for the high SES boys. For them, an additional (non-significant) trend can be noted—slight increases on the Hy and Mf scales, which suggests increased ability to manage physical aggression.

In Group Centers treatment, the low SES boys again tended to show more changes than high SES boys, though the small number of cases precludes a satisfactory analysis. No definite patterns are apparent among the changes.

At Annandale, high and low SES boys differed in their response to treatment in several interesting ways. Low SES boys decreased markedly in depression and increased markedly in hostility, suggesting that the major change for these boys was in their ability to direct aggression outward rather than inward. In spite of this change, overall level of adjustment for these boys appeared to improve. The high SES boys showed, if anything, some deterioration in their adjustment. While the only statistically significant change was a decrease in dominance (Do scale), there were sizeable increases on the Sc, Hs, and Hy scales and in overall profile elevation.

If generalizations were to be made from the above results, they would suggest that high SES boys tended to improve slightly more than low SES boys when placed on probation. At Essexfields and the Residential Group Centers, treatment may have been slightly more favorable for low SES boys, though both groups showed some positive changes. At Annandale, however, high SES boys seemed to fare poorly, becoming, if anything, more maladjusted in a passive sort of way. Low SES boys improved in adjustment, but probably not in delinquency proneness, since changes indicated a definite increase in the externalization of hostility.

Delinquency history (DH). Overall, delinquency history made a negligible difference in terms of pretreatment personality. The mean differences on this variable were generally in favor of the boys with lower DH scores, but were very small and almost entirely insignificant.

Probation boys with low DH scores fared slightly better in treatment, but the differences were quite small. The improvement pattern for low DH boys is almost exactly identical to that of high SES boys. Thus, the low DH boys showed slight improvement in anxiety, neuroticism, and social facility, and slight but definite attitude changes. High DH boys showed fewer changes, but did improve significantly in ego-strength, attitude towards self, and dominance. However, their scores on the *Re* (recidivism) scale also increased, suggesting a change towards a greater likelihood of violating probation.

At Essexfields, high and low DH boys showed about an equal degree of change, and of a fairly similar nature. Both groups showed definite improvement in anxiety, mood, and social interaction. There were also improvements in work attitude and attitude towards self. In addition, the low DH boys showed a marked decrease in hostility and an increase on the *K* scale, which together suggests a greater degree of control over the expression of hostility.

At the Group Centers, both high and low DH boys seemed to make some changes, but they were more pronounced for the latter. They showed significant changes on the *A* (anxiety), *Cy* (cynicism), *As* (attitude towards self), *De* (delinquency) and *K* scales, indicating better control over expression of feelings and improved general adjustment.

The Annandale group contained too few boys with low DH scores to permit comparisons. For the high DH boys, the only significant change was an increase on the *Re* (recidivism) scale, indicating an *increase* in the personality characteristics associated with recidivism.

To summarize for all groups, boys with low pre-treatment delinquency history scores tended to show greater improvement in personality characteristics than boys with high delinquency history scores.

Race. White and Negro boys differed slightly though definitely in pretreatment personality characteristics. The white boys tended to be better controlled and to show less direct expression of hostility (lower *Sc, Ma, F* and *Ho* scores; lower scores on the psychotic sign index), and a greater degree of sociability (higher *Hy* and *Ao* scores, lower *Si* score). However, they also scored higher on the *De* scale, indicating a greater propensity for delinquent behavior. It is possible that these differences might reflect general cultural differences as much as personality differences specific to the present groups.

For the probation group, changes were small and differed little between white and Negro boys. Both groups improved in ego strength, anxiety, attitude toward self, and in socially outgoing tendencies (lower *Sc* and *Si* scores). The Negro boys showed a notable reduction on the *Pa* scale, which, in conjunction with changes on the *Sc* and *Ao* scales, suggests a more relaxed and accepting attitude toward others. The white boys showed slight improvement in neuroticism and apathy (changes in *Ne, D,* and *Do* scales). Thus, both groups improved slightly with respect to certain characteristics which might be considered typical of them—apathy for the white boys, suspicion and resentment for the Negro boys.

At Essexfields, marked changes were shown by the Negro boys, in contrast to minor changes by the white boys. The Negro boys showed large improvements on four of the clinical scales—*D, Pa, Pt,* and *Sc,* as well as on the overall elevation score. These changes suggest considerable improvement in general adjustment and in psychiatric status. Coupled with improvement on the *Ne* and *A* scales, they also indicate greatly reduced anxiety. Taken together with changes on *Si, Wa,* and *As,* they suggest a much more conforming attitude to society, greater ability to relate to others, and the development of skills for socially facile, outgoing behavior. The white boys, in contrast, showed only minor improvements in better work attitude and slightly less neuroticism. Changes on the clinical scales were in the expected direction but not significant.

At the Group Centers, the greater changes were made by the white boys, though these were not as pronounced as those of the Negro boys at Essexfields. Significant improvement occurred in attitude toward self, attitude toward others, work attitude, and ego-strength. There were reductions in hostility, anxiety, and depression, and a number of sizeable though statistically insignificant changes on the clinical scales. These changes suggest definite increases in confidence and general feeling of well-being, as well as an increased acceptance of the modal values of society.

Changes in the Annandale boys can be evaluated only tentatively because the sample, especially in the white group, is so small. Probably the white boys showed slightly more positive change than the Negro boys, although both both groups changed minimally.

Education. Some minor differences in pre-treatment personality existed between the boys with good and poor educational backgrounds (henceforth designated GE and PE, respectively). PE boys were slightly more anxious (higher *Pt* score), more poorly socialized (lower *Sr* score), and more like a typical delinquent population (higher *De* score). These differences were minor but consistent.

In the probation group, definite improvements were shown by the PE boys, in distinct contrast to an absence of such change in the GE boys. PE boys showed improvement in general adjustment and in their orientation to the realities of life (decreases on the *Pa* and *Sc* scales, and on overall elevation and psychotic sign index). They also improved slightly in anxiety, neuroticism, and general well-being (*D, Es, A, K,* and *Ne* scales), and in attitude toward self, attitude toward others, and work attitude (*As, Ao,* and *Wa* scales). Increased social facility and conformity was indicated by changes on the *Si* and *Ho* scales. On the other hand, GE boys showed a lessening of impulse control (increased *Ma*), and other negative though insignificant changes on the clinical scales.

Among the Essexfields boys, some reasonably large changes seemed to occur. Both GE and PE boys improved in anxiety and neuroticism (*A* and *Ne* scales), and in work attitude. Other changes were slightly different: PE boys showed stable improvement in psychiatric adjustment; specifically, they became more friendly, with fewer suspicions, guilt feelings, and self-doubts (lower *Pa* and *Pt* scores, higher *As* scores, lower overall elevation). The GE boys showed a decrease in hostility (*Ho* and *Es* scales) and an improvement in general mood and social friendliness (*D* and *Si* scales).

The improvements at the Group Centers were slightly smaller and were pretty well confined to the PE boys. These boys showed some increase in interest in verbal expression (higher *Mf* scores), and some insignificant reductions on the clinical scales. The GE boys showed insignificant *increases* on most clinical scales, in addition to a poorer attitude toward others (*Ao* scale) and increased hostility (*Ho* scale).

At Annandale, PE boys made mixed changes. While changes were quite variable, general psychiatric adjustment improved, with the exception of a sizeable though statistically insignificant decrease in ability to control impulses (*Ma* scale). In addition, hostility scores increased. The GE boys made virtually no change. Although the group was extremely small, making statistical comparisons difficult, the absolute changes were also very small.

In summary, it seems that PE boys responded with some improvement when on probation, more when at Essexfields, some when in the Group Centers, and made psychiatric but no social improvement in Annandale. Curiously, GE boys showed far fewer changes. Only in Essexfields could improvement be considered to have occurred, and in some instances—on probation, for example—they may have gotten worse.

Parental status. Pre-treatment differences between boys who lived with both real parents (Group P) and those who had not been living with both real parents (Group O) were negligible.

For the probation boys, small changes occurred during treatment for both groups. The changes were basically similar—improvement in confidence (*Es, Do,* and *As* scales), self-control (*K* scale), and neuroticism (*Ne* scale). The changes for Group O boys were slightly greater, and included further improvements in attitudes and ability to relate to others (*Si, Ao, Ho,* and *Wa* scales).

For the boys at Essexfields, changes were of approximately the same order of magnitude as for boys in other groups. In each case there was a reduction in anxiety and improvement in relating to others (*Si* scale). In addition, the Group P boys showed a sizeable improvement in social conformity (*Pd* scale), while the Group O boys showed improvement on other indices of conformity and cooperation (*Es, Ho,* and *Wa* scales).

At the Group Centers, more improvement was shown by Group P than Group O boys. The former showed consistent (though mainly nonsignificant) improvements on the clinical scales, with a large decrease in depression, indicating increased optimism and enthusiasm. These boys also improved in anxiety, attitude toward self, and work attitude. Changes in Group O boys were smaller, with the only significant one being a decrease in hostility.

The small size of the Annandale sample again makes it difficult to interpret the results for this treatment. The pattern of changes is inconsistent and not clearly different for Groups P and O, except that the Group P boys seem to have become less able to control their own behavior and more likely to become recidivists over the treatment period.

To summarize, the parental status variable did not produce large differences as a result of treatment. Probation treatment seemed to favor the boys in Group O, while the Group Centers produced slightly more change in Group P boys. Annandale appeared detrimental to Group P boys, although this interpretation is a tentative one.

Personality Changes During Each Treatment Program for Matched Groups

Subgroups from each of the treatments were matched to within one T-score on the three MMPI clinical scales traditionally regarded as predictive of delinquency: *Pd, Ma,* and *Sc.* Matching on these scales resulted in the overall elevation on the clinical scales being approximately equal, although individual scale differences varied somewhat. Since the subgroups resulting from this procedure were so small, 15, and since comparisons of difference scores were being made, differences significant at the .10 level were noted. The conclusions drawn from such findings are necessarily tentative and might best be considered as guidelines for further work.

The important aspect of comparing matched groups is that it offers a more valid picture of the degree of personality change taking place over the course of each treatment, presumably as a result of the treatment. The data indicate that the changes made by the matched boys were fairly consistent with those made by the larger groups which were not matched on pre-treatment personality characteristics. On the regular clinical scales of the MMPI, the matched Probation group made fairly small changes, but these changes were entirely in accord with expectation. The largest decreases were on the *Pd, Ma,* and *Sc* scales, while the largest increase was on the *Mf* scale. No other group showed this pattern of change. Essexfields boys showed larger decreases, of a more general nature, as did Annandale boys. Changes shown by the boys at Group Centers indicated mainly a reduction in anxiety and depression.

With regard to the remainder of the scales, about the most that can be said is that Probation boys showed significantly more changes than Annandale boys, who changed not at all on these indicators. Many of these scales assess positive personality characteristics rather than pathology. Probation boys seemed to change slightly more on these scales than Essexfields and Group Centers boys, while both of these groups changed slightly more than the Annandale boys.

To summarize, the following statements are offered. Probation boys made relatively slight but definite improvements in personality characteristics specifically related to delinquency, and tended to show the most marked attitude improvements—certainly greater than the lack of attitude change shown by Annandale boys. Boys at Essexfields and Annandale did achieve sizeable reductions in general personality difficulties even though attitude improvements were negligible at Annandale and greater (though not significantly so) at Essexfields. Group Centers boys showed changes fairly similar to those at Essexfields, except that they improved only in anxiety and depression rather than in overall pathology.

III. RECIDIVISM

Although the criteria used in studying the effectiveness of correctional programs differ, one common element frequently found in evaluative research is recidivism.[11] Objections to the use of recidivism as a criterion of "success-ful" treatment may be raised on at least three grounds. First, recidivism indi-cates only one aspect of the effectiveness of a program of rehabilitation. Improvements in work habits, educational orientation, family adjustment, or personality characteristics are not necessarily indicated by the fact that a new offense is or is not committed. Second, it may be asserted that a treatment program has prepared a person for reintegration into society, but the circum-stances of the community to which he returns are such that rehabilitative effects are rapidly eroded and opportunity for reintegration is relatively closed. Third, a person may commit numerous infractions of the law or con-sort with known delinquents or criminals without arrest or conviction and still be regarded as a "success." These considerations give rise to others: what are the long range effects of treatment; what are the implications of treatment for different patterns of recidivism; on what grounds is success or failure to be ascribed to treatment; would no treatment at all give the same results?

These are valid objections and inquiries. Nevertheless, an avowed goal of corrections is to inhibit a return to crime and delinquency. Short of daily surveillance of individual cases or reliable community sources of informal information concerning them, the available evidence for estimating effective-ness in reaching this goal is the official record of court appearances and dis-positions. This evaluation, therefore, seeks to answer one major question: to what extent do those released from a program of treatment become involved in delinquency or crime again as indicated by court action? If at all possible, a much more extensive research effort than afforded here would be necessary to answer the many other queries raised by this single question.

The Indicators of Recidivism

Boys who completed a program of treatment and had no court appearances from their date of release to June of 1966 are clearly non-recidivists. Although it can be argued that they may have been delinquent but not apprehended, or apprehended but not brought to court, no problem is presented in classifying them as non-recidivists by the definition employed in this study.

Boys who had one or more court appearance after release are not so readily disposed of, since a court appearance is not sufficient to regard a case as a recidivist. A wide range of alternative dispositions are available to the court that may indicate a minor offense or even none at all. Therefore, court dis-positions were used as the basis for determining recidivism. The numerous alternative court dispositions pertinent to recidivism made during the course of this research are listed below.

1. Case dismissed
2. Petition withdrawn
3. Private placement
4. Overbrook or Trenton hospitals
5. Restitution ordered
6. Counseled
7. Adjustment to be reviewed
8. Referred to parole
9. Probation extended
10. Probation continued
11. Probation vacated
12. Referred to other states or counties
13. Bench warrant issued
14. Case pending
15. Fine
16. Jail
17. Probation
18. Essexfields
19. Group Centers
20. Reformatory
21. Prison

It is clear that these dispositions differ in degree and kind. It was decided that the first fourteen would be designated "Court Appearance: Non-recidivist" and the last seven "Court Appearance: Recidivist." This decision was made on the following grounds.

The first fourteen dispositions are of several different types, but none indicates that the court views the case as demanding more intensive correctional treatment or punitive action. When a case is dismissed or a petition withdrawn, an offense may have been committed. However, the action of the court is the only available evidence, and the presumption must be that the offense was not committed, could not reasonably be assumed to have been committed, or was so minor as to require no further action. Cases referred to Overbrook or Trenton State hospitals indicate mental observation and treatment and therefore, are not regarded as delinquencies. Similarly, "private placement" indicates private psychiatric care or private institutional placement and is not considered a recidivism. Cases pending, referred to other states or counties, and out on a bench warrant represent "lost" cases, since court disposition had not been made by the termination date of this study.

The other non-recidivist court dispositions are somewhat more marginal. Where a case was counseled or restitution ordered, it was felt that the offense was too minor to be considered a recidivism; at least, no action was taken of the order that originally brought a boy into this study. "Adjustment to be reviewed" indicates a wait-and-see policy on the part of the court; if no further action was taken, the case was not counted as a recidivist. The same is true of "referral to parole," if no other action followed. "Probation extended or continued" indicates that a boy was brought to the court while on probation; and as far as recidivism is concerned, this refers only to Essexfields and Group Centers boys. Since assignment to these facilities is a condition of probation, boys are returned to probationary supervision after treatment. A "probation extended or continued" disposition may result from a violation of the conditions of probation or some minor offense, but it does not indicate court action requiring a change in supervision or a more harsh penalty. Hence, this action was not viewed as recidivism. (It should be noted that regular Probationers who had their probation "extended" or "continued" during treatment were not counted as in-program failures on the same grounds.) "Probation vacated" refers to special cases where a boy is released from probation to join the Armed Services, live with relatives in another state, or terminate probation in some other way without serving out the full probationary period or receiving a regular discharge.

The recidivist court dispositions also vary in degree and kind, but all involve more intensive treatment or punitive action. "Fines" (except for Motor Vehicle Violations) and "jail" indicate a sentence as an adult. It might be argued that a fine suggests a minor offense and should not be considered as a recidivism. However, the offender's alternative may be either a fine or jail, and the only difference between recidivism and non-recidivism then becomes a matter of whether the fine can be paid. Furthermore, since recidivism involves both boys who are still juveniles and those who have become adults, court dispositions may vary with age. For example, the same case that is placed on probation as a juvenile may be fined as an adult. If a fine is not to be considered an indicator of recidivism, age alone would define the juvenile as a recidivist and the adult as a non-recidivist. A further consideration is the fact that the boys in this study have already experienced different types of court dispositions that are likely to affect future dispositions. Analysis of delinquency history and court assignment to the treatment programs of this research has shown that the number of past court dispositions, petitions sustained, and probation placements are associated with assignment to a treat-

ment program. In terms of recidivism, this suggests that Annandale and possibly Essexfields and Group Centers boys are more subject to institutional
confinement than a fine or short jail sentence.

This differential probability is certainly true of other recidivist court dispositions. Probationers who commit a new offense after treatment can be
placed again on probation, assigned to Essexfields or Group Centers as a
condition of probation, or sent to Annandale. Annandale boys, on the other
hand, do not have the option of Essexfields or Group Centers at all, since
they have been institutionalized. If they have previously had court dispositions
to probation, Essexfields, or Group Centers before assignment to Annandale,
there is a reasonable probability that on successive court appearances probation will be viewed as a less valid alternative by the courts. Similarly, Essexfields and Group Centers boys are unlikely candidates for these facilities
once having experienced them.

Some studies have used a sentence of a specific minimum period or more
to a correctional institution, or a felony charge leading to incarceration, as
the criterion of recidivism.[12] Neither seems appropriate for this analysis because different types of programs and cases involving both juveniles and adult
offenders are compared. Therefore, a court disposition to probation (including assignment to Essexfields or Group Centers), as well as a fine or jail sentence, constitute recidivism. In addition, of course, assignments to a reformatory or a prison are recidivisms.

Evaluation Periods

The four treatment programs being evaluated involve different periods of
treatment and different post-treatment situations. Probation and Annandale
average about nine or ten months of treatment and Essexfields and Group
Centers about four or five months. When a boy is released from probation,
his treatment is completed, and he is no longer under any supervision. When
Essexfields and Group Centers boys complete treatment, they are returned
to probation and continue to be under supervision for the duration of their
probationary period. When Annandale boys are released, they ordinarily are
placed on parole until released from parole supervision. Thus, the post-treatment conditions differ in that probationers have no further supervision after
release from treatment, while Essexfields, Group Centers, and Annandale boys
do. Furthermore, the length of time Essexfields and Group Centers boys are
in treatment and under supervision differs from that of the Annandale boys.

These different periods of treatment and supervision may have implications
for the analysis of recidivism in the four programs. However, the crucial

period of evaluation for purposes of this study is the date of release from treatment to the terminal date of the study, June 1, 1966. It is assumed that the time spent on probation, and at Essexfields, Group Centers, and Annandale represents "treatment." This discounts the fact that the period of treatment for Essexfields and Group Centers boys is about half that for probation and Annandale boys; that Essexfields, Group Centers, and Annandale boys continue under supervision (probation and parole) after treatment; and that Annandale boys have a longer period of supervision than do Essexfields and Group Centers boys. The following tabulations were made to attempt to account for these differences:

1. Recidivism from completion of treatment to termination of the study for all four programs.
2. Recidivism from completion of treatment to termination of supervision for Essexfields, Group Centers, and Annandale.
3. Recidivism from completion of supervision to termination of the study for Essexfields, Group Centers, and Annandale.

Since boys were taken into the study at different times and the possible period of time after release from treatment varied among programs, it was necessary to control for amount of time in which recidivism might take place after treatment. This was accomplished by holding constant, for all four programs, follow-up time after release from treatment. Follow-up was divided into six-month periods for a maximum of forty-seven months.

One final consideration should be mentioned at this time. Previous analysis has shown that the different treatment programs tend to draw somewhat different kinds of boys with respect to social background, delinquency history, and psychological profile. Although these differences were not, for the most part, great they may affect recidivism. Therefore, insofar as possible, it was desirable to control for these differences by matching boys across facilities. This procedure and the findings will be discussed later.

Recidivism After Treatment

Table 9 indicates that of the 894 boys who completed treatment, 212, or 24 percent, were recidivists within a period of three years from their date of release. There was no further recidivism after three years, although some boys were in the community for as long as forty-seven months. Table 9 refers to the first recidivism only. In-program failures are not included in this table or those that follow.

Setting aside for the moment the fact that boys in different programs differ in social background and delinquency history, it can be seen that Annandale

TABLE 9

Number of Recidivists, Cumulative Recidivists, and Cumulative Percent of Releasees Who Are Recidivists in Treatment Programs by Six Month Periods

Mos.	Probation (N = 671)			Essexfields (N = 77)			Group Centers (N = 49)			Annandale (N = 97)			Total (N = 894)		
	#R	CR	C%	#R	CR	C%	#R	CR	C%	#R	CR	C%	#R	CR	C%
6	50	50	7	12	12	16	8	8	16	20	20	21	90	90	10
12	37	87	13	9	21	27	5	13	27	16	36	38	67	157	18
18	9	96	14	8	29	38	5	18	37	9	45	46	31	188	21
24	5	101	15	6	35	45	2	20	41	6	51	53	19	207	23
30	1	102	15	1	36	47	–	–	–	1	52	54	3	210	23
36	–	–	–	1	37	48	–	–	–	1	53	55	2	212	24

N = Number of releasees (completed treatment)
#R = Number of recidivists
CR = Cumulative recidivists
C% = Cumulative percentage of releasees

boys have the highest recidivism rate (55 percent) and probationers, the lowest (15 percent).

Essexfields and Group Centers boys fall between these extremes, although recidivism is somewhat lower for Group Centers boys (41 percent) than for Essexfields boys (48 percent) and terminates earlier than any other program. This general pattern is also repeated when recidivism is figured by six month periods. (The differences in rates of recidivism between probation and each of the other three programs are statistically significant at a level greater than .001. The differences among the other three programs are not statistically significant.)

Table 10 shows whether the recidivisms took place during or after the supervision (probation for Essexfields and Group Centers boys and parole for Annandale boys) that followed release from treatment. Probationers are not included in this table, since they were not under supervision after release from treatment. It can be seen that recidivism for Essexfields and Group Centers boys rises sharply after supervision. This may be partially explained by the fact that they have a longer period of time within which to become recidivists after supervision than during it. However, their recidivism rates are slightly higher while under probationary supervision than failure rates while in treatment. Furthermore, as Table 11 indicates, recidivism rates for probationers for the first two six month periods after treatment (when they are no longer under supervision) are higher than either Essexfields or Group Centers

TABLE 10

**Percentage Distribution of Recidivisms after Release from
Treatment Programs during and after Supervision**

	Essexfields (N = 37)	Group Centers (N = 20)	Annandale (N = 53)
During supervision	38	30	98
After supervision	62	70	2

boys during these same two periods. This seems to indicate that delinquency increases as the degree of involvement with correctional programs decreases. This does not seem to be true of Annandale boys as far as parole is concerned. All but one of the Annandale boys became a recidivist while still on parole.

Among recidivists, the highest percentage of recidivism was within the first six months, and nearly 75 percent of the recidivism took place within a year after release (Table 11). Probation recidivists appear to have the highest rate of recidivism within the first year, which decreases strikingly thereafter. Noting the early termination of recidivism among the Group Centers boys, the other three programs appear to spread out recidivism over a longer time span. As suggested above, this difference may be indicative of the fact that boys in these three programs were under supervision after release, while probationers were not. This seems to be true of Essexfields and Group Centers but not Annandale boys.

Among recidivists, there were a considerable number of boys who had more than one recidivism during the period of time from release from treatment to the terminal date of this study. Table 12 shows, for each program, the percentage of recidivists who had one or more recidivisms. Essexfields is

TABLE 11

**Percentage Distribution of Recidivisms by Six Month Periods
for Each Treatment Program**

Mos.	Probation (N = 102)	Essexfields (N = 37)	Group Centers (N = 20)	Annandale (N = 53)	Total (N = 212)
6	49	32	40	38	42
12	36	24	25	30	32
18	9	22	25	17	15
24	5	16	10	11	9
30	1	3	–	2	1
36	–	3	–	2	1

the exception to the fact that the majority of recidivists committed only one recidivism. Group Centers recidivists appear the least likely to engage in successive recidivism. However, both probation and Annandale had some boys who were recidivistic from four to six times, while none of the Essexfields and Group Centers boys had more than three recidivisms. Since the numbers involved are small and the probability of successive recidivisms is conditioned by court disposition of the first (a boy can hardly commit an offense while incarcerated, for example), one can only speculate about these differences at this time.

TABLE 12

Percentage Distribution of Recidivisms for Recidivists in Each Treatment Program

Recidivisms	Probation (N = 102)	Essexfields (N = 37)	Group Centers (N = 20)	Annandale (N = 53)	Total (N = 212)
1	63	43	65	62	59
2	20	38	30	25	25
3	12	19	5	6	11
4	4	–	–	6	3
5	–	–	–	2	*
6	2	–	–	–	1

*Less than 0.5 percent

Fifty percent of the recidivists had at least one court appearance that was non-recidivistic, and a few boys had as many as five. Essexfields had the lowest proportion of boys without such court appearances (35 percent), while no Group Centers recidivist had more than two non-recidivistic court appearances. There does not appear to be much difference between probationers and Annandale boys.

The fact that half the recidivists appeared in court from one to five times, in addition to those appearances leading to one or more recidivisms, suggest that these boys have a relatively high involvement in delinquency. In contrast to the recidivists, only 25 percent of the non-recidivists had one or more court appearances. Among treatment programs, the court appearances of non-recidivists ranged from a low of 13 percent among probationers to a high of 32 percent among Annandale boys.

Recidivism Offenses

The distribution of offenses committed by recidivists does not appear to vary grossly from that of the pre-treatment offenses. (It should be noted that pre-treatment offenses are based on court appearances, while post-treatment offenses are based on recidivist offenses; that is, court appearances leading to a recidivist court disposition.) One notable exception is drug offenses, which rose from a total of only 2 percent to 16 percent. Some other offenses changed in the expected direction. For example, there were no "Truancy" or "Run Away" offenses among recidivists, and "Motor Vehicle Violations" increased from 2 to 11 percent. These changes would appear to be a function of age. In general, it appears that these youths continue to be involved in about the same types of delinquencies.

Recidivism Court Dispositions

Jail was the single most common court disposition (42 percent). Fines, probation, and reformatory sentences trail behind with about equal percentages (18, 16, and 18, respectively). Probationers were the only boys eligible for Essexfields and Group Centers, and only 4 percent of them were so placed by the court. This small number probably reflects the fact that many of these boys were too old for such programs by the time they had been released from probation and spent some time in the community prior to their first recidivism. Only 2 percent of all recidivists were sent to prison. Both age and offense history no doubt play a role in this court disposition.

The fact that about 80 percent of the recidivisms do not involve either a reformatory or prison sentence may indicate that these recidivistic youths have not yet become deeply involved in the more serious forms of criminality. The distribution of offenses appears to support this proposition. It may be that many of these boys will continue to receive court dispostions of this order for many years to come. If the correctional facilities have done no more than to hold the line of recidivism at this level, they have accomplished something significant, even though the goal of complete rehabilitation is not reached.

After Treatment Time

In assessing rates of recidivism for the four programs of treatment, one important consideration is the length of time boys are free in the community to commit recidivisms. Table 13 shows the number and percentage in each program who completed treatment and who were in the community for successive six month periods for a total of forty-seven months. It also indicates the percent of non-recidivists and recidivists at each six month period.

During the first year after treatment, the period of highest recidivism, all programs had approximately the same proportion of boys in the community.

TABLE 13

Percentage Distribution of Non-Recidivists and Recidivists among Boys Completing Treatment for Six Month Periods after Release for Each Treatment Program

Mos. After Treatment	Probation (N = 671)				Essexfields (N = 77)				Group Centers (N = 49)				Annandale (N = 97)			
	#Boys	%Comp.	%NR	%R	#Boys	%Comp.	%NR	%R	#Boys	%Comp.	%NR	%R	#Boys	%Comp.	%NR	%R
0-6	671	100	93	7	77	100	84	16	49	100	84	16	97	100	79	21
7-12	563	84	93	7	65	84	86	14	41	84	88	12	71	93	77	23
13-18	437	65	98	2	51	66	84	16	36	73	86	14	44	45	80	20
19-24	261	39	98	2	39	51	85	15	30	61	93	7	30	31	80	20
25-30	150	22	99	1	28	36	96	4	19	39	100	–	16	16	94	6
31-36	90	13	100	–	21	27	95	5	12	24	100	–	12	12	92	8
37-42	34	5	100	–	14	18	100	–	8	16	100	–	6	6	100	–
43-47	3	*	100	–	5	6	100	–	4	8	100	–	0	0	100	–

*Less than 0.5 percent

N = Number of boys completing treatment
#Boys = Number of boys in the community
%Comp. = Percent of all boys completing treatment (% of N)
%NR = Percent non-recidivists (% of boys in the community)
%R = Percent recidivists (% of boys in the community)

This extends somewhat into the eighteen months period, although the proportions are not as equal. The major exception is Annandale, which had 9 percent more boys exposed during the twelve months period and about 20 to 28 fewer exposures through eighteen months. Even though the proportion of boys exposed for one year is approximately the same for all programs, recidivism follows the previously established pattern. Probation has the fewest recidivists, Annandale the most. The proportion of Annandale boys in the community appears to decrease more rapidly than any other program after twelve months, and its recidivism rate remains higher at each six month period. Both Essexfields and Group Centers had a larger proportion of boys in the community for nineteen months or more than either probation or Annandale. This is to be expected, since the treatment period at Essexfields and Group Centers is shorter than the other two programs by at least four or five months. The larger proportion of Essexfields and Group Centers boys in the community after nineteen months may partially account for the higher proportion who are recidivists after nineteen months when compared with probationers. Again, Group Centers boys seem to do better than Essexfields boys, and both programs have considerably fewer recidivists after nineteen months than does Annandale.

Matched Comparisons

Since boys in the four treatment programs were found to differ with respect to social background and delinquency history, an attempt was made to match cases across programs. With the exception of probationers, the total number of boys in each program was relatively small. This meant that to match on more than two or three background variables was not feasible.

Hence, race, socio-economic status, and delinquency history were selected as matching factors[13] for several reasons. There was a clear imbalance among facilities in the distribution of Negro and white boys. This was particularly apparent among Annandale boys, since over 70 percent of them were Negro as compared with the 41 to 51 percent in the other three programs. Although race is not considered here to be a factor independent of other background variables, the nature of race in our society is such as to suggest differences not entirely encompassed by the other two matching factors. For example, the nature of the family may differ significantly by race. Indeed, such is the case with these boys. Fifty-eight percent of the whites, but only 38 percent of the Negroes, in the total sample came from homes with both parents present; 23 percent of the whites, but 36 percent of the Negroes, live with their mothers only; 26 percent of the whites, but 44 percent of the Negroes, live in families with six or more members; and 53 percent of the whites, but 85 percent of the Negroes, reside in the urban area of Newark. Similarly, although boys of both races have a relatively poor educational history, Negroes are consistently more disadvantaged with respect to number of years of school completed, number of years retarded, number of boys still in school, and number who were expelled or excluded. (Although these differences were small, ranging from 4 to 8 percent, they were consistent in each case.) This same pattern followed with respect to part-time and full-time employment history.

Socio-economic status (Social Economic Score) places these boys on a broadly defined continuum of stratification. Since data were incomplete on some of the indicators used in this Score and occupation of breadwinners was not always sufficiently specified in the available data, and because no single indicator seemed sufficient for general placement, family income and the occupation and education of family breadwinners were combined. Although combined indices of this sort are subject to criticism, it was felt that for general matching purposes this Score would differentiate boys sufficiently in terms of broad, social background considerations. No claim is made that this Score distinguishes boys systematically by "class," "white collar"-"blue collar," or other discrete categories found in traditional stratification analysis. However, since many studies have shown that such variables as income, education, and occupation are associated with a wide range of attitudes and behavior, including delinquency, the boys were matched on this Score. In addition, analysis of these variables has shown some difference in their distribution among boys in the four treatment programs.

The Delinquency History Score, used to match boys on delinquency history, attempts to equate boys in the four programs on the basis of their involvement in delinquency prior to treatment. Again, prior analysis has shown that the programs differ with respect to the delinquency history of boys in them; and to the extent that type of offenses, number of court appearances, and age of first court appearance are associated with the probability of continued delinquency, the Delinquency History Score attempts to match boys in terms of their delinquency status.

It was possible to match only forty-four boys across all four programs on the three matching factors. After elimination of in-program failures, the following rates of recidivism were obtained: Probation (N = 34), 21 percent; Essexfields (N = 35), 49 percent; Group Centers (N = 31), 45 percent; and Annandale (N = 41), 56 percent. (The differences in rates between Probation and each of the other three programs are statistically significant at a level greater than .01. The differences among the other three programs are not statistically significant.) Essexfields boys were then matched separately with probationers and Annandale boys. Ninety-nine Essexfields boys were matched with the same number of probationers. In-program failures were eliminated, and the following recidivism results were seen: Probation (N = 69), 19 percent; Essexfields (N = 76), 48 percent. Seventy-two Essexfields boys were then matched with seventy-two Annandale boys. In-program failures were eliminated to give these results for recidivism: Essexfields (N = 52), 44 percent; Annandale (N = 70), 51 percent. As these results indicate, the relative proportion of recidivists for each program does not change greatly after matching.

Background Variables and Recidivism

After the matched comparisons had been made, recidivism and non-recidivism were run against the background variables of race, socio-economic status, and delinquency history, with the following results. Eighteen percent of the white and 29 percent of the Negro boys were recidivists. This difference is significant at the .005 level ($x^2 = 16.29$). Among programs, Negroes at Essexfields and Group Centers were less recidivistic than whites, so that the higher Negro recidivism among all boys is accounted for by probation and Annandale boys. (The Negro-white difference was statistically significant only for probationers [$x^2 = 10.87$; $p = .005$].) This finding supports the conclusion of Weeks' study of Highfields and Annandale which indicated that Negroes at Highfields were more successful than Negroes at Annandale.[14] The comparison of these two studies is not precise, since Weeks included in-program failures (boys who "did not complete stay" in treatment programs) with recidivists in his comparison with non-recidivists, and he used different criteria for recidivism. Nonetheless, there is sufficient similarity to suggest again that the guided group interaction programs are especially appropriate for Negro delinquents.

The Social Economic Score was dichotomized 1.0-1.6 (low SES) and 1.7-3.0 (high SES) with a high score indicating the better social economic status. In general, there does not appear to be much difference between high and low SES boys. However, the high SES boys at Essexfields and Group Centers appear to be somewhat more recidivistic than the low scorers, and the reverse is true of the probation and Annandale boys. The differences were statistically significant only for probation ($x^2 = 16.48$; $p = .005$).

The Delinquency History Score was dichotomized 3.0-4.9 (low DHS) and 5.0-9.0 (high DHS) with high score indicating the more delinquent boys. The·

results for all boys is in the expected direction. More of the high DHS boys are recidivists (x^2 = 24.94; p = .005). However, Essexfields and Group Centers boys again reverse this pattern: the low DHS boys are more recidivistic. Differences within programs were statistically significant only for probation (x^2 = 16.0; p = .005). The direction of these findings appears to support a conclusion reached in the McCorkle, Elias, and Bixby study[15]—that, in comparison with Annandale, Highfields' rate of recidivism were more favorable for delinquents having a long history of delinquency.

In summary, two of the three matching factors are associated with recidivism in the expected direction. Negro boys and boys with a high DHS have higher rates of recidivism than whites and boys with a low DHS. There appears to be less association between recidivism and SES, although the high SES boys are slightly less recidivistic. However, this seems to be a consequence of the fact that the low SES boys from probation and Annandale are more recidivistic than the highs, while the reverse is true of the boys from Essexfields and Group Centers. Admittedly, the number of cases and the percentage differences are small, but when this pattern is combined with those found for race and delinquency history, an interesting possibility emerges. It appears that boys who may be considered poor risks generally do somewhat better at Essexfields and Group Centers than they do on probation or at Annandale.

One other combined index was available for the analysis of recidivists. This was the Educational Status Score, which involved school grade completed, educational status upon admission to this study, and number of years retarded in school. This index was dichotomized into 3-5 (low ESS) and 6-9 (high ESS). It should be noted that, in contrast to the SES and DHS, a *low* ESS indicates a *higher* or *better* educational experience. The findings indicate that boys with the better educational backgrounds (i.e., those with the *low* ESS) were less recidivistic. This is true for all of the boys and for each program of treatment. Statistical significance was found, however, for the total group (x^2 = 24.51; p = .005) and probation (x^2 = 10.01; p = .005) only.

Personality Characteristics of Recidivists

An examination was made of pre-treatment MMPI's to see what personality differences existed between boys who would subsequently become recidivists and those who would not. Taking the sample as a whole, the differences were fairly small. Recidivists scored slightly higher on the scales most relevant to degree of delinquency proneness (*Pd, Ma, Dq,* and *Ec*). They also scored lower on social responsibility, and slightly higher on overall elevation of the

MMPI profile. There was no difference on the *Rc* (recidivism) scale. Inspection of the data within each treatment facility shows that the above differences exist fairly markedly in the Annandale and Group Centers boys, and only very mildly, if at all, in the probation and Essexfields boys.

Changes during treatment were examined next. Overall, the mean changes were approximately the same for recidivists and non-recidivists. However, recidivists seemed to be somewhat more variable in their response to treatment, so that fewer of their changes were statistically significant.

Among the probation boys, changes made by recidivists and non-recidivists varied little. The main differences were a decrease in neuroticism and an increase in dominance for the non-recidivists; and an increase of the *Rc* (recidivism) scale for the recidivists. That is, the recidivists showed a personality change in the direction of greater likelihood for recidivism.

At Essexfields, both recidivists and non-recidivists showed decreases on the anxiety and neuroticism scales. However, the recidivists also showed large decreases on the *D* and *Pt* scales, indicating definite decrease in tendencies for worry, guilt feelings, pessimism, rumination, and general unhappiness. These scores might be interpreted to suggest that the recidivists tended to markedly reduce their reliance on "internalization" as a method of handling conflict.

Of the boys at Group Centers, non-recidivists showed more definite changes during treatment. These differences did not seem strongly related to the initial discrepancies between the recidivists and non-recidivists. Non-recidivists showed a considerable reduction in anxiety, accompanied by a decrease in hostility and an increase in the likelihood of verbal rather than physical acting out (*Mf* scale). For the recidivists, there were no significant changes during treatment.

It is difficult to make a meaningful interpretation of the results for boys at Annandale. Non-recidivists showed an increase in hostility, decrease in impulse control and social responsibility, and increase on the *Rc* (recidivism) scale—all unexpected changes for this group. The recidivists showed a decrease on the *Pd* (psychopathic deviate scale), although their post-treatment score on this scale was still quite high. No ready explanation is available for these findings. They cannot be adequately explained by pre-treatment differences.

In summary, recidivists prior to treatment conformed to the classic "delinquent" pattern a little more strongly than did the non-recidivists. These differences were most marked in the Annandale and Group Centers boys. The differences in the changes made during treatment were somewhat con-

sistent with what could be expected from the recidivism data for Group
Centers and Essexfields boys, but quite inconsistent for Annandale boys.
For probation boys, recidivists and non-recidivists differed only slightly in
the relatively minor changes they made.

Recidivism Among In-Program Failures

Boys who failed to complete their programs of treatment have been discussed in detail earlier. However, the outcome of in-program failures following
reassignment to another program was not taken up at that time, since it involved the analysis of recidivism. It is a significant consideration now because
recidivism rates of in-program failures may bear upon the findings concerning recidivism among boys who successfully completed treatment.

Seventy-three percent of the 296 in-program failures were recidivists. This
rate of recidivism is much higher than the 24 percent rate among all boys
who successfully completed their initial treatment program. It strongly suggests that boys who fail during treatment and are reassigned to another program are poor risks for rehabilitation. Table 14 presents a comparison, among
treatment programs, of rates of recidivism for in-program failures, successes,
and in-program failures and successes combined.

TABLE 14

Rates of Recidivism for In-Program Failures, Successes, and
Both Combined by Treatment Program

	Probation		Essexfields		Group Centers		Total	
	N	*%R*	*N*	*%R*	*N*	*%R*	*N*	*%R*
Program:								
Failures	255	76	23	48	18	55	296	73
Successes	671	15	77	48	49	41	797	20
Both	927	32	100	48	67	45	1093	34

N = Number of boys who: failed in-program, succeeded, and both combined
%R = Percent recidivistic for each N

It can readily be seen that probationers have a high rate of recidivism
among in-program failures when compared with similar Essexfields and Group
Centers boys. They also have an extraordinarily high rate in comparison with
probationers who successfully complete treatment. The difference in recidivism between probation in-program failures and successes is significant at
the .001 level ($x^2 = 314.19$). This suggests that the low rate of recidivism for
probationers who complete treatment may be partially accounted for by the
high recidivism rate of in-program failures, on the grounds that probation rids

itself of high recidivism risks. By returning high risk boys to the court for further disposition, probation may increase its chances of non-recidivism among boys who complete treatment. To a much lesser extent, this may be true of Group Centers when compared with Essexfields. Annandale, on the other hand, is not in such a favorable position to move boys into other programs; nor are the boys able to commit offenses in the community that may be the basis for in-program failure.

As Table 14 further indicates, when program successes and failures are combined, the recidivism rate for probation more than doubles, although it still remains lower than the other programs. The analysis of in-program failures and successes presented earlier adds further evidence to the contention that probation is relieved of high risk types by in-program failures. Although little difference was found between program failures and successes among Essexfields and Group Centers boys, this was not the case among probationers. Probation in-program failures were found to have less favorable social backgrounds, delinquency histories, and psychological profiles than those who completed the program. This finding, together with the differences in recidivism between program failures and successes among probationers, must be considered as a strong conditioning factor in assessing the very low 15 percent recidivism among probationers who completed treatment.

IV. SUMMARY

The rate of in-program failures within each treatment facility is quite similar, with the understandable exception of Annandale. For probation, Essexfields, and Group Centers, between 23 and 28 percent of the commitments fail to complete the program. Failure generally results from a variety of new delinquencies committed while in the program and, for Essexfields and Group Centers boys, often occurs within the first twelve weeks. Probation failures occur over a much longer time, since the average treatment period is more than twice as long as the average Essexfields and Group Centers treatment period.

Examination of pertinent background, delinquency and personality variables does not lead to a sharp differentiation between program successes and failures. In almost every case, probation successes differ significantly from probation failures, with successes being less delinquent and less delinquency-prone. However, the same relationship is not necessarily found between failures and successes in the other groups. When compared with successes, probation failures tend to be Negro, out of school, and poorly educated, with a more serious delinquency history and greater personality maladjustment. Generally speaking, failures in the other groups are similar, but do not differ as markedly from the successes in their groups.

Program successes were also evaluated in terms of their pre- to post-treatment changes on the MMPI. For the probation, Essexfields, and Group Centers successes, the changes were definite though not great. Although the changes were not necessarily the type associated with delinquency reduction, they reflected general improvement in attitudes and ego-strength and a reduction of anxiety. Annandale boys did not exhibit these positive changes and showed a greater tendency for change in a negative direction. When groups within the four programs were matched on clinical scales regarded as predictive of delinquency, changes very similar to those of the unmatched groups were noted.

In addition, the effects of selected social background variables were studied within each treatment group to see how they related to personality changes during treatment. With the exception of the finding that boys with low delinquency history scores showed greater improvement in all facilities than their peers with high scores, the results varied from program to program for each background factor.

Twenty-four percent of the 894 boys who completed treatment were recidivists within a period of three years after release. Probation had the lowest rate of recidivism (15 percent) and Annandale the highest (55 percent). Essexfields and Group Centers had a rate of 48 and 41 percent respectively. Nearly 75 percent of all recidivism took place within the first year after release from treatment. Probation recidivists had the highest rate within the first year, while Essexfields, Group Centers, and Annandale recidivism was spread over a longer time period.

Forty-one percent of the recidivists had more than one recidivistic court disposition, and a few had as many as six. Essexfields and Group Centers boys, however, had no more than three. Half of all recidivists had from one to five non-recidivistic court appearances.

The distribution of types of recidivistic offenses did not vary greatly from those committed by boys prior to treatment, although probationers appeared to have the most significant decrease in personal and property offenses after treatment. Jail was the most common court disposition for recidivists (42 percent). Eighteen percent were fined and 16 percent were placed on probation. Only 2 percent were sent to prison, and some 18 percent were given reformatory sentences.

Since exposure time in the community after treatment varied among programs, follow-up time was held constant for all programs for six month periods over a span of forty-seven months. During the first twelve months, the proportion of boys from each program in the community was approximately the same. Nevertheless, rates of recidivism followed the previously established pattern. Probation had the lowest rates, Annandale the highest. Although the proportion of Annandale boys in the community after twelve months decreased more rapidly than that for other programs, their rate of recidivism remained highest at each six month period.

When forty-four boys in each of the four treatment programs were matched by race, socio-economic status, and delinquency history, the relative proportion of recidivists in each program did not vary greatly from the pattern established by all boys who completed treatment. The same was true when ninety-nine Essexfields boys were matched with Probationers and seventy-two Essexfields boys were matched with Annandale boys.

The three background factors used in matching were examined for association with recidivism. It was found that Negro boys and boys with a poor delinquency history had higher rates of recidivism than whites and boys with a better delinquency history. There appeared to be less association between recidivism and socio-economic status, although the boys with the higher status were slightly less recidivistic. However, this appeared to be a consequence of the fact that the low status boys from probation and Annandale were more recidivistic than the highs, while the reverse was true of the boys from Essexfields and Group Centers. This same reversal of pattern was found in race and delinquency history. The educational history of the boys was also examined. Boys with the better educational history were less recidivistic in each treatment program.

Examination of MMPI data showed that prior to treatment recidivists conformed to the classic "delinquent" pattern a little more strongly than did the non-recidivists. These differences were most marked in the Annandale and Group Centers boys. The differences in the changes made during treatment were somewhat consistent with what would be expected from the recidivism data for Group Centers and Essexfields boys, but quite inconsistent for Annandale boys. For probationers, recidivists and non-recidivists differed only slightly in the relatively minor changes made.

When rates of recidivism for in-program failures were examined (excluding Annandale), it was found that 73 percent were recidivists, considerably in excess of the 24 percent rate for boys who completed treatment. Probationers

had the highest rate of recidivism among failures. When their 76 percent recidivism among failures is compared with their 15 percent redicivism among
boys who successfully completed treatment, a question is raised concerning
the very low rate of recidivism among program successes. It appears as if
probation raises its probability of non-recidivism among boys who complete the program by returning high risk boys to the court as in-program
failures. When program successes and failures were combined, the recidivism
rate for probation more than doubled, while the rate for Essexfields and
Group Centers was relatively unchanged. However, the rate was still lower
than any of the other programs.

NOTES

1. It must be kept in mind, as all tables reflect, that the success and failure groups
in probation are much larger than the comparable groups in Essexfields and Group
Centers. Hence, there is greater likelihood that differences within the former program
will be statistically reliable, whereas differences of the same magnitude within the latter
programs will not be. Under such conditions, it is important to examine the relative
differences between the groups in addition to the statistical reliability of the differences,
since statistical reliability is dependent upon sample size.

2. Educational Status Score was computed in the following way: weights of 1-3 were
assigned to each of the following education indicators and totaled.

    (a) School grade completed
        1—Ten or more
        2—Nine
        3—Eight or less or ungraded classes
    (b) School status upon admission to this study
        1—In school or graduated
        2—Quit school
        3—Expelled or excluded from school
    (c) Number of years retarded in school
        1—None
        2—One year
        3—Two or more years plus ungraded classes

3. Delinquency History Score was computed in the following way: weights of 1-3
were assigned to each of the following delinquency indicators and totaled.

    (a) Type of offenses (including offense bringing a boy into this study and all
    offenses prior to entering study; score computed by adding weights of types of
    offenses and dividing by number of offenses)
        1—Public Policy
        2—Property
        3—Personal
    (b) Number of court appearances prior to admission to this study
        1—1 or 2

   2–3 or 4
   3–5 or more
(c) Age at first court appearance
   1–15 or more
   2–12 or 14
   3–11 or less

4. The significance of pre- to post-treatment psychological changes was assessed using T-tests for correlated means. For each scale, the correlation between pre-treatment scores and post-treatment scores was assumed to be .5, which is a conservative estimate. See W. G. Dahlstrom and G. S. Welsh, *An MMPI Handbook* (Minneapolis: University of Minnesota Press, 1960), p. 475.

5. Scores on the regular MMPI scales are given in T-scores, which have a standard deviation of 10. The remaining scores are raw scores, in which differences are not directly comparable with each other.

6. For some scales, the meaning of "increase" or "decrease" is not clear from the name. In these cases, terms such as "improvement" will be used.

7. It is possible that there were reliable and stable changes for *some boys* in the personality characteristics indicative of delinquency, but that these changes were cancelled out when group means were examined. The following discussion, which examines subgroups within each treatment program, allows this hypothesis to be evaluated.

8. Social Economic Score was computed in the following way: weights of 1-3 were assigned to each of the following socio-economic indicators, totaled, and divided by 3.
   (a) Family income
      1–0 to $4,000 and welfare
      2–$4,001 to $8,000
      3–$8,001 or more
   (b) Education of family breadwinner
      1–0 to 8th grade
      2–9th, 10th, and 11th grade
      3–12th grade and over
   (c) Occupation of family breadwinner
      1–Unskilled and semiskilled
      2–Skilled and clerical
      3–Managers, owners, and professionals

Cases without data on education or occupation were given the mean weight of their income group on these items. If income data were missing, the mean weight of the case's education or occupation group (in that order) was used.

9. These scores were dichotomized as follows: socio-economic status, 1.0-1.6 and 1.7-3.0; delinquency history, 3.0-4.9 and 5.0-9.0; education, 3-5 and 6-9. Parental status was dichotomized according to whether a boy lived with both real parents or not. Race was dichotomized Negro-White.

10. Since the probation group was far larger than the others, statistical significance can be ascribed to much smaller changes in the group. Thus, the pattern of changes and their absolute magnitudes need to be considered in addition to their statistical significance.

11. Just what constitutes recidivism is determined by the criterion used. It may range

from arrests through court appearances to court dispositions, and the nature of each of these may be a further basis for defining a case as a recidivist. Whether a recidivist should be defined as a "failure" with respect to program effectiveness presents a further problem. For an instructive discussion of this matter and a review of a number of evaluative studies see Daniel Glaser, *The Effectiveness of a Prison and Parole System* (New York: The Bobbs-Merrill Company, 1964), especially Chapter 1.

12. Weeks' study of Highfields defined recidivism as a case which, "for any reason, was returned to court and/or violated probation or parole and as a result was committed to an institution" for thirty days or more. See H. Ashley Weeks, *Youthful Offenders at Highfields* (Ann Arbor: University of Michigan Press, 1958), p. 22. However, this study did not involve probation, since it evaluated only Highfields and Annandale. A parallel study of Highfields and Annandale boys considered anyone a recidivist who "had been convicted for delinquency during the exposure period regardless of the court action" or was "returned to the institution for parole violation" in the case of Annandale boys. See Lloyd W. McCorkle, Albert Elias, and F. Lovell Bixby, *The Highfields Story* (Holt, Rinehart, and Winston, 1958), p. 142. Fines, jail sentences, and probation placement were considered recidivisms. Apparently, the aforementioned study differed from the present one in only one recidivism category: "warning" by the court. Some preliminary discussion of recidivism is found in two studies that parallel the programs analyzed in this report. One study distinguished "indeterminate" from "failure" recidivists. The former did not refer to commitments, but to a criminal charge or a criminal act that was handled informally by the courts; the latter, to commitment for a criminal act. The other study apparently used one or more arrests as the criterion of recidivism. See Lovick C. Miller, *Second Progress Report: Evaluation of Southfield's Treatment Center* (The Ford Foundation, August 10, 1965); Lamar T. Empey and Maynard L. Erickson, *Annual Progress Report, 1964, The Provo Experiment in Delinquency Rehabilitation* (The Ford Foundation, 1965).

13. Race was dichotomized into Negro and white. The Social Economic Score was trichotomized as follows: 1.0 through 1.6; 1.7 through 2.3; and 2.4 through 3.0. Delinquency History Score was trichotomized as follows: 3.0 through 4.6; 4.7 through 6.3; and 6.4 through 9.0. Breaks in the trichotomy for the Delinquency History Score were conditioned by the distribution of cases (for example, the highest score was 8.0). Each case was then assigned to a cell as indicated below and a matching code number for tabulating purposes was given each case according to its cell location.

Social Economic Status Score

		10-16		17-23		24-30	
		Negro	*White*	*Negro*	*White*	*Negro*	*White*
Delinquency History Score	*30-46*	01	02	03	04	05	06
	47-63	07	08	09	10	11	12
	64-80	13	14	15	16	17	18

14. H. Ashley Weeks, *Youthful Offenders at Highfields,* pp. 42–43.
15. Lloyd W. McCorkle, *et al., The Highfields Story,* p. 151.

8

Comparative Research

In view of the theoretical basis of guided group interaction as a correctional measure, the instrumentation of theory in the elaboration of a program to act upon it, and the established feasibility of carrying out such a program, the results reported in the preceding chapter are disappointing in terms of changing delinquents to non-delinquents. Among the many speculations that might be made concerning these findings, a first consideration is the fact that the research was conducted on but a single program. It is possible that this evaluation was not a true test of program effectiveness because of inadequacies or faults in the research, the program, or both. Although residential group centers were evaluated as well as Essexfields, there is the lingering doubt that different results might be found under other conditions of time, place, or personnel. It is fortunate, therefore, that evaluative research on other guided group interaction facilities has been conducted and reported. These programs are reasonably consistent in design and content, and the research developed to evaluate them is similar enough for comparative purposes. The programs were also carried out under a variety of conditions over an extended period of time.

THE PROGRAMS

Highfields
Weeks' study of Highfields and the work of McCorkle, Elias, and Bixby represent the earliest evaluative research on the residential, guided group interaction facility.[1] Weeks compared recidivism of 229 Highfields boys with that of 116 boys sent to Annandale, the state reformatory. Defining recidivism as institutional commitment (jail for thirty days or longer or

reformatory or prison commitment) following release from Highfields for at least a year and Annandale for at least eight months, Weeks found that 63 percent of the Highfields boys had no further custodial care compared with 47 percent of the Annandale boys. Since boys were sent to Highfields as a condition of probation, they could be returned to court as "unsuitable for residence" before they completed their treatment, an option not available to Annandale boys. When only boys who completed the Highfields program were considered, the success rate rose to 77 percent. On eight scales used to measure outlook on life and attitudes toward family, law, and order, there was very little evidence that boys changed during their stay at either Highfields or Annandale. Similar findings follow from analysis of pre- to post-tests on ten scales adapted from the Army's Psychoneurotic Screening Adjunct that was used to measure personality. A sample of boys from each facility were given pre- and post-testing on the Miale-Holsopple sentence completion test; scored on a group basis, Highfields boys moved in a more favorable direction than did Annandale boys. In addition, five persons who knew the boys intimately were interviewed at the time of the boys' admission and upon release. Comparisons of these interviews indicated that, in general, the Highfields boys were thought to have improved more than the Annandale boys.

Weeks' study is subject to a deficiency common to most research on group centered programs. Boys were not sent to Highfields and Annandale on a random or stratified basis. Analysis of the background of both groups indicated that Highfields boys had somewhat more favorable social background and shorter and less intense delinquent careers. However, on the basis of prediction tables relating social backgrounds to outcome, Weeks concluded that there was no reason to believe that differences in success rates were due to differences in background variables.

The McCorkle, Elias, and Bixby study of Highfields attempted to correct for population differences among boys at Highfields and Annandale by matching boys in the two facilities on selected factors. Since too few Annandale boys were admitted during the research period to permit an adequate pool for matching with Highfields boys, matching was accomplished by selecting boys from a pool of Annandale admissions prior to the establishment of Highfields. In this way, 50 Highfields boys were matched with 49 Annandale boys (one case was dropped because of matching error) on the following factors: race, criteria of admission to Highfields (16 and 17 years of age, no prior institutional commitment, no serious mental illness or deficiency, and no known homosexuality), county of residence, and adequate adjustment to facility (Highfields boys who were returned to court during treatment and Annandale boys who were transferred to another reformatory for poor ratings were excluded from the study). Recidivism was defined as adjudication of delinquency regardless of court disposition. This included warnings, fines, and probation, in addition to the criterion of incarceration used by Weeks.

In general, this study confirmed the findings of Weeks' research. Highfields boys were found to be less recidivistic at each of four after-release periods ranging from one to five years. When adjustments were made between the two groups for differences in length of delinquency history prior to admission, age of admission, education, residence (city of Newark vs. other residence in the same county), and marital status of parents, Highfields boys still showed less recidivism for at least the first three years after release. In addition, this study suggested that boys most likely to benefit from Highfields were those usually regarded as poor risks. Highfields rates were more favorable for older boys from broken homes who had a long history of delinquency.

Southfields

Highfields opened in 1950. In 1961, the Southfields Residential Group Center, patterned after Highfields, began operation near Louisville, in Jefferson County, Kentucky. An intern from Highfields was appointed director and attempts were made to replicate the Highfields project in all respects. This provided an opportunity to determine if the Highfields concept could be applied to different settings in other parts of the country.

Continuing the excellent policy of evaluative research established at Highfields, an attempt was made to carry out a comparative recidivism study of Southfields, probation, and Kentucky Village, a traditional institution for delinquents. This study provided the additional dimension of probation not present in the earlier Highfields research. Also, aware of the problems of population comparability, the research design called for random distribution of delinquents to each of these facilities.[2]

Events, however, conspired to defeat this procedure. Largely because of changes in court personnel, random assignment was abandoned, and samples of boys placed on probation or committed to Kentucky Village during the time boys were being sent to Southfields were drawn instead. These samples were matched as closely as possible for age and criteria of admission to Southfields.[3] Research efforts were hampered further by a high rate of in-program failure relative to the Highfields experience.

Released boys from the three facilities were followed-up for recidivism for one year using the same criteria as the Weeks study. During this period,

191 Southfields boys, 162 Kentucky Village boys, and 157 probationers were available for evaluation. Boys who were not committed to an institution for one year after release were divided into Success Group A and Success Group B. Group A were those who had no commitment and no serious offenses, and Group B were those who had no commitment but were charged or convicted of a serious offense.

Results of this study showed a 70 percent Group A success rate for the 115 Southfields boys who completed the program. This compares favorably with Highfields' 77 percent success rate for similar boys. If Group B boys who completed the program are added to Group A boys, the success rate increases to 89 percent. However, since Weeks' study did not divide boys into these two success groups, the relative success of Southfields and Highfields on this index cannot be determined precisely. On the other hand, combining success Groups A and B and considering *all* of the 191 boys admitted to Southfields, 53 percent were successful compared to the 63 percent rate for comparable boys at Highfields. The 40 percent in-program failure rate at Southfields, compared to Highfields' 18 percent, indicates a major difference in the two programs. The high rate at Southfields appears to have been the result of a combination of factors which will be discussed later.

Comparison of Southfields with Kentucky Village indicated greater success among Southfields boys who completed the program. However, when Southfields in-program failures are combined with those who completed the program and considered in terms of all the boys admitted, Kentucky Village boys were more successful. This was in contrast to the greater success rate of the Highfields boys when compared with Annandale boys. This difference appears to be partly a consequence of the fact that the success rate at Kentucky Village was 67 percent, compared to Annandale's 47 percent. (If Southfields were compared with Annandale, it would have the higher success rate, i.e., 53 percent.) Another consideration is the possibility that the high in-program failure rate at Southfields may have been due to a tendency of the court to send more unsuitable boys to Southfields than the New Jersey courts sent to Highfields.

When Southfields boys were compared with probationers, it was found that boys on probation had a recidivism rate equal to the Southfields boys who completed the program and better than Southfields graduates and in-program failures combined. This comparison of the group program with probation was not carried out in the Highfields studies and raises unanswered questions concerning the comparability of populations in the three types of programs studied and the relevant effectiveness of the treatment in the facilities.

Psychological tests were carried out on Southfields boys in an attempt to determine intra-psychic changes during treatment and predict success or failure within the population. The K and Pd scales of the MMPI, indicating delinquency proneness; the Madsley scale with its two dimensions of intro-versive-extroversive and health-neuroticism; the Bendig hostility scale; and Zukerman's MAACL, which assessed depression, hostility, and anxiety, were used. In addition, the Wonderlic test was used as a short intelligence scale. Wonderlic's was the only test showing a significant difference between graduates and in-program failures, indicating that the more intelligent boys were better able to stick with the program. However, differences were not great enough to predict individual cases, and it was concluded that the psychometric data were generally unable to show initial differences between graduates and non-graduates. Comparisons of Southfields boys with general population norms on these tests did show neurotic and other intropsychic disturbances as well as psychopathic trends. Analysis of a small sample of graduates comparing initial entrance and terminal scores indicated no change on the Wonderlic and Pd scale, but a decrease in pathogenic symptoms of depression and hostility. Analysis of scores for predicting success led to the conclusion that current measures of personality variables are inadequate to predict the course of events and the complexity of processes involved in the program.

The over-all conclusion reached by this study was that Southfields should serve the dual function of a screening and therapeutic facility, standing between probation and more intensive treatment programs. It was recommended that all delinquents in need of custodial care first be sent to Southfields. Failure to complete the programs there would be evidence of need for more intensive treatment.

Pinehills

While the Southfields program was testing the feasibility of the Highfields concept in a different setting, steps were taken in the late 1950s to initiate a similar program, known as Pinehills, in Provo, Utah. Pinehills differed significantly from Southfields and Highfields, however, since it was non-residential. In this respect, it more closely approximated the Essexfields program, although Pinehills admitted boys 14 to 18 years of age. Under the direction of Dr. LaMar T. Empey, research was designed to compare Pinehills with probation and the Utah State Industrial School.[4] Initial plans were drawn to randomly select Pinehills boys from two pools composed of boys whom the judge had determined to be candidates for probation or the state training school. Those boys who were randomly selected for Pinehills would constitute the experimental group. Those who went on to probation or the training school would constitute the control groups. Thus, Pinehills would have boys who might have been placed on probation (probation experimentals) for comparison with those who were (probation controls) and boys who might have been sent to the training school (incarceration experimentals) for comparisons with those who were (incarceration controls).

This plan had to be modified when it was found that the county was unable to provide the planned quotas for all three facilities, since the court did not commit a sufficient number of boys to the state industrial school. As was the case in the Southfields study, it was necessary to select a sample of boys from the industrial school, which raised the question of sample comparability. Statistical comparisons were made among the populations in the three facilities on offense frequency, seriousness of offense, age, and socio-economic status. Because there were some significant differences between the experimentals and the controls (particularly with respect to the incarceration experimentals and the incarceration controls), it was concluded that comparative follow-up data should be treated conservatively and with reservation.

Arrest rates were used as a principal indicator of program effectiveness, and cases were followed up for a period of 4 years. In general summary, it was found that when only boys who completed their programs were considered, the probation controls (boys on probation) and the probation experimentals (Pinehills boys) were both about 60 percent successful after the first year of release and about 45 percent after the fourth year. When in-program failures (drop-outs) were combined with completers, these rates changed very little, although examination of the rates for drop-outs alone suggested that dropping out had a more deleterious effect on the experimentals than on the controls. Comparisons between the incarceration experimentals (Pinehills boys) and the incarceration controls (industrial school boys) showed a rate favoring the experimentals 55 to 40 percent after one year and 36 to 21 percent after both 3 and 4 years. The general conclusion reached on the basis of the data was that the experimental program seemed to be of greater value as an alternative to incarceration than an alternative to probation. Further examination of data or incidence of arrest, seriousness of offense, and confinement commitments after arrest led to the tentative conclusion that although none of the programs could be viewed as very successful, incarceration seemed to present the least viable alternative for the rehabilitation of delinquents.

An additional indicator of the effects of correctional intervention was used in this research when rates of delinquency prior to admission to these programs were compared with rates after release. It was found that post-intervention rates were reduced by as much as 60 to 70 percent in the probation and Pinehills groups and by 25 percent in the training school group. In every group, offenders who committed fewer offenses far exceeded those who committed more offenses. Further analysis indicated that both age and social class were independently related to correctional outcome. When the effects of these variables were controlled, it was determined that the effects of intervention were considerably greater than the effects of age and class. Furthermore, these effects differed among programs. They were helpful in reducing the delinquency of both the probation control and experimental groups; to a lesser extent they were helpful in the incarceration experimental group; but they were associated with an increase in delinquency in the incarceration control group, which were by far the largest effects found.

Essexfields

Essexfields began operation in 1961 in Newark, New Jersey. Like Pinehills, it was an experimental, non-residential program, and evaluative research was carried out as reported in earlier chapters.[5] A brief and general summary is presented here for comparison with other group centered facilities.

It was found that 73 percent of the boys who completed the Essexfields program had not had a court disposition of a fine, probation, or an institutional commitment at the end of one year from date of release. The rate for Annandale, the State Reformatory for Youth Offenders, was 62 percent. By the end of three years of follow-up after release, these figures had decreased to 52 percent for Essexfields and 45 percent for Annandale. Combining Essexfield in-program failures with those who completed the program did not effect the Essexfields success rate. Although these differences in success rates are small, there was other inferential evidence that Essexfields boys may have made the more satisfactory community adjustment. Fewer Essexfields than Annandale boys had non-recidivistic court appearances, committed personal and property offenses, committed more than three recidivistic offenses, and were unemployed or employed part-time upon completion of probation or parole. After the first 12 months of follow-up, Essexfields had a greater proportion of boys released to the community than did Annandale, but Annandale's recidivism rate was higher at each six month period for the next 24 months. Furthermore, although 38 percent of the Essexfields recidivists became recidivists while completing their term of probation upon release from Essexfields, 98 percent of the Annandale recidivists became recidivists while on parole after release from Annandale.

Unlike the other studies, Essexfields was compared with three residential group centers located in the State of New Jersey. Group centers were found to have a 7 percent better success rate than Essexfields. In comparison with the group centers recidivists, Essexfields recidivists committed more recidivisms and had more non-recidivistic court appearances. Essexfields non-recidivists also had more court appearances.

In conformity with the Southfields and Pinehills studies, Essexfields was compared with probation. Probation produced a remarkable 85 percent success rate at the end of three years after release from probation. When boys who failed to complete probation were added to those who did, the failure rate increased markedly, but the success rate, 68 percent, was still better than either group centers or Essexfields.

Because analysis of social background and delinquency histories demonstrated progressively poorer "risks" from probation through the group programs to the reformatory, attempts were made to match boys across facilities on race, socio-economic background, and delinquency history. Although differences among programs changed slightly as a result of matching, the relative proportion of recidivists for each program remained substantially the same.

The MMPI was used to measure personality change during treatment in this study. Changes were not dramatic in any of the facilities. The major findings indicated general improvement in attitude and ego-strength and decrease in anxiety in all programs except the reformatory. Essexfields and the residential centers seemed especially effective in reduction of hostility, while the reformatory boys actually increased on this index and probationers changed very little. Pre-treatment test indicators on recidivists and non-recidivists were slight but in the expected direction, recidivists scoring higher on scales associated with delinquency proneness. In-program failures among probationers tended to be more delinquency prone, but this was not found in any clear pattern among boys in the other programs.

Silverlake

In 1964, Silverlake was opened in Los Angeles, California, in cooperation with a private institution for delinquents at Chino, known as the Boys

Republic, and the Youth Studies Center of the University of Southern California.[6] The group program included the general characteristics of other residential, group centered facilities, but boys attended public school from approximately 7:30 A.M. to 4:00 P.M. and were free to go home weekends if they so desired. The boys were also responsible for maintaining the grounds and residential facilities.

In the evaluative research, Silverlake was compared with Boys Republic, a relatively self-contained, open, non-custodial oriented, residential facility established in 1907. Located on a 215 acre farm, its program consists of cottage living, vocational and academic education, organized recreation, work activities on the farm, buildings, and grounds, and a system of student government. Length of residence varies from six months to two years, with an average stay of 16 months. Boys placed in the two facilities were chosen by the following common criteria: 15½ to 18 years of age, no psychotics, mentally retarded, addicts, or serious sex offenders, common residence in Los Angeles County, and representative ethnicity. Boys who qualified in these respects were randomly placed in Silverlake or Boys Republic by the Admissions Counselor of Boys Republic.

In addition to a number of other purposes, the research was designed to indicate differential impact of the two programs on boys having different kinds of social and personal characteristics, to test delinquency theory upon which the Silverlake program was based, and to assess Silverlake's program processes. This research, like the others, experienced some difficulties in carrying out random assignment. However, comparison on a number of variables led to the conclusion that the two groups were reasonably comparable.

Recidivism was measured in terms of any new recorded arrests indicated in either police or probation records. Based on 140 Silverlake and 121 Boys Republic admissions who had been released for at least one year, it was found that 60 percent of the Silverlake and 56 percent of the Boys Republic cases were free from arrest. An additional 25 and 24 percent, respectively, had only one arrest. A significant number of these boys, however, failed to successfully complete their programs (54 percent for Silverlake and 50 percent for Boys Republic). When only boys who completed their programs were considered, success rates increased to 73 percent for Silverlake and 82 percent for Boys Republic. An additional indicator of program effectiveness was available in this study. The number of offenses committed one year before admission was compared with the number for a similar period after release, and a substantial decrease in the volume of offenses was found. There was an 84 percent reduction for Silverlake boys who completed the program and a 63 to 64 percent reduction for those who did not. There was also a significant reduction in the seriousness of offenses committed. Relatively similar reductions were found among the cases from Boys Republic. Since the focus of much of the Silverlake research was on program processes and implementation rather than personality or attitude change that might have resulted from program impact, the results of this aspect of the study will not be taken up here but will be reserved for later comment.

Collegefields

In 1965, a non-residential group program called Collegefields was initiated under the supervision of Dr. Saul Pilnick, who directed Essexfields.[7] This facility differed in two respects from those reported above. Boys were younger (14 and 15) and because of their age were subject to school attendance. Since delinquency and poor school adjustment frequently go together, the program was designed not only to reduce delinquent behavior but to improve the boy's educational experience. With the cooperation of the Laboratory for Applied Behavioral Science of Newark State College of New Jersey, the Newark School System, the Newark Family Service Bureau, and Essex County Juvenile Court, the program was organized to provide specially designed school work from 9:00 to 12:30 in the morning at Newark State College, accompanied by group interaction meetings in the afternoon. This program was supplemented by light clean-up duties at the college, informal interaction from 7:30 A.M. to class time, use of the college library, planned trips to local communities for learning and enjoyment, publication of a school newspaper, and a daily hot lunch provided by the college cafeteria. Nights and week ends were spent at home.

The evaluative research compared Collegefields boys with boys placed on probation, most of whom remained in school. Both groups were given a series of pre-treatment and six months follow-up tests. A third group of non-tested probationers was also used for comparative purposes. All boys met the criteria of admissions to Collegefields (no prior institutionalization, 14 and 15 years of age, and no clear evidence of sub-normal intelligence or psychosis). Boys were followed up for recidivism after release for a period of from six to twenty months, depending upon their date of admission to Collegefields or probation. The original design of random selection had to be abandoned because not enough boys could be assigned randomly to the Collegefields group. However, it was felt that such differences as a larger number of boys with previous court histories in the Collegefields group would, if anything, put this group to a more severe test than the other two.

At the end of a maximum of 20 months follow-up for recidivism, it was found that of the 55 Collegefields boys in the study, 66 percent had not been placed in "penal custody." Comparable results for the 54 tested probationers were 56 percent, and for the 52 non-tested probationers 60 percent. When recidivism was examined by month, it was found that there was no consistent difference in offense rates during the early months, but offenses among Collegefields boys became rare in later months in contrast to the continued offense pattern of the two probation groups.

A variety of pre-treatment and six months follow-up tests were used in an attempt to evaluate the impact of the Collegefields program. In general, these tests were calculated to compare treatment changes in Collegefields boys and the tested probationers on such items as mental ability, vocational orientation, attitude towards school and teachers, self-concept, and delinquent street norms. The findings indicated that compared with the tested probationers, the Collegefields boys made larger gains in reading and mental ability, anticipated years of schooling, upgrading in social status of anticipated vocation, and favorable attitudes towards self. The Collegefields graduates (those who completed the program) showed the greatest gains in reading comprehension, the largest reduction in unfavorable attitudes towards teachers, less fantasy in occupation choice, more definite rise in achievement motivation, and a reduction in negativistic street norms. The research results indicated that the Collegefields graduates made consistent gains in all these respects, while the non-graduates or in-program failures were inconsistent (they improved in some measures and became more vulnerable in others). After the six month testing, the non-graduates scored much like the graduates did on entering the program. This suggested to the researchers that the Collegefields experience increased the readiness of the non-graduates for rehabilitation.

COMMENTS

Other experimental correctional programs that involve some use of the group concept have been developed or are in operation.[8] These are not reported here since they vary considerably as to age of inmates, the extent to which they replicate the Highfields model, the degree to which adequate and comparable research has accompanied the program, and the stage of reportability of research findings.

In the six studies reported here, differences in program and research design should be noted. Length of follow-up and criteria of recidivism varied. In addition, programs differed by location of facility (rural or urban), composition of populations (age, delinquency history, social background), type of program accompanying the core of the guided group interaction sessions (residential or non-residential; work or school), and type of control facility used for comparative purposes (probation, reformatory, residential group centers, Boys Republic). Although such differences are useful for evaluating the group approach under differing conditions, they should be kept in mind in attempting to draw general conclusions concerning the effectiveness of guided group interaction.

Despite these differences, the results of the studies are reasonably consistent. Boys who successfully completed treatment in the group programs had lower rates of recidivism than boys released from the more traditional, reformatory type facilities. Success rates approximately one year after release are reasonably similar among the group programs. The Essexfields study, which had a three year follow-up, suggests that these rates decrease over time. (Similar evidence is indicated in the 6 to 20 months follow-up comparison of Collegefields with probation and the 4-year follow-up in the Pinehills study.) However, they are still somewhat better than the rates of recidivism for the reformatory type facility. With the exception of Southfields, when in-program failures and program completers are combined, comparisons with reformatories still favor the group programs. However, success rates are generally higher when only successful program completers are considered. It is perhaps unfair to include the in-program failures in calculating the success of the group programs, since many of them failed in the first few weeks and had little or no exposure to the treatment processes. These data generally seem to indicate that the short but intensive treatment in the guided group interaction facilities is more effective than the usual longer-term and more expensive full confinement, reformatory program.

Serious questions concerning the over-all effectiveness of group centered programs are raised, however, when they are compared with probation. Although the economics of corrections would seem to favor the group facilities over the reformatory type of institution even when the results are the same, this cannot be said of probation. Either probation usually possesses the most effective correctional program among those compared, or the samples in the compared programs are not comparable as to recidivism risk. As indicated earlier, four of these studies planned to control for sample differences by random distribution in assignment to facilities. Despite every effort to insure random distribution, however, none of them was able to carry it out completely. This sound, scientific procedure was defeated by unanticipated or unpredictable events. *Ad hoc* methods worked out to overcome possible differences among samples, although ingenious and varied, are not entirely convincing to the skeptic, even though the researchers give assurance of reasonable comparability.

Recidivism is certainly not the only, or necessarily the most suitable, index of program effectiveness or impact. Favorable changes in personality or attitudes, as indicated by research that accompanied the recidivism studies, is another. Yet, the results of this research, with some notable exceptions, are modest at best. Few signficant changes were found in before-and-after tests of attitudes and values, and tests of personality change were not dramatic. Furthermore, none of these studies indicated a strong relationship between proven favorable changes and recidivism. It is quite possible that the tests used were inadequate. Weeks, for example, concluded that the Miale-Holsopple sentence completion test probably better revealed the more subtle kinds of change than the extensive battery of other tests used in the Highfields study. It is also true that we know little specifically about which attitudes or values and what psychological states play a role in delinquency, and how they fit into the complex set of conditions that result in delinquency. Nevertheless, these studies provide some evidence and clues for informal speculation, and we shall return to them in the comments that follow.

NOTES

1. H. Ashley Weeks, *Youthful Offenders at Highfields* (Ann Arbor: The University of Michigan Press, 1958) and Lloyd W. McCorkle, Albert Elias, and F. Lovell Bixby, *The Highfields Story* (New York: Holt, Rinehart, and Winston, 1958).

2. John M. Wall, Albert Elias, and Albert Axelrod, "Southfields Residential Group Center: A Four Year Report," March, 1966 (Mimeographed). This report contains the original research design and detailed discussion of the program.

3. Lovick C. Miller, "Evaluation of Southfields: A Short-Term Inpatient Treatment Center for Delinquents," no date (Mimeographed). The findings that follow are taken from this study.

4. LaMar T. Empey, Maynard L. Erickson, and Max L. Scott, "Pinehills," Annual Progress Report, 1964, The Provo Experiment in Delinquency Rehabilitation, to the Ford Foundation (Mimeographed) and LaMar T. Empey and Maynard L. Erickson, *The Provo Experiment* (Lexington, Mass.: Lexington Books, 1972). Discussion that follows is based on these reports.

5. Richard M. Stephenson and Frank M. Scarpitti, "The Rehabilitation of De-linquent Boys," report to the Ford Foundation, 1967 (Mimeographed).

6. LaMar T. Empey and Steven G. Lubeck, *The Silverlake Experiment* (Chicago: Aldine Publishing Co., 1971). Conclusions drawn are based on this book.

7. Saul Pilnick, *et al.,* "Collegefields: From Delinquency to Freedom," report to U.S. Department of Health, Education, and Welfare, Office of Juvenile Delinquency, 1967. Discussion follows from this report.

8. See, for example, Maurice A. Harmon, "Community Rehabilitation of the Younger Delinquent Boy: Parkland Non-Residential Group Center," Final Report to the U.S. Department of Health, Education, and Welfare, Kentucky Child Welfare Research Foundation, Inc., 1967; Theodore B. Palmer and others, "Community Treatment Project, Seventh Progress Report, Part I: The Sacramento-Stockton and the San Francisco Experiments," CTP Research Report No. 9, Part I, October, 1968; Bernard C. Kirby, "Crofton House: An Experiment with a County Halfway House," *Federal Probation* 33:1 (March 1969): 53-58; Charles Larsen, "Guided Group Interaction: Theory and Method," Department of Court Services, Hennepin County, Minneapolis, Minnesota, Report No. 1, July, 1970; Doug Knight, "The Marshall Program: Assess-ment of a Short-Term Institutional Treatment Program, Part II: Amenability to Con-frontive Peer-Group Treatment," California Youth Authority, Research Report No. 59, August, 1970; and John M. Flackett and Gail Flackett, "Criswell House: An Alternative to Institutional Treatment for Juvenile Offenders," *Federal Probation* (December 1970): 30-37. Also see Oliver J. Keller, Jr. and Benedict S. Alper, *Halfway Houses: Community-Centered Correction and Treatment* (Lexington, Massachusetts: D. C. Heath and Co., 1970). For a special program within a prison system emphasizing "resocialization" through the group approach see Elliot Studt, Sheldon L. Messinger, and Thomas P. Wilson, *C-Unit: Search for Community in Prison* (New York: Russell Sage Foundation, 1968).

9

Conclusions

The comparative research on guided group interaction programs confirms, with considerable consistency, the findings of the Essexfields study. Taken together, the evidence from these studies is not impressive with respect to the general efficacy of guided group interaction when compared with alternative programs of correction. What remains to be analyzed is the apparent incongruity between the observed operation of the program described in preceding chapters and the limited results of these efforts in achieving their intended goals. Bound by limited resources and practical needs in the comparative assessment of facilities in terms of deterring delinquency, the Essexfields research, like most of the other studies, was not designed to answer this question in depth. However, the various studies provide sufficient collective evidence to indicate how these programs might be improved to more effectively achieve the desired results, to isolate some results of the programs that seem to have special merit, and to suggest some limitation and weakness of this correctional approach.

SELECTION

Scattered and fragmentary evidence suggests that the group programs may be especially suitable for certain types or categories of delinquents. The McCorkle, Elias, and Bixby study indicated that Highfields had greater post-release success than Annandale with older boys, boys having a long history of delinquency, and boys from broken homes. Weeks found that, although there was no statistically significant difference in success rates between whites at Highfields and Annandale, Negroes were considerably more successful at Highfields. In fact, the difference in success rates between the two facilities was almost wholly accounted for by the success rate of Highfields Negroes. An analysis of race in the Essexfields study showed that Negroes at Essexfields and Group Centers were less recidivistic than whites, while the reverse was true for probation and Annandale. It was also found that Essexfields and Group Centers were more successful with boys of low socio-economic status and with boys having high delinquency history scores; the reverse was true of Annandale and probation. In comparing success rates at Collegefields with tested and non-tested probationers, it was found that Collegefields boys who had prior court appearance were more successful than similar boys in the probation control groups. The Pinehills study also indicated that, for experimental and control probationers, the experimental program was somewhat more successful with boys with a longer history of delinquincy. It might be noted further that the Wall, Elias, and Axelrod report on Southfields recommended that boys who had less than three court appearances be excluded from the program on an experimental basis.

Although the number of cases and the magnitude of difference was not uniformly great, the general pattern in these studies suggests that the guided group interaction programs are relatively successful with boys usually thought to be poor risks. In interpreting this pattern, it should be recalled that the theoretical basis of guided group interaction called for boys with considerable involvement in the "sub-culture of delinquency" and the interpersonal relations associated with it. Early experience at Highfields lent some credence to this theoretical assumption. The response of "apron strings delinquents"—boys with little experience with traditional, street oriented delinquents—indicated that they were likely candidates for return to the courts as unsuitables.[1] This suggests that boys more involved in delinquent group experiences were more adept at the social relations and more suitable for the processes of the group program. Such boys are likely to possess the social characteristics and possible psychological correlates associated with the "poor risk" delinquent.

Some firmer evidence for this interpretation is provided by the research accompanying the Marshall Program, a facility operating at the Youth Authority's Southern Reception Center-Clinic at Norwalk, California.[2] Although differing in some respects from the group programs discussed here, this program makes use of group based interpersonal relations and self-confrontation to induce attitudinal and behavioral change. When an

18½ months post-release comparison was made between Marshall boys and boys in other programs at any one of four institutions, it was found that, on a case-matching basis, there was virtually no difference in parole violation. A later 15 months follow-up showed even less favorable results. However, further investigation determined that older Marshall boys who had two or more companions in the offense that brought them to the study showed superior post-release performance when compared with "(1) any other subcategory of wards released from Marshall and (2) any reasonably-sized subcategory from a matched comparison group of 'regular program' releases."[3] (With respect to age, it should be noted that the Marshall Program includes boys from 15 to 18.) The older, multiple co-offender boys also were less likely to be in-program failures than younger, lone offenders and boys with escape histories. Furthermore, some evidence indicated poor results with boys without prior delinquency commitments. It was also found that the Marshall population was under-represented by boys from below-average socio-economic background when compared with similar court commitments to the Youth Authority.

When statistical estimates of Interpersonal-Maturity Level (I Level) subtype were made, it was found that the older, multiple co-offender Marshall boys who were also "stronger, less readily intimidated, and more self-sufficient" (the I_4 Na subtype I Level) did especially well upon release. When age and co-offender status were disregarded, boys of this I Level subtype did better than the "seemingly less socially assertive, perhaps retreatist" boys (I_4 Nx subtype I Level).[4] The stronger boys also tended to show less alienation from authority during treatment, while the more threat-sensitive boys showed more alienation; and increased alienation was associated with post-release failure.

Based on these and related findings, the Marshall Program report reached the following speculative conclusions:

> Insofar as Marshall's confrontive treatment was concerned, different "kinds" of delinquents seemed to respond in different ways. Some delinquents more than others may be amenable to peer-group-centered (or staff-directed) appeals to any underlying ambivalence about deviant behavior. Boys with a certain personal and social strength may have better capacity to face problems in confrontive situations. They may be better able to engage in potentially threatening interactions and yet still be oriented to

solving problems, to testing new behaviors and relationships, to
trying "new ways of being me," to *attaining* successes—rather
than to *avoiding* failure or threat. . . .

Certain other delinquents, then, may be *less* amenable to treatment in confrontive situations . . . . For these boys, confrontation
may provoke increased resistance—or worse. Possibly feeling a
diminished sense of social adequacy and personal control, some
of these less adequate boys may react to a focus on deviant aspects
of their identity by drifting even more deeply into a failure-
identity.[5]

These conclusions parallel those reached by the Silverlake study. In an analysis of recidivism and its correlates, it was found that different kinds of boys
responded differently to the treatment programs at Silverlake and Boys Republic. Supportive findings followed from the analysis of runaways and program failures. Through the use of simulating techniques drawing upon research data, preliminary attempts were made at matching offender types to
types of treatment by (1) simulating subjects from the control program (Boys
Republic) through the experimental program (Silverlake) and vice versa and
(2) simulating through both programs hypothetical delinquent types based on
causation theory underlying the Silverlake program. Examination of the results of a simulation of 135 experimental subjects through the control program showed that nearly a quarter probably would have succeeded and fully
a quarter apparently would have failed in either program. Thirty-four percent succeeded in the experimental program, but might have failed if placed
in the control program. Sixteen percent, while they failed in the experimental program, might have succeeded in the control program. Particularly
relevant to a consideration of delinquents and guided group interaction was
the finding of the simulation of theoretical types. The delinquency type most
nearly conforming to the theory upon which Silverlake was based (lower-
class, low achievement, high strain, high identification with peers, and high
delinquency) performed relatively well in the experimental program, but very
poorly in the control. The reverse was true of the opposite theoretical type.[6]

Taken together, the evidence from these various studies, while by no means
entirely firm or conclusive, presents convincing support for the selection criteria for guided group interaction as originally conceived. No one program
of corrections can be expected to bear the burden of rehabilitation of all
kinds of delinquents. Poor matching of offenders to programs may not

only raise the rates of in-program failure and recidivism, but may do more harm than good for those cases unsuitable for the program. As the Silverlake study repeatedly concluded, and other studies reported here appear to confirm, social and personal characteristics of offenders may have significant predictive value for success or failure only in combination with a consideration of differences in treatment programs (and, it should be added, organizational changes in them that may take place over time). What may appear to be poor risks when only the variables associated with success and failure are considered may prove to be more favorable risks when treatment variables are taken into account, and may be far more successful in one program than another. Furthermore, a careful consideration of the pattern of variables associated with success in a given program and a specification of particulars that may be masked by a single factor or more general ones would very likely give even better results. The present state of knowledge is such that precision in selection criteria for treatment are crude at best, but it seems apparent that the group programs received many unsuitable boys, among them those who appeared to have relatively good prognoses based on general personal and social characteristics.

The matter of selection also applies to the criteria of admission governing age, intelligence, and psychiatric status. Most programs managed to meet the age requirement. (The Marshall Program admitted boys 15 to 18, but the research findings did not support the utility of including the younger boys.) The exception seems to be Southfields, where 15 year olds represented 21 percent of the total intake. These boys were found to be the most unstable age group in the program, they had the most difficult period of adjustment afterwards, and only about a third completed the program. It was thought that boys of this age lacked sufficient maturity concerning the reality of their total situation to work well in the program. Pinehills admitted boys from 14 to 18 years of age. Research findings indicated greater success with older boys in this experimental program, which seemed to accelerate the pace of maturational reform and have a longer effect than either probation or the training school. Results were unfavorable for 14 to 16 year olds when compared with both the older boys in the experimental program and with the younger boys in the probation control group. Collegefields' comparative success with 14 and 15 year old boys indicates that this age group is amenable to treatment under a program specifically designed for them. The age span from 14 or 15 to nearly 18 is very probably too great to be bridged by a single program, and the wisdom of the original age criterion of admission seems sound.

The programs clearly were not designed to accommodate the intellectually sub-normal or the severely disturbed. The Southfields research indicated that graduates had a higher score on the Wonderlic Test used to measure intelligence than the non-graduates, and that over 50 percent of the boys returned to court as unsuitables for the program had I.Q.'s below 90. It seems reasonable to conclude that the very nature of the group programs demands a reasonable level of intelligence. Boys who suffer from psychotic or severe neurotic conditions are similarly unsuited to such programs. Six such boys in the Southfields program were returned to the court as unsuitables, and other programs also experienced problems with such boys. It is clear that these boys are inappropriate for the kind of pressure, anxiety, and stress that accompanies the processes of group living and interaction implicit in the group programs.

RELATIONS WITH THE COMMUNITY AND THE COURTS

It is apparent that relations with the community, the courts, and related facilities play an important role in the success of the group programs. Although community support for any correctional effort is desirable, it is especially so for the group programs because of their experimental nature, the absence of security measures in the residential centers, and the freedom boys have in the community in the non-residential facilities. This support involves both the continued existence of the programs and the community reintegration of the boys after they leave them. The New Jersey programs, especially Essexfields, have been relatively successful in this respect, largely through such efforts as the organization of citizen committees which were involved in the early planning and continued to function thereafter, contact with community service clubs and organizations, thorough briefings of personnel from the courts and probation, an open policy of public visitations, a willingness to be evaluated by outside research, the maintenance of good press relations, and a program flexible enough to change when change was called for.

At Silverlake, mutually beneficial relations with probation personnel were maintained by inviting case workers and their supervisors to observe Silverlake in operation and to discuss the research and the program. Similar meetings were held periodically with representatives of the juvenile court, the police, the schools, and Boys Republic. Because of the size and impersonality of the court system, linkage with the Juvenile Court was not adequate. Although supportive of the Silverlake experiment, the courts could have been more flexible and responsive to program needs, particularly with respect to boys returned to the court and to those held in detention. Relatively good relationships were maintained in the neighborhood, despite some resistance, by the use of public meetings and open house visits to acquaint people with the program and allay fears or rumors about the boys' activities.

Failure to get adequate support may seriously jeopardize the program. One factor that partially accounts for the high rate of in-program failure at Southfields appears to have been a problem of communication with the court. A significant number of boys had to be returned to the court as unsuitable because of psychiatric or intellectual inadequacies. Furthermore, many boys who ran away and were returned to the court were placed on probation with no further penalty. This gave little support to the program's attempts to hold boys long enough to integrate them into group controls and processes, since shortly after admission a boy could opt for greater freedom and less supervision by running away and being placed on probation or, if he were 18 years of age, perhaps securing release.

The Pinehills report indicates parallel problems in its relations with the court and probation. The program design called for placing boys in detention if they continued delinquency or failed to participate, the purpose being to use negative sanctions as a means for involving boys more effectively in the program rather than a means of punishment. Although initial permission was granted for this plan, subsequent changes in probation personnel, with differing practices and philosophies, resulted in discontinuing detention. Another problem arose from the nature of the experimental design. The report indicates the nature of this difficulty as follows.

[The court staff] could not escape its impact. One very obvious reason is that the Experimental design put them in competition, in one sense, with the Experiment. The boys who were members of the probation control group were members of probation officers' case loads. Consequently, it was impossible for the Chief Probation Officer and his deputies to ignore the possibility that those for whom they were responsible might do more poorly than boys who attended the experimental program. No amount of discussion regarding the scientific need to try different methods or to recognize that the treatment approaches were vastly different could do away with a sense of competition.[7]

All of this placed the juvenile court judge in a very difficult position in attempting to support both his staff and the Pinehills program. In retrospect, the Pinehills staff indicated their failure to devote enough time to court personnel in discussing the nature of the program and the evaluative research accompanying it.

Despite considerable citizen and state political support, Pinehills also experienced serious resistance from state and county officials, which ultimately resulted in a failure to renew funds to continue the program. In addition to the matter of financial support, some officials apparently accepted the impression that the group programs denied youths their individuality in favor of rigid conformity to group values, and assumed that adolescent boys were incapable of making appropriate decisions for themselves and others.

Severe problems may arise in attempts to incorporate public school education into the program. Collegefields was established with the active cooperation of educational institutions as part of its design and demonstrated rather effectively the positive results of such a working relationship. Silverlake, on the other hand, made use of public schools rather than the special educational program worked out at Collegefields. As a result, Silverlake encountered problems associated with community acceptance, truancy, imposition of extra work on school staff, differences in life style permitted boys at Silverlake but not possible in school, the extent to which the school could sustain and contain deviance, and the like. There was also the problem of what to do with a boy who for whatever reason was no longer eligible for school attendance. Furthermore, it was felt that school pressures may have contributed to the high rate of runaways. As a result of these experiences, it was concluded that advanced preparation and liaison with the schools and some means for dealing with academic retardation are necessary if public school education is included in the total program.

Essexfields made it possible for boys who made sufficient progress to arrange school attendance while in the program. This screening of candidates for school attendance seemed to overcome some of the difficulties encountered at Silverlake, since it selected boys who were motivated to attend school and who were likely to present few problems. Through group discussion at Pinehills, the boys concluded that education was more important than job placement and efforts were made to help them remain in school. Liaison with school officials was established, a tutorial program was added, school problems became an important issue for discussion in the meetings, and school progress was made a consideration for judging progress in the program. It was tentatively concluded that some boys who otherwise would have dropped from school remained in, and that boys seemed to get along better in school as a consequence of improved conduct. School staff, in turn, were among those who most actively supported the continuance of Pinehills. Nevertheless, it was felt that future programs might be more successful if schools rather than work were integrated more closely into the program. Presumably, this would be especially appropriate for younger boys.

The support of their families—who are also part of the community—is essential to the boys and the program; this may be ignored in the effort to integrate the program with larger, more powerful organizations. Experience at Essexfields led to the realization that deteriorating home and family relations impede a boy's rehabilitation, that families were largely ignorant of the nature of the program, and that they might unwittingly subvert program efforts through distrust or misunderstanding. Consequently, procedures were worked out for a staff member to interview parents upon a boy's admission to Essexfields. This was followed by home visitations, utilizing the initial contact established by the interview. As a result, staff consensus was that families became more cooperative and interested in the program and their boy's progress.[8] Collegefields worked directly with the Newark Family Service Bureau, and two staff social workers provided a "reaching-out" effort to involve otherwise disinterested or suspicious families. Based upon this experience, one of these social workers was later appointed a full-time case work consultant to the county juvenile court. Although not part of the original design, Silverlake found it helpful to introduce conferences involving a staff member, a boy, and his family into the program, because in many cases unresolved family difficulties precluded the boy's successful adjustment. In some cases, a boy's family was requested to attend one or more of the group meetings. As the number of families requesting help increased, weekly meetings were held to which all families experiencing problems were invited. On the assumption that family difficulties are rarely the function of the individual delinquent, efforts were made by these means to help family members see difficulties in the context of the family as a whole and work towards a collective solution. Failure to include the family was viewed as a major omission in the original design of the program. Similar conclusions were made as a result of the Pinehills experience.

INTERNAL ORGANIZATION

The staff appears to play a crucial role in both the feasibility and effectiveness of the group programs. Because of the innovative nature of the programs and the amorphous state of treatment oriented correctional work in general, there are no clear guidelines for selection and training of staff. Highfields had the advantage of its first director having had prior experience in group work. Highfields also initiated a residential internship for the training of future directors, some of whom are presently working in group centered facilities. Essexfields was started by using Highfields boys as a seed bed into which new boys were gradually planted. Collegefields was organized and partially staffed by Essexfields personnel. More recently, the possibility of using successful program graduates as part of the staff has emerged.

When a new program is started without such advantages, there is the very real hazard of failure or difficulty, particularly in the early stages. Even though Southfields was directed by a former Highfields intern, one of the major problems centered around the development of an effective group early in the program. In a perhaps overly harsh self-evaluation, Wall, Elias, and Axelrod's report on Southfields concluded that a poorly designed program and inadequate staff were partly responsible for what was felt to be the poor results there. Miller's report on Southfields pointed out that the drop-out rate improved considerably in the last year of the program, suggesting that it had begun to stabilize. The Silverlake research made a two year study of critical incidents, including fighting, theft, use of drugs or alcohol, sex activities, school problems, and unauthorized absences from the program. It was found that critical incidents decreased from slightly more than four per boy to less than one per boy over the two year period. Furthermore, early in the program, well over half of the incidents were perpetrated by groups of boys rather than by individuals. This was reduced to less than a third towards the end of the period. It seems reasonable to assume that these changes were at least partly a result of the emergence of a strong and effective treatment culture.

One problem emphasized by the Silverlake research was the relative absence of effective rewards for conformity. This became a crucial issue when negative sanctions were developed that tended to increase solidarity among conformers but appeared to increase the rate of runaways among new boys and exacerbate in-program failure among boys with personal problems. The low in-program failure rate at Essexfields compared with some of the other programs indicates that high failure rates are not an inevitable consequence of program pressure and strain. Since a major source of rewards flows from group approval and making progress, it is important that strong group solidarity, morale, and institutional pride be developed. It seems likely that Essexfields managed to evolve a structure in support of these objectives. As indicated in earlier discussion, effort was made to highlight progress and develop group concern by such means as ceremonial transition from new to old group status, extension of options to school or work outside the program for helped boys, printing of cards indicating successful completion of the program (this was requested by the boys themselves as partial validation of their readiness to assume community roles), extension of concern to graduates by maintaining a record of their community adjustment, visitation by graduates who were successful in the community, and the like. Since sources of rewards are scarce and the need for some measure of negative sanction is pressing in any correctional setting, every effort should be made to develop positive inducement in programs organized for help rather than punishment.

Some of the problems here and elsewhere center around building, in the early stages of the program, an adequate group culture in support of program goals. If the initial group of new boys, for example, does not progress beyond the first few stages of development described in Chapter 4 and produce an effective group of "old boys," the program is in serious jeopardy. The same is true thereafter, which is one reason a program may be seriously weakened by a change in admissions that fails to meet the basic criteria of suitability. Similarly, a sudden loss or influx of boys, for whatever reason, may create a crisis in the continuity of the program. This is why intake and discharge procedures are so important and should not be subject to court calendars, change in court personnel, or other administrative considerations if a fair test of effectiveness is to be made.

Because of the small group nature of these facilities and the pressures and anxieties that develop, every member of the staff plays an important role in the treatment processes. Even a pet dog may be important to a shy and withdrawn boy who has difficulty early in the program, and many of the facilities had pets by chance or design. The presence of women as cooks or secretaries adds a special dimension, and some boys develop helpful relations with female staff members. The work supervisor is a key member of the staff. At Pinehills there was continual friction between the various work supervisors and the boys, since supervisors were either rigidly authoritarian or too easily manipulated by the boys. Essexfields was fortunate in having a black work supervisor who, out of his own life experience, was able to communicate effectively with the boys and gain their respect. In retrospect, it was recommended that a black work supervisor be hired for Southfields, which, like Essexfields, had a considerable number of black admissions.

As well as playing a supportive role, staff can also provide an important learning experience for the boys. The natural and varied interpersonal environment provided by their presence, and the inevitable difficulties that arise, are useful in the meetings for identifying boys' problems, ways of coping with others, and means for avoiding or handling trouble.

IN-PROGRAM FAILURES

Experience in several of the programs indicated that in-program failure was not solely a function of inadequacies in program design. It has been pointed out that proper selection of suitable boys may reduce drop-out rates and that family contact may increase support in holding boys to the program. There is also evidence that policy governing return of boys to the court as unsuitable may affect the rate of in-program failure. Since it is clear that recidivism is lower among boys who complete treatment, such policy plays an important role in the success of the program.

The rate of boys returned to the court for running away varied among programs and within a given program at different times. It is apparent that this is not only a consequence of the number of runaways, but of the way in which the staff responds to running away. A substantial proportion of AWOL takes place during the first few weeks after a boy is admitted. Not infrequently, boys will return of their own accord. A rigid policy of "unsuitability" may return some boys to the court who might have been integrated into the program. This was the conclusion of the Silverlake study; the Wall, Elias, and Axelrod report, particularly sensitive to the AWOL problem, pointed to the need for a well thought out program change at Southfields to handle run-aways. It was suggested that the problem be attacked before a boy's departure, when there is some evidence of his intention to leave. At Silverlake, it was found that instituting AWOL sanctions had an immediate but not a long range effect in decreasing run-aways. It was concluded that sanctions were needed from time to time to reinforce the norm of compliance to the program, but that flexibility was also needed in the use and form of sanctions. This is a special instance of the general need for a policy of program flexibility that leaves open the response to deviance so that sophisticated delinquents cannot readily learn to "beat the system," on the one hand, and boys with special problems can be helped, on the other.

The Silverlake study also indicated that AWOL's were partly a result of the increasing strength and development of the group culture, which became more difficult for some new boys to tolerate. Experience at Essexfields suggests that use of the "weak boy" role is one way of meeting this problem. As indicated earlier, this role was designed for the boy who was withdrawn or found difficulty in relating to the group, and required that other boys "go easy on him" and make special effort to integrate him into the group. Similarly, effort was made to hold boys to the program who were in a period of crisis as, for example, when a boy who was likely to get into trouble was accompanied home on week-ends by another boy, or when "easy days" or special meetings were arranged. The Essexfields study found that this non-residential program had a somewhat lower in-program failure rate than the residential group centers, and this seemed to be true of non-residential Pinehills as well. It may be that a chance to return home evenings and weekends provides sufficient relief from group pressure to encourage boys to stick with the program. Since it is also possible that non-residence dilutes the therapeutic effects of the group, a sequence of non-residential and residential programming might be considered.

LENGTH OF TREATMENT

Although there is little systematic study of the relationship between length of treatment and rates of recidivism (other than the fact that boys who complete the program are much less recidivistic than those who do not), there is indication that some of the boys might profit by more extended exposure to the program. Most boys released from the program have had four to five months experience in it. Not many are held longer, even though they do not present any particular problem. Some are sent home "on a humble," which to Essexfields boys means a boy was released even though he had not been "helped." It was felt that there was nothing more the group could do for him, and that such boys only took up space that might be occupied by a boy who wanted to be helped. There is also the danger that unhelped old boys might dilute the therapeutic group culture. In addition, the program was designed as short-term therapy, and its validity was partially based on the assumption that such intensive treatment would give positive results. The further assumption seems to have been that extension beyond a reasonable time span would only bring diminishing returns.

Despite these considerations, the Wall, Elias, and Axelrod report recommended an extension of the time a boy be permitted to remain at Southfields. This might apply particularly to "late starters" who have difficulty integrating into the group processes. The Collegefields study found that in-program failures made some improvement after they left the program. The six months follow-up testing of these boys showed that they scored much like the graduates did on entering the program, and the researchers concluded that the Collegefields experience had increased their readiness for rehabilitation. Had they been retained by the program and their stay extended, they might have shown the same rates of improvement and success found among the graduates. Although caution should be taken on extension of stay lest dependency on the program replace effective return to the community, experimentation with, and research evaluation of, extension seems warranted.[9]

FOLLOW-UP

Beginning with Weeks' study of Highfields, it has been suggested frequently that boys released from the programs would benefit by follow-up guided group interaction sessions. The case for some kind of follow-up after release might be made for any treatment program. However, there is a good deal of impressionistic and some firmer empirical evidence in the reports reviewed here that boys who complete the group programs are better candidates for community reintegration than those in alternative programs. Changes that seem to have been accomplished involved improvements in diffuse feelings centering around hostility, asociality, openness to alternatives, self-confidence, and attitudes towards others. Such considerations suggest a receptiveness to significant behavioral change, but indicate a need for support and continuing structure sufficient to make the final leap from intent to action. Readiness for change, and even a deep commitment to it, can be gradually extinguished once moved from a supportive structure into a hostile or indifferent environment.

A more general case for follow-up may be made from speculations based on analysis of attitudes and personality and changes taking place in them. Generally speaking, attitudes and personality characteristics indicated by pre-treatment tests did not prove to be very effective prognosticators of after-release performance. (The Silverlake data suggested, however, that personality variables may be affected differently by different types of programs, and, hence, their predictive value may depend upon program variables.) Furthermore, where favorable change was found between pre- and post-release tests and run against recidivism, little significant relationship was demonstrated. These findings suggest that the role attitudes and personality characteristics play in delinquency may be over-emphasized by some analysts. Reducing hostility or depression, for example, may succeed in producing a "happier," rather than a less delinquent, boy. Such states are neither necessary nor sufficient conditions for deviant *behavior* or for being officially processed as a "delinquent." The same is true of attitudes. Primary focus on motivation to deviance may obscure the role that factors such as opportunity to deviate, social control, and exposure to strain play in activating and expressing that motivation in behavior.

It seems probable that the boys in these studies are likely to have a high motivational potential for deviance when compared with general population norms, and much of the data indicates they do. It also is likely, however, that they are more exposed to deviance, less subject to conventional, informal controls (but more subject to formal, official scrutiny), and experience greater stress and pressure. Therefore, to treat the motivation without considering the factors involved in its behavioral activation may not give much assurance of desired results. This appears to be a major weakness in the general theory upon which the group treatment approach is based.

Precisely what form follow-up aftercare should take is not specified in any of the reports. The Southfields report called for an aftercare program that would involve the boys for at least one year and recommended that preparing boys for it be worked into the ongoing program. It would appear that every effort should be made after release to engage the boys in the more conventional activities and groups formerly denied them or rejected by them and to provide the boys, on a gradually diminishing basis, with the kind of mutual help, critical evaluation, and search for alternatives they experienced in the program. It would seem equally necessary for them to have some assurance that their commitment to more conventional behavior would receive reasonable rewards, so that they would have a "stake in conformity" previously denied or ignored by them.

THE PROGRAM AS A HUMAN ENVIRONMENT

Although the recidivism of inmates released from correctional programs cannot be lightly turned aside, the experience of inmates (and staff as well) in a program should not be neglected as unimportant. Experience has shown that informal inmate systems are likely to develop in any correctional institution. In security and custodial oriented facilities, they are frequently organized against administrative and therapeutic efforts, and may be predatory and antisocial with respect to the inmates themselves. Recent investigations of treatment oriented facilities, however, have indicated that they can offer a correctional setting that fosters more positive inmate attitudes towards staff and program, less hostile and authoritarian inmate systems, and an inmate perception of less deprivation and greater freedom.[10] Rather than attempting to control or destroy inmate systems, the guided group interaction facilities attempt to organize and use these informal relations as a natural vehicle for staff-inmate integration and for carrying out a program of treatment in a humane setting.

Unless the boys were playing some grotesque charade at Essexfields, the example used in this book to describe the program and process of guided group interaction, one cannot but gain the impression from the boys and the staff members that the quality of their relations were more intimate, personal, free, and involving than usually experienced in traditional correctional institutions. The boys seemed more positively oriented towards the program and the staff directing it, and there was greater mutual trust and respect.

The research on program processes at Silverlake gives some empirical evidence that confirms the impressions gained at Essexfields. Although all of the objectives of the Silverlake program were by no means fully implemented, in comparison with Boys Republic (a facility far more liberal than most traditional, correctional institutions), Silverlake showed relatively more favorable attitudes towards change objectives, more open communication and collaboration, less separation of staff and boys, and more inclination to perceive organizational rules as helpful. In addition, there was considerable sharing of critical incidences at Silverlake, and a program culture developed that became increasingly effective in revealing and controlling these program deviances.

Where carefully planned and instrumented, the feasibility of the short term, group programs has been firmly established. It is also clear that such facilities present no serious threat to the community. Nor do they appear to increase the risk of potential failure, particularly if candidates are carefully selected. Admittedly, there are potential dangers to the individual in any program that involves the manipulation of group processes, and adequate protection of the rights and dignity of the individual must be assured.[11] However, there is no evidence that the group program staffs are less sensitive to this potential than personnel in other programs, or that their wards experience greater constraint on personal liberty or more severe threat to individual dignity. Indeed, quite the opposite seems to be the case.

Given these considerations, there is a strong humanitarian case for continuing these programs rather than abandoning them for more constrictive or harsher methods.[12] This is entirely in the spirit of the general movement for more humane treatment of offenders. Furthermore, the need for experimentation and innovation in the field of corrections is supported by results regarding feasibility, community protection, and failure risk. No program of correction presently in operation gives the desired results and, as indicated in the discussion of the need for follow-up services, it is unlikely that correctional efforts alone will do so. Since it is even less likely that delinquency will be reduced to inconsequential proportions in the foreseeable future, society will continue to be faced with the problem of what to do with or for the delinquents it has. While serious effort should be given to delinquency prevention and after-care, we are in equal need of programs of intervention that can effectively prepare youths who do become delinquent for successful reintegration into the society to which they will return.[13]

The guided group interaction programs have demonstrated the feasibility of experimentation in correctional methods. They have shown that delinquents usually thought to be serious risks can be given short term treatment involving considerable personal freedom and active participation in correctional processes, and that such programs can be carried out in the community. Those in charge of these programs have had the courage to subject them to research investigation which is essential for evaluation and developing knowledge of correctional processes. The research has indicated guidelines for program improvement, innovation, and extension, without dismissing alternative approaches. These are worthy accomplishments. It can only be hoped that the pattern set by experimental guided group interaction programs will continue to be followed and elaborated in the field of corrections, and will be expanded to encourage similar efforts in seeking solutions to the general problem of crime and delinquency in our society.

NOTES

1. The significance of a boy's relationship to others in the group programs is under-scored by research on sociometric types at Silverlake. It revealed that boys who neither liked nor were liked by others were least likely to complete the program; boys who liked and were liked by others were most likely to finish. See LaMar T. Empey and Steven G. Lubeck, *The Silverlake Experiment* (Chicago: Aldine Publishing Co., 1971), p. 249.

2. Doug Knight, "The Marshall Program: Assessment of a Short-Term Institutional Treatment Program, Part II: Amenability to Confrontive Peer-Group Treatment," California Youth Authority, Research Report No. 59, August 1970.

3. Knight, "The Marshall Program."

4. Knight, "The Marshall Program." The Interpersonal-Maturity Level system of classification is used to distinguish types of delinquents for treatment purposes. As elaborated by Marguerite Q. Warren and associates, it has been used extensively in re-search involving California Youth Authority wards. For references on I Level theory and research see "Status of Current Research in the California Youth Authority," Annual Report, California Youth Authority, July 1970.

5. Knight, "The Marshall Program," pp. 64-65.

6. Empey, *The Silverlake Experiment,* pp. 326-330.

7. LaMar T. Empey, Maynard L. Erickson, and Max L. Scott, "Pinehills," Annual Progress Report, 1964, The Provo Experiment in Delinquency Rehabilitation, to the Ford Foundation (Mimeographed), p. 16.

8. Albert Elias and Saul Pilnick, "The Essexfields Group Rehabilitation Project for Youthful Offenders," in *Correction in the Community: Alternatives to Incarceration,* Youth and Adult Corrections Agency, Board of Correction, State of California, Mono-graph No. 4, June, 1967, pp. 51-57.

9. For a penetrating discussion of program dependency and implications for group centered correctional programs see David Sternberg, "Synanon House—A Consideration of its Implications for American Correction," *Journal of Criminal Law, Criminology and Police Science* 54:4 (December 1963): 447-455.

10. For example, see David Street, "The Inmate Group in Custodial and Treatment Settings," *American Sociological Review* 20:1 (February 1965): 40-55 and Bernard S. Berk, "Organizational Goals and Inmate Organization," *American Journal of Sociology* 71:5 (March 1966): 522-534.

11. For one discussion of these potentials see Whitney H. Gordon's comments and LaMar T. Empey's rejoinder in "Communications." *American Sociological Review* 27:2 (April 1962): 256-258.

12. A trenchant case for divorcing evaluation of programs by recidivism from humane considerations, where risk of failure is relatively constant, is made by Paul Lerman, "Evaluative Studies of Institutions for Delinquents: Implications for Research and Social Policy," *Social Work* 13:3 (July 1968): 55-64.

13. Prevention, intervention, and re-entry are separate but intimately related dimen-sions of delinquency. The few comparative studies of prevention that have been made in-dicate no greater success than the intervention program discussed here. See, for example, Edwin Powers and Helen Whitmer, *An Experiment in the Prevention of Delinquency* (New York: Columbia University Press, 1951) and Walter B. Miller, "The Impact of a 'Total-Community' Delinquency Control Project," *Social Problems* 10:2 (Fall 1962):168-191.

Appendix A:
Essexfields Argot

Boy—impersonal term applied to a particular boy under discussion in a meeting; name of boy not ordinarily used. Also used as a control so that boy doesn't get "false idea of his importance" or get "superiority complex."

Boy, helped—boy who is making progress in program.

Boy, new—boy entering program.

Boy, old—boy who is towards end of program. Usually ten oldest boys.

Boy, weak—boy who is shy, has difficulty relating with other boys, can't take harsh or severe pressure or others getting on him. Not necessarily derogatory.

Bogarding—boisterous monopoly of meeting; boisterous behavior to get what boy wants; physical or vocal.

Bull-shitting—not giving straight answers; covering up; talking without purpose in the meeting.

Busted—getting apprehended for delinquency; caught breaking a law. (see role, busting a)

Checking—self and others; boy should check self, i.e., should learn to inhibit initial responses; if boy doesn't do this, others should check him by saying "check yourself."

Checking up—visiting or telephoning a boy's home to make sure he is doing what he says.

Cliquing—(pronounced "clicking")—general term for deviance in and outside program.

Cliquing in program—not "confessing on" boys; holding anything back that could help self or other boys.

Cliquing, group—group trying to "look good" in eyes of staff without sincerity.

Cliquing together—boys getting together to stick up for one another or cover each other's program violations.

Cliquing with self—failing to confess on self; not telling the boys what they should know so they can help.

Clowning——not taking program seriously.

Comparing——boy trying to take the pressure off himself by accusing other boys of engaging in the same deviance he is being questioned about.

Confess (on self and others)——reporting deviances in and outside the program to the group.

Confidence, self——boy must gain confidence in self and believe he can be helped, expressed through participation in program, speaking up, defending opinions and impressions.

Confidence of others—boy must gain confidence of group and staff. Group trusts a boy because he levels with them and wants to be helped.

Confused——a boy who doesn't understand the program; group says one thing, but he thinks they said something else; not paying attention to what's going on in the program.

Defying——not doing what the group legitimately tells a boy to do.

Dodging criticism——defensive maneuvers to avoid or fend off group criticism; failure to admit faults.

Easily aggravated——too easily angered by individual or group criticism.

Easily discouraged——giving up; not trying; backing down; dropping opinion without good reason.

Easily influenced——going along with boys; ready to do what someone else does without questioning the consequences.

Easy day——old boy is assigned to a new boy so that they can talk over new boy's problems; new boy is not required to do any work but is expected to talk about his problems with other group members.

Extra duty——giving extra hours of work or taking away smoking privileges or dessert for infraction of group norms.

Getting on a boy——finding out about a boy, finding his problem, helping him; verbally abusing a boy. (Situation determines whether this is positive or negative behavior. Also, sometimes called ball busting, hiking, or hiking a boy.)

Going along with the boys—not thinking for self.

Group—a number of boys, used variously as below:

> Group leader—work leader, usually old boy, assigned by boys or work supervisor to oversee small groups of boys in the work program.
>
> Group, new—group made up predominantly of new boys in the meeting.
>
> Group, old—group consisting predominantly of old boys in the meeting.

Help—what boy gets from the program at Essexfields; learning to handle problems; better understanding of self and others.

> Helped boy—(see boy)
>
> Helping others—program participation that helps other boys.
>
> Helping self—self-reliance and responsibility in handling one's own problems.

Hiding behind the program—taking advantage of group norms in order to pursue individual needs or desires. For example, aggravating other boys knowing that the norm is that they should not fight back physically.

Hours—extra work for infraction of group norms, for doing things boy wouldn't do at home (spitting on floor, putting butts on floor, etc.); may have to sand floors, wash woodwork, etc. Time to think about why one broke a requirement and why he won't do it again.

Humble, being sent home on a—not really earning one's way out of Essexfields. (Boys feel they have done all they can for a boy, but haven't changed him; should be released to take in a new boy who wants to be helped. On the outside, getting arrested for something you didn't do is called a "humble.")

Impressing—giving group or staff a false image of self; trying to be a big shot; adjunct to playing a role. Trying to give staff or boys a good impression without changing or improving.

Impressions—boy's statement about self and others: how program is progressing, what boys' problems are; what a boy honestly feels about another.

Inconsiderate (of self or others)—not wanting to be helped or thinking or acting in ways that inhibit being helped; acting in ways that fail to help or interfere with other boys; behavior that hurts a boy's family.

Lacking effort—not participating sufficiently in program.

Loud—boisterousness that interferes with the program.

Meeting—the evening guided group interaction sessions.

> Getting the meeting—discussion concerning who is to have the meeting; boys are expected to ask for it and explain why they should have it.

Giving the meeting—boy is given the meeting even though he does not ask for it if group feels he needs it.

Help meeting—Saturday morning meetings with boys who have been released from Essexfields and voluntarily return to help a boy currently in the program or one with a problem who has been released.

Meeting's meeting—meeting devoted to discussion of the group and its problems as a group; elected by consent of group. Boys discuss specific problems such as poor meetings or other program weaknesses.

Split meeting—when more than one boy needs the meeting; sharing the meeting.

Summarize the meeting—staff asks boy to review meeting; staff may participate in summary; indicates what was brought out at meeting; keeps boys "on toes" at meeting since anyone may be called to summarize; helps new boys learn how meetings work.

Mocking——making fun of boy in the program.

Monthly Report——written report on boy's progress submitted to the court by the Program Director. Staff reads the monthly report at a meeting and the group discusses it before forwarding to court.

On report——loss of pay for infraction of group norms.

On trial——new boys are in probationary period with group until they gain group's confidence.

Office patrol——boys clean office twice a day. Boys usually make a list of who is to do the cleaning and rotate the job. If they do not do adequate job, the staff will make up a list of who is on office patrol.

Opinions——boys' statements regarding other boys, the group, the meeting, or any aspect of the program; usually given in the process of arriving at group discussions. (Who gets the meeting, whether a boy is ready for release, should a boy work on the outside, etc.).

Dropping a boy's opinion—group may veto boy's opinion if it agrees he is bull-headed, impressing, bogarding, or role playing.

Dropping opinion—a boy may change or drop his opinion but must state reasons why.

Outside——what goes on outside the program.

Outside the meeting—activities that take place in program outside the meeting.

Outside ways—delinquent ways of behaving, street ways.

Pressure——getting on a boy, but not overdoing it, is legitimate pressure. Bad pressure implies not really wanting to help a boy; getting him to confess just to punish him; staying on boy constantly.

Problems—roots of boy's difficulty; delinquency redefined in terms of problems; boy must discover his problems with the help of the group; behavior or action which a boy and/or the group consider needs analysis and understanding.

Program—term applied to the total structure of Essexfields.

Progress—getting helped in the program.

Psyching—teasing a boy to get adverse reaction; tempting a boy to deviate from program in order to test him; seeing if he is role playing. Psyching a boy to get him to confess on himself is better than other boys confessing on him. This is "good" psyching. "Bad" psyching is just trying to get boy in trouble.

Punk—a boy who fights when he knows he can win and runs away when he knows he will lose; boy who plays the role of a tough.

Punked out—quitting when things get tough.

Revenge squad—coalition of boys who seek to dominate the program or "get even" with other boys. (Also see, "Taking out revenge.")

Role playing—acting out program norms without internalizing them; not being your true self; acting for approval without changing.
  Busting a role—demonstrating to a boy that he is playing a role.
  Meeting playing a role—boys in a meeting trying to impress new boys or the staff by loud and active participation; also may be done in order to inhibit boys from "getting on" each other in the meeting.
  Playing a role with yourself—unconscious role playing; conforming but not sure it is because one has changed or helped his problems; may ask other boys to find out at a meeting.

Runaway—failing to show up for any aspect of the program without proper excuse.

Self—referring to oneself.
  Not revealing true self—playing a role or hiding your feelings.
  Self confidence—see "confidence."
  Showing yourself—communicating true feelings so that you can be helped; opposite of playing a role.
  True self—what a boy really is; his "normal self."

Slicking—goofing off at work; not working at group rate; loafing when you should be working.

Sneaky—not being straight with boys; underhanded; doing something unacceptable to the group and hoping not to be found out.

Sponge—currying favor with staff or other boys; trying to "get in good" with staff and boys but not gaining their confidence.

Sponging——when two or more boys clique and withhold information from the group.

Story, telling your——new boy relates in the meeting the sequence that led to being sent to Essexfields.

Going deep into your story—probing a boy's story after he has related it and when group knows more about him and how he acts in program.

Street ways——deviant or delinquent ways of behaving "on the outside"; behavior before coming to Essexfields; behavior of boys who are not helped.

Taking out revenge——getting on other boys simply because they got on you. (Also see "revenge squad.")

Talk up——boys must participate in meetings, take initiative to speak, raise questions, express opinions and impressions.

Touch off——very aggressive boy who may hit or shove other boys.

Touching——any physical contact that indicates physical aggression.

Undesirables——prior delinquent associates; boys outside the program with whom boys should not interact; anybody who can get a boy busted.

Consorting with undesirables—contacting in any way boys who might get one into trouble.

Appendix B:
Description of MMPI
Scales and Indices

Basic information about all the measures employed in the study may be found in W. G. Dahlstrom and G. S. Welsh, *An MMPI Handbook* (Minneapolis: University of Minnesota Press, 1960), and/or in the references cited. The origin and meaning of the first 14 basic scales are widely documented, and only a brief description is repeated here. The 18 additional measures used in this study are described below, together with a rating of the extent to which their validity has previously been established. A rating of 3 indicates that the authors consider the scale to have been adequately validated. The basic MMPI scales are assigned a rating of 3. A rating of 2 indicates that the scale or index holds good promise of adequate validity, but has not been used widely enough to be considered thoroughly validated. Scales are given a rating of 1 if little or no evidence exists for validity other than the initial construction technique, or if the validity evidence is conflicting. It is thus not at all certain that such scales are evaluating what their names indicate, and they are therefore used in an exploratory vein.

MMPI SCALES

1. Hs (hypochondriasis).
   This scale is related to psychosomatic illness and a high score characterizes those who express their emotional conflicts through somatic channels, are generally self-centered, and demand a great deal of attention.
2. *D* (depression).
   Depression, unhappiness, hopelessness or sorrow are measured by this

scale. A high score may also indicate that the person feels unsure of himself and of the future. Scale is sensitive to changing emotional states.

3. *Hy* (hysteria).

   Closely related to scale 1. High scorers tend to avoid or run away from crises rather than face them realistically. In avoiding them, they may develop a physical or psychological illness as a solution.

4. *Pd* (psychopathic deviancy)

   This scale is related to the ability of the ordinary mores of the society to control the individual. Persons with high scores are not affected by remorse, have difficulty maintaining satisfactory personal relationships, are easily angered and often act hostilely and impulsively. They are likely to commit asocial acts and are often immune from experiencing guilt or shame.

5. *Mf* (masculinity-feminity)

   This scale is related to masculine-feminine interests. High scores do not necessarily indicate homosexuality, but a general interest in things not usually identified with one's sex. In men, a high score may characterize a passive, dependent person with aesthetic, bookish interests.

6. *Pa* (paranoia).

   This is a measure of undue personal sensitivity which in its extreme form may be manifested as suspicion or feelings of persecution. The high scorer may feel threatened or mistreated.

7. *Pt* (psychasthenia).

   The psychasthenia scale is related to compulsions and obsessions. High scorers may be excessively meticulous or overly conscientious, perform ritualistic acts and be perfectionists. They often tend to worry and engage in self-criticism beyond justifiable limits.

8. *Sc* (schizophrenia).

   This measure is related to the degree to which one thinks and acts like others. At the extremes, the scale is an indicator of schizophrenia. More generally, it measures the way in which one may distort his social world, see it and react to it in unusual ways.

9. *Ma* (hypomania).

   This scale is related to enthusiasm and energy. High scorers are readily interested in things and approach problems with enthusiasm. In abnormal cases, this scale may indicate irrational manic behavior.

10. *Si* (social introversion).

    The degree of social introversion-extroversion is measured by this scale, with a high score indicating the former and a low score the latter. High scorers tend to withdraw and not become involved in social contact and social activity.

11. *?*

This is a validity scale obtained by counting the number of items for which neither or both alternatives were indicated. A high score indicates that no conclusions can be safely drawn from the inventory.

12. *L* (lie)

The lie scale indicates an excessive amount of naive lying in a socially desirable direction. The high scorer attempts to put himself in a good light, especially with reference to personal ethics and social behavior.

13. *F*

Opposite of the *L* score, indicating an attempt by the respondent to show himself in a bad light. In addition, the *F* scale will be high if the subject has inadequate reading ability, answers carelessly, or makes random responses to the questions.

14. *K*

The *K* score suggests the presence of a set toward subtle distortion or defensiveness in a socially desirable direction. In general, it is like the *L* scale but in a more subtle way.

15. *A* (first or anxiety factor).

This scale was derived by first listing all the items which were scored (in the same direction) on three or more of the clinical scales. The MMPI responses of high and low extreme scores on this initial "general maladjustment" scale were compared, and 39 items were identified which showed at least a 75 percent separation. This 39 item *A* scale was shown to load .99 on the first factor identified by Welsh in his factor analysis of the MMPI responses of VA medical patients. A similar factor has been reported by other workers as the main source of variance among responses on the MMPI and other inventories. It has been variously named ego-resiliency, social desirability (for low scorers), and neuroticism. There is reasonable agreement that it is a valid measure of psychological comfort and health, provided deliberate distortion can be ruled out. (Rating of 3.) G. S. Welsh, "Factor Dimensions A and R," in G. S. Welsh and W. S. Dahlstrom (eds.), *Basic Readings on the MMPI in Psychology and Education* (Minneapolis: University of Minnesota Press, 1956).

16. *Ao* (attitude toward others) and
17. *As* (attitude toward self).

These measures were originally constructed to assess the effects of client-centered therapy on clients seen by advanced graduate students in a college counseling center. To quote:

> . . . . (the scales) were constructed from MMPI items selected on the basis of judgments made by trained judges. For an item to be retained, seven judges from a total of eleven had to agree on the proper scoring direction. The 20 items having the highest point-correlations with the total score were then selected for each scale.

In each case, a high score indicates a positive attitude. The scales were used in a factor-analytic study of change and no empirical validity data were reported. (Rating of 1 for both scales). R. L. Gibson, W. V. Snyder and W. S. Ray, "A Factor Analysis of Measures of Changing Following Client-Centered Therapy," *Journal of Counseling Psychology* 2 (1955): 83-90.

18. *Cy* (cynicism factor)

Comrey carried out separate factor analyses of eight MMPI clinical scales, and reported the existence of approximately 40 factors, though few were well defined. The factors were named according to the content of items with high loadings. A factor named "cynicism" was identified within the *D, Hy,* and *Pa* scales; the scale contains those items with high loadings on the factor. Little or no validity evidence exists for the scale. (Rating of 1.) A. L. Comrey, "A Factor Analysis of Items of the MMPI Paranoia Scale," *Educational and Psychological Measurement* 18 (1958): 99-107.

19. *Do* (dominance).

Criterion groups for high and low dominance were obtained by asking college fraternity and sorority members to nominate the five most dominant and five least dominant members of their group. "Dominant" was defined, in part, as "stronger in face-to-face situations," "forceful," "masterful," "confident," "authoritative," and "sure of himself." By this procedure, 15 high and 25 low dominant subjects were obtained. Similar groups of high school students were selected. Out of an initial pool of about 250 items, 60 discriminated significantly between both groups. Twenty-eight of the items came from the MMPI: these comprised the *Do* scale. Several cross-validation studies for the longer 60-item *Do* scale are reported in the *California Psychological Inventory Manual.* (Rating of 2.) H. G. Gough, H. McCloskey and P. E. Meehl, " A Personality Scale for Dominance," *Journal of Abnormal and Social Psychology* 46 (1951): 360-366.

20. *Dq* (delinquency).

This 33 item scale was constructed as part of a longitudinal study in predicting delinquency among adolescent boys. A relatively unselected sample of 1,958 ninth grade boys was administered the MMPI. Follow-up two and four years later identified those who had subsequently engaged in more than a very minimal amount of delinquent behavior. Those items which empirically discriminated the subsequent delinquents from the nondelinquents were identified from the original MMPIs. Thirty-three items "...stood up in a double cross-validation both as against all delinquents and as predicting delinquency that occurred after the time of testing" (p. 161). Hathaway and Monachesi (*Adolescent Personality and Behavior*, Minneapolis: University of Minnesota Press, 1963, p. 90) later refined the *Dq* scale, but were dissatisfied with its ability to separate delinquents from nondelinquents. (Rating of 2.) S. R. Hathaway and E. D. Monachesi, "The Personalities of Predelinquent Boys," *Journal of Criminal Law, Criminology and Police Science* 48 (1957): 149-163.

21. *Ec* (escapism).

The escapism scale contains 42 items which differentiated 103 male felons who had at some time escaped from custody from 100 felons who had neither escaped nor were considered likely to do so. The scale also discriminated between cross-validation escape (N = 57) and non-escapee (N = 46) groups beyond the .01 level of confidence. (Rating of 2.) H. S. Beall and J. H. Panton, "The Use of the MMPI as an Index to Escapism," *Journal of Clinical Psychology* 12 (1956): 392-394.

22. *Es* (ego strength).

This is one of the more popular MMPI additional measures, probably on account of its name. It consists of 68 items which discriminated 47 psychoneurotic patients who were judged to have improved after six months of individual psychotherapy and 16 patients who were considered not to have improved. Although the criterion samples were small, subsequent evidence has shown it to predict response in other psychotherapeutic settings. Positive correlations have also been reported with intelligence, breadth of interest, and courage. Dahlstrom and Welsh ((p. 356) have characterized it as assessing "overall personality strength" and "ability to deal with environmental pressures." They have also regarded it as the best single MMPI measure of emotional control (p. 303). There is also some indication that

high *Es* scores may in some cases suggest hostility, aggression and competi-
tiveness (Barron, 1956). (Rating of 3.) F. Barron, "An Ego-Strength Scale
which Predicts Response to Psychotherapy," *Journal of Consulting Psychology* 17 (1953): 327-333 and F. Barron, "Ego-Strength and the
Management of Aggression," in G. S. Welsh and W. G. Dahlstrom, (eds.),
Basic Readings on the MMPI in Psychology and Medicine (Minneapolis:
University of Minnesota Press, 1956).

23. *Ho* (hostility).

The *Ho* scale was derived in an attempt to measure one aspect of a person's ability to get along well with others. The Minnesota Teaching Attitude Inventory was used to define this ability. High and low scorers (the
top and bottom 8 percent) were used as criterion groups (N = 112 and 100
respectively), and the 250 MMPI items which discriminated between them
were inspected. A group of 77 items which most obviously reflected hostility was reduced to 60 on the basis of agreement among five clinical
psychologists. The item content suggests that the scale is reflecting a dis-
like for and a distrust of others. Dahlstrom and Welsh (p. 251) could find
no direct evidence that important degrees of *overt* hostility were reflected
by this measure. The *Ho* scale was chosen over several other hostility scales
because it held promise of assessing covert aspects of hostility. (Rating of
1.) W. W. Cook and D. M. Medley, "Proposed Hostility and Pharisaic-
Virtue Scales for the MMPI," *Journal of Applied Psychology* 38 (1954):
414-418.

24. *Iq* (intelligence).

This 59-item scale was constructed in somewhat the same manner as the
Do scale. It consists of 39 items which appear on the *Ie* (intellectual ef-
ficiency) scale of Gough's California Psychological Inventory (CPI), plus
another 20 items specific to the MMPI. Several cross-validation studies for
Ie scale are reported in the CPI Manual. (Rating of 1.) H. G. Gough,
California Psychological Inventory Manual (Palo Alto: Consulting Psychologists Press, 1957).

25. *Ne* (neurosis).

The 30 items on the neurosis scale were those out of the 117 items on
the three MMPI "neurotic" scales (*Hs, D,* and *Hy*) which discriminated
best between 140 normal and 140 psychiatrically ill veterans. Groups
were matched for intelligence, age, education, occupation, and marital
status. All items discriminated beyond the .01 level of confidence. Cross-
validity was established for two further pairs of samples, drawn from the

same general population, and some additional validity data are summarized by Dahlstrom and Welsh (1960). (Rating of 2.) J. F. Winne, "A Scale of Neuroticism: An Adaptation of the MMPI," *Journal of Clinical Psychology* 7 (1951): 117-122.

26. *Pc* (prediction of change).

This scale consists of 24 "therapy-susceptible" items; that is, neurotic and psychotic patients who responded favorably to psychotherapy tended to change their responses (in post-therapy testing) significantly more than did normals in an equivalent retest. An independent sample of hospitalized neurotics showed a significant decrease on this scale after treatment; however, two additional cross-validation studies failed to produce significant results. (Rating of 1.) W. Schofield, "Changes in Responses to the MMPI Following Certain Therapies," *Psychological Monographs* 64, No. 5 (1950).

27. *Rc* (recidivism).

The Rc scale consists of 24 items which discriminated (absolute difference of 10 or more) between 45 Army trainee AWOL first offenders and 55 who had been AWOL more than once. This scale was not cross-validated by Clark and a later attempt to do so (R. A. Freeman and H. M. Mason, "Construction of a Key to Determine Recidivists from Non-Recidivists Using the MMPI," *Journal of Clinical Psychology* 8 (1952): 207-208) proved unsuccessful. (Rating of 1.) J. H. Clark, "Application of the MMPI in Differentiating A.W.O.L. Recidivists from Non-Recidivists," *Journal of Psychology* 26 (1948): 229-234.

28. *Re-r* (social responsibility).

This scale was constructed in much the same manner as the *Do* scale. Four sets of high and low responsibility subjects were identified, by means of teacher and peer ratings, among high school and college students. Fifty-six items were identified which revealed the "...best discriminations among all the groups." Of these, 32, which came from the MMPI, comprised the present *Re* scale. A responsible person was defined in part as one showing "...ready willingness to accept the consequences of his own behavior, dependability, trustworthiness, and a sense of obligation to the group." Some validity evidence is reported in the form of correlations between the *Re* score of three additional samples and ratings of expert assessors. The *Re* scale was later revised into the shorter (20-item) *Re-r* scale. (Rating of 2.) H. G. Gough, H. McCloskey and P. E. Meehl, "A Personality Scale for Social Responsibility," *Journal of Abnormal and Social Psychology* 47 (1952): 73-80.

29. *Wa* (work attitude).

The 37 items on the *Wa* scale were those which discriminated between 50 industrial employees with a "good work attitude" (two or more years of satisfactory service) and 60 Air Force personnel with a "poor work attitude" (AWOL cases, disciplinary problems, etc.). The groups were matched on intelligence, age, education, general occupational level, and marital status. Later cross-validation showed that the scale also discriminated among college student samples who had been assessed by faculty members as having good and poor work attitudes. (Rating of 1.) Mary Tydlaska and R. Mengel, "A Work Attitude Scale for the MMPI," *Journal of Applied Psychology* 37 (1953): 474-477.

30. *Ah* (index of active hostility).

This index was derived from a study of actively hostile and passive aggressive patients in a mental hygiene clinic. Therapists nominated patients in treatment who characteristically manifested these forms of hostility and aggression. The configural characteristics of the MMPI profiles of the 19 actively hostile patients seemed on informal inspection to be best represented by the sum of the T scores on the *Pd* and *Ma* scales. (Rating of 2.) G. S. Welsh and P. L. Sullivan, "MMPI Configurations in Passive-Aggressive Personality Problems." Unpublished materials, 1952. Cited in Dahlstrom and Welsh, *An MMPI Handbook*.

31. *OE* (overall elevation index).

This index, consisting of the sum of the T scores on the eight clinical scales *Hs, D, Hy, Pd, Pa, Pt, Sc,* and *Ma*, is commonly used clinically as an indicator of severity of illness. The *Mf* scale, sometimes regarded as indicating direction of interests rather than pathology, is omitted from the index in the present study. Dahlstrom and Welsh (p. 283), while commenting on the wide clinical use of this index, warn that acuteness of psychological upset or lack of test defensiveness may contribute to profile elevation, as may positive personality characteristics in some instances. (Rating of 2.)

32. *PS* (psychotic signs).

P. E. Meehl ("Profile Analysis of the Minnesota Multiphasic Personality Inventory in Differential Diagnosis," *Journal of Applied Psychology* 30 (1946): 517-524), wrote a qualitative description of criteria which were commonly used to identify the MMPI profiles of psychotic patients, as opposed to those whose psychiatric diagnosis was conduct disorder or neurosis. He showed that the psychotics could be discriminated with better than chance accuracy by means of these criteria. Peterson quantified the signs, and showed that all six of them significantly discriminated between psychoneurotics and a group of patients diagnosed neurotic who later turned out to be schizophrenic. Further validity evidence for Peterson's version of the signs has been reported. (Rating of 2.) D. R. Peterson, "The Diagnosis of Subclinical Schizophrenia," *Journal of Consulting Psychology* 18 (1954): 198-200.

Selected Bibliography

BOOKS

Akers, Ronald L., *Deviant Behavior: A Social Learning Approach* (Belmont, Calif.: Wadsworth Publishing Company, 1973).

Cloward, Richard A., et al., *Theoretical Studies in Social Organization of the Prison* (New York: Social Science Research Council, Pamphlet 15, 1960).

——, and Lloyd E. Ohlin, *Delinquency and Opportunity* (Glencoe: The Free Press, 1960).

Cohen, Albert K., *Delinquent Boys: The Culture of the Gang* (Glencoe: The Free Press, 1955).

——, *Deviance and Control* (Englewood Cliffs, N. J.: Prentice-Hall, Inc., 1966).

Cressey, Donald R., ed., *The Prison* (New York: Holt, Rinehart and Winston, 1961).

Empey, LaMar T., and Steven G. Lubeck, *The Silverlake Experiment: Testing Delinquency Theory and Community Intervention* (Chicago: Aldine-Atherton Press, 1971).

——, and Maynard L. Erickson, *The Provo Experiment: Evaluating Community Control of Delinquency* (Lexington, Mass.: D. C. Heath and Co., 1972).

Fenton, Norman, Ernest Reimer, and Harry A. Wilmer, *The Correctional Community: An Introduction and Guide* (Berkeley: University of California Press, 1967).

Galvin, John J., ed., *Re-Educating Confined Delinquents* (Washington, D.C.: Bureau of Prisons, U.S. Department of Justice, 1965).

Gibbons, Don C., *Changing the Lawbreaker* (Englewood Cliffs, N. J.: Prentice-Hall, Inc., 1965).

Glaser, Daniel, *The Effectiveness of a Prison and Parole System,* (New York: The Bobbs-Merril Company, Inc., 1964).

Goffman, Erving, *Asylums* (New York: Doubleday, 1961).

Gold, Martin, *Status Forces in Delinquent Boys* (Ann Arbor: University of Michigan, Institute for Social Research, 1963).

Hirshi, Travis, *Causes of Delinquency* (Berkeley: University of California Press, 1972).

Keller, Oliver J., Jr., and Benedict S. Alper, *Halfway Houses: Community-Centered Correction and Treatment* (Lexington, Mass.: D. C. Heath & Co., 1970).

Kvaraceus, William C., and Walter B. Miller, *Delinquent Behavior: Culture and the Individual* (Washington, D.C.: National Education Association, 1959).

Lemert, Edwin M., *Human Deviance, Social Problems and Social Control,* 2d ed. (Englewood Cliffs, N. J.: Prentice-Hall Inc., 1972).

McCorkle, Lloyd W., Albert Elias, and F. Lovell Bixby, *The Highfields Story: A Unique Experiment in the Treatment of Juvenile Delinquency* (New York: Henry Holt & Co. 1958).

Matza, David, *Delinquency and Drift* (New York: John Wiley & Sons, Inc., 1964).

Merton, Robert K., *Social Theory and Social Structure,* Rev. and enl. ed. (Glencoe: The Free Press, 1957).

Rubington, Earl, and Martin S. Weinberg, *Deviance: The Interactionist Perspective,* 2d ed. (New York: The MacMillan Company, 1973).

Schur, Edwin M., *Labeling Deviant Behavior* (New York: Harper and Row, 1971).

Shaw, Clifford R., and Henry D. McKay, *Juvenile Delinquency and Urban Areas* (Chicago: University of Chicago Press, 1942).

Short, James F., Jr., and Fred Strodtbeck, *Group Process and Gang Delinquency* (Chicago; University of Chicago Press, 1965).

Street, David, Robert D. Vinter, and Charles Perrow, *Organization for Treatment* (New York: Free Press, 1966).

Studt, Elliot, Sheldon L. Messinger, and Thomas P. Wilson, *C-Unit: Search for Community in Prison* (New York: Russell Sage Foundation, 1968).

Sutherland, Edwin H., and Donald R. Cressey, *Criminology,* 8th ed. (Philadelphia: J. B. Lippincott Company, 1970).
Weeks, H. Ashley, *Youthful Offenders at Highfields* (Ann Arbor: University of Michigan Press, 1958).
Wheeler, Stanton, ed., *Controlling Delinquents* (New York: John Wiley & Sons, 1968).
Whyte, William F., *Street Corner Society: The Social Structure of an Italian Slum,* Enl. ed. (Chicago: The University of Chicago Press, 1955).

ARTICLES

Akman, Donald D., Andre Normandau, and Marvin E. Wolfgang, "The Group Treatment Literature in Correctional Institutions: An International Bibliography, 1945-1967," *The Journal of Criminal Law, Criminology and Police Science* 59 (1968): 41-56.
Bixby, F. Lovell, and Lloyd W. McCorkle, "Guided Group Interaction and Correctional Work," *American Sociological Review 16* (August 1951): 455-459.
Bordua, David J., "A Critique of Sociological Interpretations of Gang Delinquency," *Annals of the American Academy of Political and Social Science* 338 (November 1961): 120-136.
——, "Some Comments on Theories of Group Delinquency," *Sociological Inquiry* 32, no. 2 (Spring 1962): 245-260.
Cartwright, Dorwin, "Achieving Change in People: Applications of Group Dynamics Theory," *Human Relations* 4 (1951): 381-392.
Cressey, Donald R., "Contradictory Theories in Correctional Group Therapy Programs," *Federal Probation* 18, no. 2 (June 1954): 20-26.
——, "Changing Criminals: The Application of the Theory of Differential Association," *American Journal of Sociology* 61 (September 1955): 116-120.
Elias, Albert, and Saul Pilnick, "The Essexfields Group Rehabilitation Project for Youthful Offenders," *Correction in the Community: Alternative to Incarceration,* Monograph No. 4, Board of Corrections, State of California (June 1964): 51-57.
Empey, LaMar T, and Jerome Rabow, "The Provo Experiment in Delinquency Rehabilitation," *American Sociological Review* 26 (October 1961): 679-695.

Flackett, John M., and Gail Flackett, "Criswell House: An Alternative to Institutional Treatment for Juvenile Offenders," *Federal Probation* 34, no. 4 (December 1970): 30-37.

Gordon, Whitney H., and LaMar T. Empey, "Communications," *American Sociological Review* 27, no. 2 (April 1962): 256-258.

Kirby, Bernard C., "Crofton House: An Experiment with a County Halfway House," *Federal Probation* 33, no. 1 (March 1969): 53-58.

McCorkle, Lloyd W., "Group Therapy," *Contemporary Corrections*, Paul W. Tappen, ed. (New York: McGraw-Hill Book Co., 1951).

———, "Group Therapy in the Treatment of Offenders," *Federal Probation* 16, no. 4 (December 1952): 11-27.

———, and Richard Korn, "Resocialization within Walls," *Annals of the American Academy of Political Science* 293 (May 1954): 88-98.

Miller, Walter B., "Lower Class Culture as a Generating Milieu of Gang Delinquency," *Journal of Social Issues* 14 (1958): 5-19.

Pilnick, Saul, Albert Elias, and Neale W. Clapp, "The Essexfields Concept: A New Approach to the Social Treatment of Juvenile Delinquents," *The Journal of Applied Behavioral Science* 2, no. 3 (1966): 109-124.

Reckless, Walter C., Simon Dinitz, and Ellen Murray, "Self Concept as an Insulator against Delinquency," *American Sociological Review* 21 (December 1956): 744-746.

Reiss, Albert J., Jr., "Delinquency as the Failure of Personal and Social Controls," *American Sociological Review* 16 (April 1951): 196-207.

Robinson, James, and Gerald Smith, "The Effectiveness of Correctional Programs," *Crime and Delinquency* 17 (January 1971): 67-80.

Sarri, Rosemary C., and Robert D. Vinter, "Group Treatment Strategies in Juvenile Correctional Programs," *Crime and Delinquency* 11, no. 4 (October 1965): 326-340.

Scarpitti, Frank R., and Richard M. Stephenson, "The Use of the Small Group in the Rehabilitation of Delinquents," *Federal Probation* 30, no. 3 (September 1966): 45-50.

Stephenson, Richard M., and Frank R. Scarpitti, "Establishing a Therapeutic Milieu in a Noninstitutional Setting for Delinquent Boys," *Corrective Psychiatry and Journal of Social Therapy* 14, no. 1 (Spring 1968): 10-23.

———, and Frank R. Scarpitti, "Argot in a Therapeutic Correctional Milieu," *Social Problems* 15 (Winter 1968): 384-395.

Sternberg, David, "Synanon House—A Consideration of Its Implications for
  American Correction," *Journal of Criminal Law, Criminology and
  Police Science* 54, no. 4 (December 1963): 447-455.
Street, David, "The Inmate Group in Custodial and Treatment Settings,"
  American Sociological Review 30 (February 1965): 40-55.
Sykes, Gresham M., and David Matza, "Techniques of Neutralization: A
  Theory of Delinquency," *American Sociological Review* 22 (December
  1957): 664-670.

REPORTS

Harmon, Maurice A., "Community Rehabilitation of the Younger De-
  linquent Boy: Parkland Non-Residential Group Center," Final Report
  to the U. S. Department of Health, Education and Welfare, Kentucky
  Child Welfare Research Foundation, Inc., 1967.
Knight, Doug, "The Marshall Program: Assessment of a Short Term Institutional
  Treatment Program, Part II: Amenability to Confrontive Peer-Group
  Treatment," California Youth Authority, Research Report No. 59,
  August 1970.
Larsen, Charles, "Guided Group Interaction: Theory and Method," Depart-
  ment of Court Services, Hennepin County, Minneapolis, Minnesota,
  Report No. 1, July 1970.
Miller, Lovick C., "Evaluation of Southfields: A Short Term Inpatient Treat-
  ment Center for Delinquents," no date (mimeographed).
——, Second Progress Report: *Evaluation of Southfields's Treatment Center,*
  The Ford Foundation, August 10, 1965.
Palmer, Theodore, et al., "Community Treatment Project, Seventh Progress
  Report, Part I: The Sacramento-Stockton and the San Francisco Ex-
  periments," CTP Research Report No. 9, Part I, October 1968.
Pilnick, Saul, et al., "Collegefields: From Delinquency to Freedom," Report
  to U. S. Department of Health, Education and Welfare, Office of
  Juvenile Delinquency, 1967.
Stephenson, Richard M., and Frank R. Scarpitti, "The Rehabilitation of De-
  linquent Boys," Final Report to the Ford Foundation, 1967, (mimeo-
  graphed).
Wall, John M., Albert Elias, and Albert Axelrod, "Southfields Residential
  Group Center: A Four Year Report," March 1966 (mimeographed).

——, "The Residential Group Center as a Treatment Method for Selected Youthful Offenders Aged 16 and 17," A four-year report on the Southfields Residential Group Center, March 1966 (mimeographed).

Warren, Marquerite Q., and Theodore Palmer, "The Community Treatment Project After Five Years," Sacramento, California Youth Authority, 1966.

Index

DATE DUE